Democratic Struggle, Institutional Reform, and State Resilience in the African Sahel

Democratic Struggle, Institutional Reform, and State Resilience in the African Sahel

Edited by
Leonardo A. Villalón and
Rahmane Idrissa

LEXINGTON BOOKS
Lanham • Boulder • New York • London

Published by Lexington Books
An imprint of The Rowman & Littlefield Publishing Group, Inc.
4501 Forbes Boulevard, Suite 200, Lanham, Maryland 20706
www.rowman.com

6 Tinworth Street, London SE11 5AL, United Kingdom

British Library Cataloguing in Publication Information Available

Library of Congress Cataloging-in-Publication Data

Names: Villalón, Leonardo Alfonso, 1957- editor. | Idrissa, Abdourahmane, 1971- editor.
Title: Democratic struggle, institutional reform, and state resilience in the African Sahel / edited by Leonardo A. Villalón and Rahmane Idrissa.
Description: Lanham : Lexington Books, 2020. | Includes bibliographical references and index. | Summary: "This book examines how the struggles for democracy over the past quarter century have affected the resilience of states in the region of the West African Sahel. Distinguished scholar-practitioners from the region provide detailed insights into these processes in Senegal, Mauritania, Mali, Burkina Faso, Niger and Chad"—Provided by publisher.
Identifiers: LCCN 2019057450 (print) | LCCN 2019057451 (ebook) | ISBN 9781498569996 (cloth) | ISBN 9781498570008 (epub) | ISBN 9781498570015 (pbk)
Subjects: LCSH: Democratization—Sahel. | Sahel—Politics and government.
Classification: LCC DT532.6 .D46 2020 (print) | LCC DT532.6 (ebook) | DDC 320.9660917541—dc23
LC record available at https://lccn.loc.gov/2019057450
LC ebook record available at https://lccn.loc.gov/2019057451

Contents

Acknowledgments

This book has had a long gestation, for many reasons. Not the least of these are the extraordinary commitments of the authors of the country studies. They are not only academic scholars, nor are they simple observers of the many events that have marked their countries in recent years, but in myriad ways our authors have been actors directly involved in these events. In the years since the initial 2013 conference that brought the group together at the University of Florida, they have served as presidential advisors, members of national commissions and electoral bodies, consultants to major international organizations, members of constitution-writing commissions, ministers in governments, and even in one case as a hostage in a military plot to derail democratization. We are grateful for their commitment to this project, and we express our deep admiration for their collective capacity to bring an academic and analytical approach to issues of such direct and dramatic impact in the political trajectories of their countries, and in their own lives.

This book was conceived in the context of the Center for African Studies at the University of Florida, and specifically within the Sahel Research Group. We are grateful for the support and the intellectually exciting climate sustained by director Brenda Chalfin, associate director Todd Leedy, and Ikeade Akinyemi of the Center for African Studies. Within the Sahel Research Group, we are fortunate to have a set of colleagues and graduate students who share a strong interest in and commitment to the six francophone Sahelian countries discussed in this volume. For frequent intense discussions, regular exchange of information and ideas, and more than occasional social gatherings, we thank Sebastian Elischer, Abdoulaye Kane, Sarah McKune, Fiona Mc Laughlin, Renata Serra, Benjamin Soares, Alioune Sow, and Olivier Walther.

A special thanks and recognition goes to the team of the extensive research project funded by the Minerva Initiative, under the title "Institutional Reform, Social Change, and Stability in Sahelian Africa." It was our great fortune to have been able to recruit not one but three outstanding PhD students, now all doctors themselves, to the project team. Mamadou Bodian, Daniel Eizenga, and Ibrahim Yahaya Ibrahim collectively spent the equivalent of over four years doing fieldwork across all six Sahelian countries in the years since we began this book project, and contributed to it in many ways. They participated in and helped organize our initial conference, and many other Sahel Research Group events. And they read and commented on drafts of the chapters that follow. This work, like so many other Sahel Research Group projects, truly represents a collective effort.

Other colleagues and students, as well as numerous visitors and guests, have also contributed to our understanding of the region during the lifetime of this project. At the risk of an inadvertent omission, we thank Marjatta Eilittä, El Hadji Sarr, John Hames, Benjamin Burgen, Isabelle Walther Duc, Isaie Dougnon, Oumar Ba, Antoinette Tidjani Alou, Zekeria ould Ahmed Salem, Bakary Sambe, Fatoumata Hane, Ladiba Gondeu, Mamadou Cissé, Awa Doucouré, and Frédérick Madore. A key priority for the Sahel Research Group is to work collaboratively with colleagues in the region, and in each of the six countries an entire network of colleagues have contributed to our efforts in various ways. In addition to the authors of the chapters in this volume, we are indebted to the numerous other colleagues from across the region who participated in our Trans-Saharan Elections Project, as well as in other collaborative research projects on religion and educational reform, on religious movements on university campuses, and on the future of *laïcité* in the Sahel.

All of the country chapters in this book were initially drafted in French. El Hadji Sarr kindly undertook the translation of one of the chapters into English. The other country chapters were translated by the editors. For help with subsequent editing, formatting, and rooting out the occasional remaining gallicisms, we thank Jordan MacKenzie, as well as Emily Moore and, as the book was being finalized, Luke Whittingham. We must acknowledge the extraordinary financial support of the Minerva Initiative Grant, not only in directly making this book possible but more broadly in institutionalizing the Sahel Research Group as an academic center for the study of this crucial and long-neglected region. We thank program officers Erin Fitzgerald, David Montgomery, and Lisa Troyer not only for their efficient administrative support of the project but more importantly for their commitment to ensuring the high standards of academic freedom and scholarly independence of the Minerva program.

Chapter 1

The Politics of Democratization and State Building in the Sahel

Leonardo A. Villalón

On March 22, 2012, an unplanned and indeed almost accidental coup d'état against Malian president Amadou Toumani Touré put an end to two decades of what had been widely hailed as one of Africa's most successful democratic experiments. The incident grew out of a military mutiny by disgruntled soldiers, unhappy about the government's handling of a rebellion in the country's north. This rebellion was itself linked to a long history of conflict, but its immediate iteration was sparked by the return of Tuareg fighters from Libya after the fall of Qaddafi in late 2011. The coup was actually welcomed among many Malians, long frustrated with the limitations of this Western "donor darling" (Bergamaschi 2014), and the widespread assumption in its immediate wake was that there would be a relatively quick restoration of an elected government and a return to the status quo ante (Whitehouse 2017).

That was not to be. On the contrary, in a bewilderingly rapid series of events that caught both international and domestic actors by surprise, the Malian state largely collapsed. The ethno-nationalist Tuareg movement that initially took the major urban settlements of the north—Timbuktu, Kidal, and Gao—was quickly displaced by an assortment of Islamist jihadi groups that occupied virtually half the national territory, and threatened to take the rest in the face of the incapacity of the Malian government or military to stop them. Only a French-led intervention in early 2013, eventually complemented by the United Nations (in the form of the UN Multidimensional Integrated Stabilization Mission in Mali, MINUSMA) and other outside actors, has managed to prop up the shell of a state in Mali. To be sure, there have been efforts to rebuild, including the holding of elections and inauguration of new governments in 2013 and 2018. But by the end of the decade, it was very clear that whatever might be labeled the Malian state had virtually no substantive power, a fact reflected in its almost complete incapacity to address the spread

1

of violent intercommunal conflict in much of the country. Whatever the two earlier decades of democracy had accomplished in Mali, they had not built a capable state.

Some thirty months after the Mali coup, a set of equally unexpected events in neighboring Burkina Faso offered a striking contrast to the Malian story. Under the continuous presidency of Blaise Compaoré since the coup that brought him to power in 1987, Burkina Faso was widely regarded as a pro-totypical "competitive authoritarian" regime (Levitsky and Way 2010), and likely to remain as such. Yet in October 2014, when the government moved to introduce a long-anticipated constitutional reform to further prolong Com-paoré's tenure, massive protests broke out on the streets of Ouagadougou and the National Assembly was set on fire to prevent the vote. In a rapidly escalating and startling twist, the regime quickly lost control of the uprising, and within forty-eight hours, Compaoré had resigned from office and fled the country, putting an abrupt end to his twenty-seven years of rule. The speed at which these events unfolded stunned outside observers and, indeed, caught the participants themselves by surprise (Eizenga and Villalón 2020). The year that followed witnessed a series of more dramatic events, includ-ing an attempted coup against the transitional government by disgruntled elements of the old presidential guard. Yet despite the disruption resulting from the failed coup, and with the specter of Mali's collapse casting a long shadow, the state in Burkina Faso continued to function, and the transitional government managed the significant feat of organizing joint presidential and legislative elections in November 2015, widely acknowledged as the fairest and most competitive in the country's history. Despite the severe democratic limitations of Burkina Faso, the two decades of democratic struggle against the entrenched regime seem to have been accompanied by a process of sub-stantive state building.

The contrast must be nuanced, of course; both countries face significant challenges. In particular, the subsequent expansion of violence and the rise of new and unconventional actors—jihadi or terrorist groups prime among them—in both Mali and Burkina Faso and across the region, have produced the situation now almost universally described as the "crisis" in the Sahel. And, indeed, it is important to note that while significant variations exist in the capacity of states to manage it, the future of all of the countries of the region remains clouded by the spread of religious and intercommunal violence.

The efforts to understand and make sense of this violence and the some-times-bewildering collapse of social order and the disintegration of state insti-tutions have resulted in a proliferation of analyses, primarily in the form of reports by international organizations and think tanks, attempting to identify the causes and drivers of violence. At the current juncture, works of this sort have been valuable contributions to the policy community and to governments as they struggle to respond to rapidly changing landscapes. From a somewhat longer-term analytic perspective, however, a focus on the proximate causes of conflict can obscure the more fundamental political dynamics that have produced the varied degrees of state resilience and fragility that characterize the region. It is the premise of this book that both the commonalities and the variations in the ways in which states have been able to navigate the challenging forces of destabilization that mark the contemporary Sahel can only be understood via analyses of the core political dynamics that have shaped the historical process of state building in the region. The relative reliance or fragility of states is a product of long and protracted processes of building—or undermining—institutions.

The *longue-durée* of African state building is of course colonial in its origins and passes through the years of attempted nation building around single parties and founding fathers, before entering the period of intentional state-*weakening* via structural adjustment, as mandated by the outside world. But most centrally for the contemporary political systems of the region, the institutions of governance have been shaped over some three decades by the play of political struggles around the central declared goal of democracy. In each country, and despite how elusive its substance has often been, the framework within which institutions have been debated, attacked, manipulated, reinforced, or appropriated has remained the declared normative goal of a democratic state.

With this observation in mind, this book seeks to address a core analytic question: *How have the politics of democratization across the Francophone Sahel since the early 1990s shaped processes of state building, and with what effects on the resilience of state institutions?* The empirical focus is on six countries: Senegal, Mauritania, Mali, Burkina Faso, Niger, and Chad. The goal is to consider this question comparatively and, hence, to attempt to understand which political processes have tended to strengthen state institutions, and which have weakened them, in any given case. Such an understanding, I argue, is central to understanding the varied resilience of states in the region and, hence, to their potential to manage and react to the current Sahelian crisis.

I use the term "politics of democratization" broadly to refer to the complete set of political dynamics—both for and against—set in motion by the pressures on states to undertake institutional reforms under the banner of democracy. There has been, of course, much variation in the extent to which regimes that might be qualified in any way as "democratic" have in fact emerged. The politics of democratization, in Africa as elsewhere, include no end of efforts by some actors to manipulate, harness, or subvert institutions so as to consolidate power and limit contestation. Indeed, the processes leading to the instauration of "electoral authoritarian" regimes have themselves been a hallmark of the politics of democratization in the Sahel, and indeed across Africa (see Eizenga 2018). These dynamics, however, should not occult the fact that in any given country some political actors have continuously exerted pressure to reform institutions in keeping with a vision of what democracy requires. And in each country, periodic moments of intense politics, whether resulting from ruptures such as a coup d'état, or from moments such as those provided by mass popular mobilization following contested elections, have opened up new opportunities for substantial reform: new electoral codes, term limit changes, or even new constitutions (see Bodian 2016).

With the paradox of Mali at the center of concerns—how the country that had arguably made the greatest progress toward democracy had simultaneously weakened the state to the point of collapse—there is an urgent need to address the question of whether and how the politics of creating or reforming institutions in the name of "democracy" have weakened or strengthened states themselves. Considering the likelihood that they have actually done both at the same time, a more precise question might thus be *Which aspects of state structures were strengthened, and which weakened, by the politics of institutional reform over the past three decades?*

Asked in the context of the unprecedented and ever-deepening political crisis in the Sahel, these questions are formulated on several assumptions. The first is that states matter, fundamentally, and will continue to do so. While often framed as a security crisis brought about by social phenomena—by identity-based rebellions or by the rise of "radical" or "extremist" religious movements—in fact those social developments are clearly parasitic on a more fundamental failing of the state, a failing that was in itself much longer in the making than the current crisis. States must be understood in large part as a collection of interrelated institutions for attempting to shape behavior, and specific institutions thus also matter. Too often in studies of Africa, states are described as if they are only fictive shells of "neo-patrimonial" networks, shaped only by informal or culturally bound rules. These characteristics are a part of the mix, of course, but as seminal empirical work on the state by such scholars as Thomas Bierschenk and Jean-Pierre Olivier de Sardan (2014) has documented, specific state institutions do matter on the ground in Africa, and this by their role in shaping the behavior of civil servants and other agents of the state. The norms and modes of local politics that emerge from these behaviors in turn reshape state structures at their foundation—where they intersect with their citizens. The effects of the crisis in the Sahel are thus uneven and varied given the different institutional capacities of the states that make up the region.

An important caveat is in order: Our purpose in this book is not to call into question the value of research on democracy or democratization, as either an empirical phenomenon or a normative goal. It is simply that in the effort to think about the likely resilience of the Sahelian states in the face of the enormous pressures they now face, a focus on their progress toward democracy has many analytic limitations. In what follows, then, I attempt to propose a framework by which we might instead consider the effects on state institutions of the ways in which the issue of democracy was posed in the early 1990s, and has been debated and fought over since then.

A CONCEPTUAL FRAMEWORK

Democratization as it was undertaken in Africa in the early 1990s was not a uniform process. Rather the term refers to an interrelated, but not always cohesive, set of political reforms, with consequences in the institutional, social, economic, and policy realms, and pushed by diverse sets of actors, both domestic and international, with varying agendas. Some actors were more concerned with one set of reforms than with others—for example, gender issues, economics, electoral institutions, and media freedoms. In all cases, it initially involved an electoral process, but this was only intended to be the point of departure for much more fundamental and long-term changes. Crucial to it all, however, was some form of liberalization, in the sense of reduced state power to structure politics, society, and economies.

In the first years of the 1990s, all the Sahelian states—like virtually every African regime—were forced to make concessions, whether substantive or symbolic, to demands for the democratization of political systems. In the optimism that accompanied those events, political scientists throughout the 1990s made the study of "transitions to democracy" their core concern in Africa, with particular attention to the conditions under which elections were carried out. By the end of a decade, however, two things were already clear: first that very little substantive democracy had in fact resulted, and second that the nature of the "transition"—which was the focus of much initial study—had only limited explanatory value in predicting the subsequent configurations of political systems. Thus, the initial optimism about a "second liberation" heralded by the promise of African transitions to democracy (see e.g., Hyden and Bratton 1992) quickly gave way to pessimism about democracy's prospects, and even before the end of the decade to "a growing sense . . . that the promotion of rapid democratization in Africa at the beginning of the 1990s—with its emphasis on competitive, multiparty elections—was misguided at best, a fundamental mistake at worst" (Reynolds and Sisk 1998).

Whether democratization was a "good" or "bad" idea, however, and whether in fact something identifiable as "democracy" emerged in any given case, the fact is that historical forces thrust political reform in the name of democracy onto the agenda in Africa, and regimes had no choice but to react. As a consequence, important transformations in the very basis of political order on the continent were set in motion, and the seeds of more fundamental future transformations were sown. Rather than actually defining new rules of the game, the reforms of the 1990s were most significant in three ways: (1) they put the issue of elaborating new rules on the agenda; (2) they politicized the forces attempting to weigh in on the process; and (3) they effected an initial distribution of power among these competing forces. With the hindsight of almost thirty years, this period does seem to continue to merit the label of "critical juncture" (Villalón and Huxtable 1998).

At the current juncture, the crucial question might thus be: What have been the long-term political consequences of the reforms undertaken in Africa in the name of an ideal of democracy? Taking the democratic "wave" of the early 1990s as a point of departure, we need to ask what debates the democratic agenda gave rise to, what social and political factors were mobilized to attempt to shape these debates as they unfolded, and how these dynamics have cumulated to shape contemporary states. Events of the early 1990s called existing political systems and state structures into question everywhere, and mobilized social groups of all sorts in attempting to redefine these systems, or create new ones. But in few, if any, cases were the key issues resolved. Neither did these issues fade away; in country after country they have continued to define political struggle. The task at hand now, therefore, is to attempt to sort out analytically how the prolonged efforts to reform or build new institutions and to define new relations of power among social groups have continued to evolve in reciprocal interaction with each other under the liberalized contexts post-1990, and with what consequences for state capacity.

For years, much of the emphasis in the study of the democratic question in Africa was focused on the nature of the political transition, and in particular on the factors influencing whether elections deemed "free and fair" resulted in a change of government. The typologies of transitions were largely constructed on these criteria. (e.g., Bratton and van de Walle 1997). Yet it is now clear that the occurrence or not of an "electoral transition" (i.e., the inauguration of a new government via an election) was at best a very imperfect predictor of the subsequent outlines of reconfigured state structures (see Villalón and VonDoepp 2005). Most often transitions via an election in Africa left the processes of restructuring state institutions unaddressed or incomplete; post-transition governments were still faced with the need to elaborate and create key institutions and structures central to the political order. Elections and the processes leading to them, however, had consequences of their own: they politicized issues and set agendas, provoked the formation of different kinds of groups and mobilized them politically, and influenced the initial distribution of power among social actors. The particular pattern of such politicization in any given case, and how the interaction of these forces plays out, may be the more significant variables in determining the shape of political structures over the longer run.

The impact of liberalization was most strongly felt, and its effects are most clearly visible, in the transformations of associational life that began in the early 1990s, namely in the explosive burst of organization, mobilization, and politicization of an extraordinary array of social groups. The Malian example is indicative of this initial explosion. With the demise of the old single party and the opening of the political system in 1991, some fifty-six parties were formally recognized in short order. By 1995, eighty-seven women's associations were already officially registered with the Ministry of the Interior, and the monopoly of the state media had given way to over hundred newspapers and over twenty independent radio stations operating in the country. The former official Islamic association was challenged by some fifty other registered groups claiming to represent Islamic interests. In each of these cases, these groups had replaced a *single* such group only four years earlier, at the end of the old regime. Many of these associations, of course, were to prove rather ephemeral, and in most domains, only a handful remain strong. Nevertheless, the rapid proliferation of organized groups in response to the opening of the space available for associational life remains the most noteworthy social legacy of that decade, and its effects persist today.

Strikingly, this phenomenon was replicated throughout the region, and this despite differences in terms of whether an electoral "transition" occurred or not: in Burkina Faso's "flawed" transition no less than in the successful case of Mali, and somewhat later in the highly questionable "transition" in Chad. Even more tellingly, the strength of liberalization in terms of the impact on social formations remained consistently evident in Niger throughout the turbulent reversals that have followed. Even following the overthrow of the elected government in the 1996 coup which ended that country's first "successful transition," there was no containing the social groups—students, human rights groups, women's groups, religious associations, and ethnic associations—which continued to agitate and shape political events in the country. The press remained widely diverse and critical, and the issues that were put on the agenda in the debate on democratization in the early 1990s remained at the center of political life in the country throughout the turbulent two decades that led from the Third (1992) to the Seventh (2010) Republic.

In the most important early work on Africa's "democratic experiments," Bratton and Van de Walle suggested that "In many respects, political transitions center on struggles over the rules of the political game, with alternate clusters of rules representing opposing regime options" (1997, 42–43). In fact, however these battles usually continued to be fought *post* transition, that is *after* a founding election had been held and often even after a new government had been put in place. Most often, the first struggle over rules was only a struggle for the rules of "transitions" themselves; that is, for how the first set of elections were to be organized. In most cases, however, very fundamental issues concerning the state itself were left unresolved, and to be decided by the subsequent elected governments. Precisely because elections took place in a mood of urgency and in a context of very weak or incomplete state structures, new governments tended to claim that making significant and fundamental changes to the nature of the regime and to the shape of the state were their right—indeed even their mandate. The losers in the transition process, however, overwhelmingly refused to accept these claims, and constant acrimony between governments and opposition—including frequent boycott of elections—has continued to mark politics in the region. Despite constant negotiation and struggle and reiterated elections over two decades, state structures themselves are still very much in question in much of Africa. In the Sahelian cases, we thus see years of ongoing and continuous debate about political and constitutional reform in even the most "successful" of cases; Mali and Senegal were each in the midst of debates on such fundamental reforms in 2011, as the current crisis loomed, and in each case, these debates continued into the end of the decade (Bodian 2016; Fall in this volume).

How then to conceptualize the factors shaping politics in the region today? A useful point of departure is to analyze the specific patterns of political change on two distinct dimensions, as these were set in motion in the early 1990s and have evolved since then. We need to consider first the nature of the questions about the state itself that were raised at the point of response to pressures for democratic change. That is, what were the issues concerning the state that were put on the agenda in a given country? Second, we need to consider the social transformations sparked by the era of liberalization; what were the social forces born or reinvented in the new contexts and organized to weigh in on items of the agenda, and how have these evolved? The ongoing intersection of variations on these two dimensions has been central to defining the trajectories and outcomes of efforts at state building since the 1990s, with direct impact on the evolving capacities of states today.

Two main kinds of questions concerning the state were raised in the critical period of transitions. Most fundamental were those questions about the very *nature of the state*. What is the purpose of the state, and what functions and whose interests should it be designed to serve? Most centrally in the Sahel, this at times took the form of questions about the place of religion: Is the state's role to be the neutral arbiter of societal and cultural diversity, or is to be the representative institution of religious (Muslim) majorities? That is, should the state be an "Islamic" or a "secular" one? Debates about the nature of the state can also take on an ethnic or racial cast. The "Arab" nature of Mauritania has been squarely at the center of politics in that country (tellingly, despite virtually no disagreement on its Islamic nature). With rather different political dynamics, Chadian politics have also been shaped by questions of national identity, often expressed in linguistic terms: "Arabophone" vs. "Francophone."

Second, transitions (virtually by definition) raised questions everywhere about the *shape of the state*, that is, about what institutional forms should define it. This of course initially centered on debates about electoral systems and institutions, but it also included key debates on such issues as the presidency and other executive institutions of the state; the shape and power of legislatures; the judiciary; key legal provisions often seen as central to "the rule of law," such as family codes, land tenure codes, and press codes; and the decentralized units of the state. What is striking in the Sahel in general (and indeed across Africa) is the degree to which so little consensus has emerged around institutions, even in the cases of relatively "successful" democratic experiments. Thus fundamental decisions about the rules of the political game continued to be fought out in highly politicized environments well after the first electoral cycle had allocated the power to impose decisions, and have continued over the following decades (Bodian and Villalón 2020). As the chapters in this volume document, the politics of democratization in the Sahel since the early 1990s have been less about the struggle for power within established institutions than about the effort to rework those institutions so as to accede or hold on to power. The consequences of these dynamics are enormous. In the case of Mali, and despite two decades of experience as a "model democracy," fundamental and unresolved questions about electoral institutions loomed large just a couple of months before the planned 2012 elections, and before the 22 March coup put an end to that process (Bodian 2016).

The struggles that have continued to shape political systems have been intertwined with the politics of social formations as they emerged and have been shaped in the process. On the dimension of social transformations, it is useful to distinguish between the politics of group interests and the politics of group identities. By "interest"-based groups, we refer broadly to what has been most frequently called "civil society": human rights groups, women's groups, journalists, jurists, and business associations, and such. Much of the early attention on democratization in Africa focused on the important role of such groups in promoting democracy by "fixing" state structures gone wrong (see, e.g., Harbeson, Rothchild and Chazan 1994). This focus, however, was quickly the subject of various critiques. Pointing to the opportunistic proliferation of groups attempting to carve out a stake for themselves in the emerging political order, their democratic commitment was called into question very early (e.g., Fatton 1995). The international connections of such groups also raised critiques that they responded more directly to external phenomena (and sources of funding) than to domestic concerns. Related to this, and perhaps more significantly, was the observation that even collectively the groups of "civil society" represented only a small minority of the population, and most frequently (at least in the Sahel) a distinct social stratum composed of the more "westernized" and "secularized" elements of society.

The institutions of civil society in the Sahel have been neither mass-based nor popular organizations. Clearly, such groups played important, at times central, roles in shaping political processes in the 1990s, and to varying degrees among countries and at specific crucial moments, they have remained important in the democratization struggle. But it is striking that in the liberalized contexts that opened doors more broadly to societal forces, their weight gradually eroded, and they consequently and incrementally shifted their foci and tactics.

Those groups that *do* represent larger social categories, and that thus emerged as more influential in shaping outcomes in the longer term, were those organized around the politics of identity. Much attention in the democratization literature was dedicated to the need to avoid the politicization of such groups, especially ethnic or religious ones, as "pathologies" of democratization (for any early statement see Glickman, 1995). Tellingly, however, it is toward such groups that political parties have an inherent tendency to make appeals; numbers (votes)—the currency of democratic systems—are more likely to be found in such support. In any case, what became quickly clear in the region was that such groups must be taken seriously into account for their role in shaping political systems.

The explosion of associational life with liberalization in much of the Sahel has been most significantly felt in the religious sphere. Across the region, religion has consistently increased in importance in defining the emergence of points of contention, and in framing key debates and shaping the parameters of discussion. Most fundamentally, we have witnessed the emergence of an "Islamic public sphere" and the rise of what we might call an "Islamic civil society" (Holder 2009; Tayob 2007). The proliferation of varied religious voices has in turn led to new dynamics and indeed, in many ways to a "democratization" of religion itself, in the sense of new possibilities for individual voices to challenge established authorities. As democratization put policy issues on the public agenda, debates about the appropriate religious position on any given issue leads naturally to interpretation, and thus opens the door to religious change driven by these public discussions (Villalón 2010).

In the Francophone Sahel, this process has led to wide-ranging debates on policy issues. In this process, religious voices have made themselves heard more loudly than ever before in the political domain, leading to tensions with secularists. Sahelian prodemocracy movements, while fed by popular frustration and economic grievances, were in fact initially led by the small educated elite of people with formal French-language education. These prodemocracy activists took their inspiration for the design of new regimes from the model they knew best, namely the French Fifth Republic (Cabanis 1999). Crucially, their normative approach to the democracy they sought to build suggested the need to focus on social transformation so as to build cultures compatible with their vision of democracy, rather than on the elaboration of institutions to reflect local values in public policy. The question the prodemocracy activists tended to ask themselves was not, "How do we build a democracy that reflects an African Muslim society?" but rather, "How do we transform an African Muslim society so that it is compatible with democracy?"

Not surprisingly, this approach led rather quickly to clashes with representatives of Muslim groups. While there was initially an important element of rivalry and occasional conflict among different religious groups, to varying degrees, they also often learned to make common cause in opposition to specific items in the agenda of the secular prodemocracy forces. The 1990s thus saw a number of conflicts and protests between Muslim groups and new governments on both substantive and symbolic moral issues such as the holding of fashion shows or the opening of bars during Ramadan. These conflicts were often colored by critiques of the very notion of democracy by religious groups, given the normative content with which it was proposed. The most significant feature of Muslim politics in the region today, however, is the fact that rather quickly religious society learned to play the democratic game to its advantage. This was facilitated by the demographic advantage of Islamic associations in the confrontation with the secular "civil society" forces, given the much broader appeal of those groups to popular sentiment in deeply religious countries.

As politics evolved in the era of democracy, then, there has been an increased presence of religion not only in public life in the form of participation in debates but also in protests and public pressuring, in favor or against policy issues of concern to religious sensibilities (Idrissa 2017). Throughout most of the period, however, and despite many fears to the contrary, there has been very limited direct electoral involvement by religious movements. Rather the rise of religion in the public sphere in the context of democratization has moved from a series of confrontations between secular "prodemocracy" activists and Islamic actors to a much more fluid and wide-ranging debate about how politics and state structures and policies should be organized in Muslim societies. These debates have taken place within both the political and the religious arenas. Of particular importance in these debates has been the rise of Francophone Muslim intellectuals, often organized into new Islamic associations, who espouse a commitment to democracy and the capacity to engage in public policy debate, but who also argue that in a democracy these policy issues should reflect popular (religious) sentiment. In addition these debates led to new forms of Muslim women's politics, as Muslim women's associations weighed in on debates (see Alidou 2005; Augis 2005; Masquelier 2009). The intersection of political reform and social mobilization in these countries, then, sparked significant internal religious discussion and a wide range of religious ideologies that compete with each other for dominance in the public sphere.

Unsurprisingly, on many issues, there has been no agreement on the limits of religion in public policy, and some debates have proven rather intractable. This is particularly the case on issues that concern clashes between what secular activists present as "international" or "universal" values that cannot be compromised, and prevailing values in religious society. The core disagreement driving such conflicts is on whether a given position is an "inalienable" element of democracy, *regardless* of what the majority might want, or whether it is subject to democratic majority rule. The most noteworthy and difficult policy issues that have led to such standoffs have been those concerning family law, and issues regarding sexuality more broadly. In the Sahelian countries, there have thus been long, intense, and ultimately unresolved debates about "family codes" (Villalón 1996; Soares 2009; Brossier 2004). These remain significant points of contention and sources of intense social conflict, and religious groups have remained capable of mobilizing large numbers of protesters on the issue in most countries.

The efforts to reconfigure African states in the 1990s were everywhere launched in the name of democratization, and democracy quickly emerged as the leitmotif of the decade. But this very process was brought about in large part by a profound and systemic crisis of collapsing or unsustainable political institutions, and this weakness continues to plague virtually every case, in some form or other. At the same time, the efforts at political reform that these crises produced sparked significant mobilization and at times unexpected politicization of social groups and issues. The intersection of continued efforts to reform state structures under difficult circumstances with social formations that remain in flux leaves the future of political systems tenuous and contingent. Yet the variations in the play of forces as reform and social change have interacted in the intervening years have also had distinct impacts on political institutions in each country.

Asking why events in the Middle East and North Africa caught so many by surprise, Ellen Lust (2011) proposed the concept of "micro-transitions" to refer to the longer-term causal factors behind the "Arab spring." Her suggestion is that such large-scale tumultuous political change was largely unpredicted by political scientists because insufficient attention was paid to the consequences of the accumulation of many small social changes over time, at the "micro" level. In an edited book growing out of a comparative project on social change and governance reform in Africa, Lust and Ndegwa (2012) further suggested the importance of considering gradual and episodic societal transformations in Africa and "the ways in which they have reshaped the context of power and politics and, ultimately, the fortune of attempted reforms." They argue for the need to try to understand how incremental changes "cumulate to re-shape the contours of state power and the emergence of new actors and arenas of contestation."

Within the parameters of the dimensions described above—debates about the nature and the shape of state institutions, and the forms of social mobilizations and transformations that have marked individual cases—the concept of micro-transitions helps provide a fruitful framework within which we can begin to analyze the varying evolution of state structures in the Sahel in the era of democracy. In the chapters that follow, authors carefully trace how the interaction of debates about institutions and the politicization of social groups have cumulatively and over time shaped processes of state building in each specific case. Echoing the analytic framework suggested by Lust and Ndegwa, collectively they suggest that the relative resilience or fragility of contemporary states in the Sahel has been constructed since the early 1990s via incremental institutional changes, themselves shaped by debates about political reform in the name of democratization. A comparative overview of the patterns that have characterized the region, to which I now turn, can help to contextualize the analyses of individual cases.

DEMOCRATIC POLITICS ON THE DESERT'S EDGE: THE SAHELIAN CASES

Over a fifteen-month period from late 1991 to early 1993, Mali, Niger, Burkina Faso, Mauritania, and Senegal all held presidential elections; Chad was to follow in 1996. This wave of elections in the region was the direct result of the global wave of democratization ushered in by the end of the Cold War. The ways in which incumbent regimes responded to the pressures, and how elections were organized in each country, however, varied widely.

Mali and Niger's elections concluded transitions that had grown out of "national conferences," following the much-hailed model successfully pioneered by Benin and imitated across the region. In both cases, the transition process and the elections brought to power new regimes to replace long-standing autocratic ones, via the collapse of Moussa Traoré's regime in Mali and the marginalization of Ali Saïbou's during the Nigerien national conference (Villalón and Idrissa 2005a; Villalón and Idrissa 2005b). Reading the writing on the walls, regimes in Burkina Faso and in Mauritania maneuvered to avoid a national conference by preemptively declaring a democratic opening and organizing elections that were carefully controlled to assure their own victory (Ould Ahmed Salem 1999; Harsch 2017). In Senegal, often described as the exception, the *Parti Socialiste* also faced intense opposition to its thirty years of rule in the early 1990s, and after a number of important reforms, the regularly scheduled elections of 1993 were for the first time held under conditions that might be reasonably labeled "democratic" (Villalón 1994). And even in Chad, where a new regime under Idriss Déby had taken power by force in 1990, prodemocracy activists were able to force the convening of a national conference in 1993 (Buijtenhuijs 1993). The regime managed to retain control of the process, however, and eventually to ensure Déby's victory in the country's first-ever democratic presidential elections in 1996 (Buijtenhuijs 1998).

Retrospectively, as the region approached the thirtieth anniversary of these transitions, the trajectories that they set in motion have also proven to be quite varied. Mali's "success" was to last for twenty years, under two elected presidents, but then collapsed in 2012, in the face of its incapacity to confront rebellious forces and jihadi challenges. The return to an elected government that was made possible under international tutelage in 2013 only produced a fragile regime with very limited authority over the national territory. Niger's roller-coaster trajectory has been marked by three coups, three more democratic transitions, and four new constitutions as the country moved from its "Third Republic" to its Seventh in the space of twenty years. In Mauritania, Burkina Faso, and Chad, the regimes that had managed to survive the wave transformed themselves into electoral authoritarian regimes and proved quite resilient in the face of regular contestation. Such regimes can nevertheless be gradually undermined by processes of change. Mauritania's regime was thus to collapse in 2008, ushering in a period of democratic instability (N'Diaye 2009; Foster 2011), followed by the Burkinabé "revolution" in 2014 (see Loada in this volume). Chad's Idris Déby, alone in the region, managed to cling to power while maintaining some limited pretense of democracy via institutional manipulation. And at the other end of the spectrum, after the significant reforms of the early 1990s, incumbent presidents in Senegal have twice been defeated at the polls, in 2000 and 2012, meeting the definition for some scholars of a consolidated democracy.

As the contrasting stories of Mali and Burkina Faso that open this chapter suggest, intersecting the variations in the democratic dimension of politics in the region were equally significant variations in the strength and resilience of states. Strikingly, however, the continuum of the democratic dimension does not correlate in any clear way with that of state resilience. The direction of democratic trajectories does not help us predict either the weakening or the strengthening of states in the region. The effects—if any—of a quarter century of the politics of democratization on state institutions and resilience are instead messy, indirect, and highly contingent. The case study chapters in this book wade directly into these muddy waters to attempt to shed light on these complex dynamics.

A couple of important caveats are in order in attempting a comparison of the relative resilience of states in the Francophone Sahelian countries. First is the perhaps obvious but crucial observation that *all* of the states of the region are in some ways highly fragile, and hence none might be described as "resilient" in a broader comparative sense; an effort to distinguish among them on these grounds may be splitting hairs analytically. Yet we must also recognize that these fine distinctions are highly relevant to the lives of those who live in one state context rather than another. They are also relevant for policymakers attempting to foresee points of vulnerability and issues likely to destabilize political systems. A second related caveat is the recognition that regardless of their relative resiliency, all states are subject to the possibility of contingent factors and events that are very difficult if not impossible to predict, particularly in the form of external shocks or pressures, and the weak states of the Sahel particularly so. The comparison offered below cannot claim to predictive power for the future of the region.

On the eve of the current Sahelian crisis in 2011, as the Arab Spring unfolded to the north and as events played out in Libya, an effort to create a typology of the Sahelian countries according to their *democratic trajectory* over the two decades from 1991 to 2011 might reasonably have grouped the countries into three pairs, as follows:

1. *Democratic trajectories: Senegal and Mali.* Both of these countries were widely regarded as having made and sustained successful democratic transitions over two decades. In both cases, the frequent assumption was also that this trajectory had produced more resilient states. In 2010, for example, one analyst of the risk of terrorism in the region described these two as "states with considerable legitimacy" and a "balanced approach" that had proven effective in "maintaining stability while mitigating extremism" (Devlin-Foltz 2010, 5–6).

2. *Unstable democratic trajectories: Niger and Mauritania.* Despite some notable differences (Niger was an early—and frequent—transitioner, while Mauritania took much longer), the trajectory of each of these countries was characterized by coups that interrupted efforts at creating democratic systems, before undertaking new transitions.

3. *Electoral authoritarian regimes: Burkina Faso and Chad.* In both of these cases, incumbent authoritarian regimes that had earlier come to power in coups managed to hang on to power while officially launching processes of "democratization" that in fact entailed periodic elections and varying degrees of liberalization. In 2011, both still had the same president in power as in 1991, but each claimed the legitimacy of having been elected.

Table 1.1 Tracking Democracy in the Sahel: Polity IV Scores

	Senegal	Mali	Niger	Mauritania	Burkina Faso	Chad
1991	−1	Transition	Transition	−6	−5	Transition
1992	−1	7	8	−6	−5	−4
1993	−1	7	8	−6	−5	−4
1994	−1	7	8	−6	−5	−4
1995	−1	7	8	−6	−5	−4
1996	−1	7	−6	−6	−5	−2
1997	−1	6	−6	−6	−4	−2
1998	−1	6	−6	−6	−4	−2
1999	−1	6	Transition	−6	−4	−2
2000	8	6	5	−6	−3	−2
2001	8	6	5	−6	0	−2
2002	8	7	5	−6	0	−2
2003	8	7	5	−6	0	−2
2004	8	7	6	−6	0	−2
2005	8	7	6	−5	0	−2
2006	8	7	6	−3	0	−2
2007	7	7	6	4	0	−2
2008	7	7	6	−5	0	−2
2009	7	7	−3	−2	0	−2
2010	7	7	3	−2	0	−2
2011	7	7	6	−2	0	−2

Higher scores indicate higher level of democracy, where 10 is the highest possible value and −10 is the lowest possible value.

Somewhat roughly, as table 1.1 shows, a comparison of these trajectories using one the widely used indices of democratic progress by political scientists suggests the validity of these paired sets.

Considering our paired comparisons or the scores in table 1.1 from the perspective of even a few years later, however, it is quickly evident that efforts to compare states in terms of degrees of democratization tell us very little about the capacities of individual states to handle the pressures that rapidly built up in the region from 2011 to 2012. Our typology, and these numbers, in fact hide much more than they reveal about the underlying processes of state building that had occurred in any given case. And if it was possible to have any doubts about the dubious connection between apparent progress toward "democratization" and state resilience or capacity, the dramatic collapse of Mali in 2012 underlined and brought this paradox front and center. Clearly, whatever democratization had taken place in Mali—and until the day it ended many thought it was a lot—this process had not in any sense built resilient institutions. Yet on the eve of its collapse, there were actually more concerns expressed about Mali's neighbors.

In retrospect, it is possible—as various people have done—to point to weaknesses and failings of Malian politics that led to the collapse (Bergamaschi

2014; van Vliet 2014; Bleck and Michelitch 2015; Craven-Matthews and Englebert 2018). But it is important to emphasize that as the pressures on the Sahel heightened with the events of the Arab Spring, and then in particular with the fall of Qaddafi and the flows of arms and men southward into the Sahara, the loudest alarm bells were sounded about the looming threats for Niger, a country much more directly tied to Libya than Mali (not least by a shared border). In April 2011, Niger found itself under a new government tentatively attempting to establish itself following another coup in 2010, a yearlong transition, and a new round of elections. Niger seemed to many to be the weakest link in the Sahel, and hence the most likely candidate for destabilization from Libya. Yet in fact, and despite the turbulent trajectory of democratization that had led from the "Third Republic" in 1992 to the inauguration of the "Seventh Republic" in 2010, Niger's political system—under siege though it was—proved relatively resilient to the pressures.

Indeed, if we consider the concerns being expressed about possible destabilization from another source of pressure in the region—namely the conduct of national elections in the face of wide popular dissatisfaction—in the first months of 2012, Mali's prospects seemed no worse (and to many even better) than those of Senegal. Many analysts, myself among them (Villalón 2011), described potentially catastrophic scenarios for the destabilization of Senegal in 2012 as incumbent President Abdoulaye Wade attempted to stay in power via the manipulation of electoral institutions. Mali's looming elections, by contrast, elicited few concerns of this sort, even in the face of their poor preparation.

On closer analysis, not only did the politics of democratization as they played out in Mali not build state capacity, but in many ways, they seem to have ultimately been a prime *cause* of the weakening of the state. The Malian collapse must be understood as the outcome of the cumulative effects of political dynamics over an extended period of time as these added up to undermine the institutional capacity of the state. In retrospect, it is rather easy to see the significant weaknesses of president Amadou Toumani Touré's (ATT) decade-long tenure in office, from his first election in 2002 until the coup of March 22, 2012. While now taking much of the blame, it is also clear that these weaknesses themselves grew out of the failure of the first decade of Malian democracy to set in motion a process of building institutions. The collapse of Mali was long in the making, as chapter 4 by Soumano in this volume clearly demonstrates. For our purposes here, some key factors merit underlining.

"Democracy" in Mali was never built on acceptable electoral institutions. The first two national elections (1992, 1997) were deeply flawed and not consensually accepted. Given ATT's candidacy and his stature as hero of the 1991 overthrow of the authoritarian regime, the next two elections (2002,

2007) were not substantively competitive. None of these elections were even minimally acceptable at a technical level. In addition, the first decade of rule under a strong dominant party (ADEMA) did little to create institutions as political competition was displaced by cronyism and cooptation as a means of governance. The international rents from democracy aid and assistance comfortably supported a class of political actors, and elites were careful to resolve conflict or settle disputes personally and informally so as to avoid tarnishing the image that sustained financial flows. This dynamic was only strengthened from 2002 to 2012 given the de facto suspension of democratic competition under ATT in the name of "consensus politics." By contrast, massive international aid was invested in a drive to develop institutions that, at best, did not strengthen the central state, and at worst undermined it—most significantly a highly elaborate scheme for decentralization that eventually created a stunning 703 local governments. The domestic dynamics were sustained by the ambivalent role of the international community and a lack of focus on building real state capacity. In the eager search for a "success" and a democratic model for Africa, the outside world and the aid industry were at the very least complicit in a charade.

This cursory consideration of Malian state capacity in comparison to its neighbors, and a schematic look at what seems to have gone wrong in Mali, would seem to support the two main arguments I advance here. First, the apparent relative success in progress on "democratization" is not directly correlated with any progress on building state institutions. In fact, the relationship between these two dimensions is complex and multifaceted; the devil is in the details. And second, it seems clear that there has been significant variation across the region in the ways in which the processes of institutional reform in the name of democracy have affected the resilience and capacity of states.

Extending these comparative considerations of the six countries in the two decades of the democratic era, we can propose a rough schema for capturing the variations in the Sahel on the two dimensions of democracy and state building. While this represents a rather significant simplification, a categorization of the six countries along two dimensions as in table 1.2 may provide an analytic point of departure. For each of the three patterns or trajectories of democracy, we have identified earlier, the actual politics of democratization

Table 1.2 Trajectories of Sahelian Democracy Compared, 1991–2011

	Democratic	Unstable Democratic	Electoral Authoritarian
Higher institutionalization	Senegal	Niger	Burkina Faso
Lower institutionalization	Mali	Mauritania	Chad

over the two decades would seem to have had very different effects on the institutionalization of states within each pair. To be sure, the comparison here is relative and within the set of Sahelian countries; in a broader international comparison, *all* of the Sahelian states have rather low institutionalization. But there is nevertheless significant variation within the group.

One important domain in which we can see this variation is in electoral institutions. These, of course, are in themselves central to the democratic process, and their functioning (or disfunctioning) is a very likely source of the pressures that at times destabilize states. The results of an extensive qualitative examination of electoral systems in the six countries on ten distinct dimensions carried out between 2011 and 2013 strongly suggested that three countries—Senegal, Niger, and Burkina Faso—had managed to develop quite strong and well-institutionalized electoral systems, *despite* their very different positions on the scale of democratic trajectories since the early 1990s. By contrast, and despite the same variation in their apparent democratic trajectories, over the same period three of the six countries—Mali, Mauritania, and Chad—had not managed to elaborate and institutionalize robust electoral systems.[1]

The detailed discussions of individual cases in the chapters that follow collectively suggest a number of other institutional domains within which there is significant variation among pairs of countries. These might include for example, the rather surprising strengthening of judicial institutions—notably in the constitutional and political realm—over the course of Niger's unstable democratic trajectory, as compared to Mauritania. Similarly, we note a significant difference in the institutional management of civil–military relations in the two electoral authoritarian regimes of Burkina Faso and Chad, despite their common origins in military coups. One might also point to the differences in the ways in which Senegal and Mali were able to manage legislative policy conflicts pitting civil society organizations against religious movements on such contentious issues as family law reform.

While such comparisons are suggestive of the variations in state building under democratic politics in the region, we should be cautious in the conclusions to be drawn. We cannot assume that institutionalization in one domain will necessarily translate into institutionalization across the board. Variations in state resilience are certainly multidimensional, and can be relatively independent from each other. That is, we can well envisage that specific aspects of the politics of democratization in any given country might have strengthened some institutional domains, while leaving other domains weak or underdeveloped. An attempt to examine the relative effects of the politics of democratization on strengthening or weakening state institutions must nuance and disaggregate those effects across different institutional domains. As the chapters that follow suggest, besides electoral system, judiciaries, or civil–military relations, these might include legislative bodies, political parties, executive institutions, as well as the institutions for managing the realm of civil society organizations, trade unions, and the world of NGOs—all crucially important actors in the political contexts of the Sahel.

Clearly, the challenges of governance in the Sahel are among the most difficult in the world. These challenges have a long history and many structural sources, and they have also changed and been magnified over time, rather dramatically in recent years. They include economic constraints, demographic pressures, social cleavages and identity-based grievances, geographic limitations and environmental pressures, and more recently, the rise of religiously inspired insurgencies and violence. Since independence, states in the region struggled to govern this political space as they were progressively weakened by both domestic and international forces. And, starting in the 1990s, outside pressures combined with internal ones to leave few options but to attempt to restructure states in the name of democratic reforms. These reform processes have played out in different ways in each case, and crucial decisions or steps in each have had consequences that have led to new challenges, producing distinct trajectories that have cumulatively influenced the capacity of each state to manage tensions, and the resilience of its institutions in doing so. While all states in the region will remain fragile and vulnerable, it is also the case that the relative degrees of fragility and vulnerability will vary. And that too matters.

DEMOCRACY AND STATE RESILIENCE
IN THE SAHELIAN CRISIS

As the Sahelian crisis extends into a new decade, the longer-term consequences for the region remain far from clear. Nevertheless, and building on the framework proposed above, in lieu of a conclusion, I offer here six observations about some ways in which the current context of crisis is affecting political and social dynamics, and hence further reshaping the parameters likely to define the future of the region.

First, the ongoing and worsening security crisis does not seem to have significantly eroded the norm of democracy; in no case have regimes or even outside actors openly argued that the crisis demands nondemocratic "strong" governance. At the same time, the authoritarian turns of, say, Idriss Déby in Chad have been widely tolerated, no doubt due to his perceived utility in fighting the jihadi threats. To a different degree, Niger also seems to benefit from this dynamic. Yet even in Chad, Déby's manipulations of institutions are presented as "reforms" in the name of democratic politics. More broadly, the region has seen little convergence on institutional structures that might help to stabilize democratic politics. Institutions remain sources of ongoing experimentation, in a context of contestation and conflict, and with seemingly significant impact on state resilience. Recent examples abound: another constitutional referendum following debates about presidential terms in Senegal; the attempts to abolish a Senate in Mauritania, and to create one in Mali; or the establishment of a contested commission to draft a new constitution in Burkina—despite the fact that the revolution of 2014 was driven by the call to defend the existing constitution *against* attempted changes.

Second, and as I have argued above, democratic politics over the 1990s and 2000s gradually but significantly eroded the position of the small elite class that dominated the political system in each country. The consequences of this were seen, for example, in shifts in public policies, such as the abandonment of the firm commitment to francophone and secular education (Villalón and Bodian 2020), or the failures to impose the versions of family law promoted by the alliance of small civil society groups and outside donors. In the process, "politics" emerged as a pejorative term at the popular level, referring to electoral and related behavior, and often seen as the game of elites in the capital city with only tangential relevance for the vast rural areas. In the context of growing insecurity in the peripheral areas in time of crisis, this chasm between urban elite and the rural areas appears to be growing rapidly—most strikingly in Mali, but also, say, in eastern Niger or northern Burkina. There appears to be an ever-widening disconnect between political actors in Bamako hotly debating institutional reforms such as a Senate, and the concerns of the varied claimants for authority in Gao, Kidal or Mopti.

Third, and related to the point above, variations in the types of democratic institutions that were pursued in the post 1990s era, and especially variations in the forms of "decentralization" and allocation of power to local institutions, produced changing landscapes of authority in peripheral areas. The changed role of chiefs and other traditional authorities, as well as the emergence of new authorities as shaped by processes and forms of decentralization, had significant impact on central state capacity and control of peripheral regions. The consequences of these variations are now being illustrated in the varied capacity to ensure security and to control contestatory social movements. An important example might be the effects of variations in local forms of authority on either side of the Niger–Mali border, and indeed in the neighboring border zones of Burkina Faso.

Fourth, the decline in state capacity for governance of the religious sphere which resulted from the initial liberalization in the era of democratization has been further complicated by the changing religious landscape in the era of jihad. Beyond the obvious weakness of states to control jihadi activity by small violent groups, there is significant variation in the region in terms of state capacity to effectively govern and channel mass-based public religious dynamics and movements (Elischer 2019). In this context, states are engaged in ongoing experimentation, reacting to social forces over which they have limited influence. These often require efforts to balance conflicting ends: ensuring religious freedom and maintaining secularism; making concessions to "Arabophones" without undercutting the dominance of the Francophone elite; upholding democratic norms of speech and assembly while controlling radicalization. In the resulting tensions, we see a continued emergence and strengthening of new poles of religious authority, and increased religious contestation of the state and of dominant sociopolitical paradigms.

Fifth, while in comparative African terms, the Sahel has historically been a zone of relatively limited politicization of social and religious cleavages, some important fault lines have existed and, as I have argued, these were at times politicized in era of democracy. The most significant of these have been the ethno-racial divides seen in Mauritania and Saharan societies, and the related distinctions between free-born and servile groups in the hierarchical social structures of the region (Jourde 2020). In addition, in many locales ethnically linked economic distinctions between pastoralists and farmers have been sources of political and social conflict. These social identities and hierarchical cleavages have been very resilient, yet states had gradually and to varying degrees found means to manage the resulting tensions. In the context of a deepening security crisis, however, the cleavages show signs of intersecting with new political and religious dynamics, particularly in zones of tension and conflict. Thus ethnic, caste, or tribal affiliation may intersect with religious ideology in defining the cleavages pitting various jihadi groups against others, as the conflicts in the Gao or Mopti regions of Mali seem to illustrate. And across the region "farmer-herder" conflict has intensified and been transformed in the zones of jihadi activity (Benjaminsen and Ba 2019).

Finally, and centrally important, the dramatic and rapid increase in new forms of international intervention in the region has, of course, created new resources—and constraints—for governments. It has also skewed priorities for other social actors. There has thus been a profound shift in the "strategies of extraversion" in the region, that is, in the ways in which local regimes can convert "their dependent relations with the external world into domestic resources and authority" (Peiffer and Englebert 2012, 355). Across the region, the "good governance" strategy of extraversion of the democratic era has been replaced by "countering violent extremism" (CVE) as the game that governments as well as local "civil society" entrepreneurs need to play in the constant search for external patronage and support. While in some cases, the same groups and familiar activities are simply reframed as efforts at CVE rather than "development," it is also clear that the declared agendas and priorities of both governments and social groups have shifted, and that new actors have emerged or been reinforced by the changing outside concerns.

The politics of democratization, in the broad sense in which I have presented them in this chapter, have been central factors shaping the state-building process in the Sahel since the early 1990s. The variations in the institutions and in the resilience of states that have resulted are in many ways shaping their respective abilities to manage the new era of jihadism and insecurity that define the current crisis. At the same time, core elements of the crisis itself and the rise of the new politics of security have become factors reshaping the effects of politics of democratization. These new dynamics are fueling the ongoing "dialectics of democratization and stability," which Idrissa describes in the concluding chapter of this book, and which are analyzed in detail in the case studies in this volume.

NOTE

1. This research was carried out as part of the Trans-Saharan Elections project (TSEP), funded by a grant from the U.S. Department of State and involving seminars and exchanges in all six Sahelian countries as well as in the United States. I thank my collaborator in that project, Daniel A. Smith, as well as Mamadou Bodian, Ibrahim Yahaya Ibrahim, and Daniel Eizenga for their help in executing the project. For more information on TSEP and the dimensions of electoral systems in the Sahel, see the project website at: http://tsep.africa.ufl.edu/.

REFERENCES

Alidou, Ousseina. 2005. *Engaging Modernity: Muslim Women and the Politics of Agency in Post-Colonial Niger.* Madison, WI: University of Wisconsin Press.

Augis, Erin. 2005. "Dakar's Sunnite Women: The Politics of Person." In *L'Islam politique au sud du Sahara: Identités, discours et enjeux*, ed. Muriel Gomez-Perez. Paris: Karthala, 309–326.

Benjaminsen, Tor A. and Boubacar Ba. 2019. "Why Do Pastoralists in Mali Join Jihadist Groups? A Political Ecological Explanation." *The Journal of Peasant Studies, 46*(1), 1–20.

Bergamaschi, Isaline. 2014. "The Fall of a Donor Darling: The Role of Aid in Mali's Crisis." *The Journal of Modern African Studies, 52*(3), 347–378.

Bierschenk, Thomas and Jean-Pierre Olivier de Sardan, eds. 2014. *States at Work: Dynamics of African Bureaucracies.* Leiden, Netherlands: Brill.

Bleck, Jaimie and Kristin Michelitch. 2015. "The 2012 Crisis in Mali: Ongoing Empirical State Failure." *African Affairs, 114*(457), October 2015, 598–623.

Bodian, Mamadou. 2016. *The Politics of Electoral Reform in Francophone West Africa: The Birth and Change of Electoral Rules in Mali, Niger, and Senegal.* University of Florida, PhD diss., Political Science.

Bodian, Mamadou and Leonardo A. Villalón. 2020 (forthcoming). "The Democratic Struggle in the Sahel." In *The Oxford Handbook of the African Sahel*, ed. Leonardo A. Villalón. Oxford: Oxford University Press.

Bratton, Michael and Nicolas van de Walle. 1997. *Democratic Experiments in Africa: Regime Transitions in Comparative Perspective.* Cambridge: Cambridge University Press.

Brossier, Marie. 2004. "Les Débats sur la reforme du Code de la Famille au Sénégal: La Redéfinition de la laïcité comme enjeu du processus de démocratisation." Mémoire DEA Université Paris I.

Buijtenhuijs, Robert. 1993. *La Conference nationale souveraine du Tchad: Un essai d'histoire immediate.* Paris: Karthala.

Buijtenhuijs, Robert. 1998. *Transition et elections au Tchad, 1993-1997: Restauration autoritaire et recomposition politique.* Paris: Karthala.

Cabanis, André and Michel Louis Martin. 1999. *Les Constitutions d'Afrique francophone: Evolutions récentes.* Paris: Karthala.

Craven-Matthews, Catriona and Pierre Englebert. 2018. "A Potemkin State in the Sahel? The Empirical and the Fictional in Malian State Reconstruction." *African Security, 11*(1), 1–31.

Devlin-Foltz, Zachary. 2010. *Africa's Fragile States: Empowering Extremists, Exporting Terrorism.* Africa Center for Strategic Studies. Africa Security Brief No. 6, August 2010.

Eizenga, Daniel. 2018. *Managing Political Liberalization after Multiparty Elecitons: Regime Trajectories in Burkina Faso, Chad and Senegal.* PhD diss., University of Florida.

Eizenga, Daniel and Leonardo A. Villalón. 2020 (forthcoming). "The Undoing of a Semi-Authoritarian Regime: The Term Limit Debate and the Fall of Blaise Compaoré in Burkina Faso." In *The Politics of Presidential Term Limits in Africa*, ed. Jack Mangala. New York: Palgrave Macmillan.

Elischer, Sebastian. 2019. "Governing the Faithful: State Management of Salafi Activity in the Francophone Sahel." *Comparative Politics*, *51*(2), 199–218.

Fatton, Robert. 1995. "Africa in the Age of Democratization: The Civic Limitations of Civil Society." *African Studies Review*, *38*(2), 67–99.

Foster, Noel. 2011. *Mauritania: The Struggle for Democracy.* Boulder, CO: FirstForumPress, a division of Lynne Rienner Publishers, Inc.

Galilou, Abdoulaye. 2002. "The Graduates of Islamic Universities in Benin: A Modern Elite Seeking Social, Religious and Political Recognition." In *Islam in Africa*, eds. Thomas Bierschenk and Georg Stauth, 129–146. Yearbook of the Sociology of Islam 4. Münster: Lit.

Glickman, Harvey. 1995. *Ethnic Conflict and Democratization in Africa.* Atlanta: African Studies Association Press.

Harbeson, John, Donald Rothchild and Naomi Chazan, eds. 1994. *Civil Society and the State in Africa.* Boulder, CO: Lynne Rienner Publishers.

Harsch, Ernest. 2017. *Burkina Faso: A History of Power, Protest and Revolution.* London: Zed Books.

Holder, Gilles, ed. 2009. *L'Islam, nouvel espace public en Afrique.* Paris: Karthala.

Hyden, Goran and Michael Bratton, eds. 1992. *Governance and Politics in Africa.* Boulder, CO: Lynne Rienner.

Idrissa, Rahmane. 2017. *The Politics of Islam in the Sahel: Between Persuasion and Violence.* London and New York: Routledge.

Jourde, Cédric. 2020 (forthcoming). "Caste, Slavery, and Inequality in the Sahel." In *The Oxford Handbook of the African Sahel*, ed. Leonardo A. Villalón. Oxford: Oxford University Press.

Levitsky, Steven and Way, Lucan A. 2010. *Competitive Authoritarianism: Hybrid Regimes After the Cold War.* Cambridge: Cambridge University.

Lust, Ellen. 2011. "Why Now? Micro-transitions and the Arab Uprisings." *APSA-CD, the Newsletter of the Comparative Democratization Section of the American Political Science Association*, 9(3), 1, 3–8, October 2011.

Lust, Ellen and Stephen Ndegwa, eds. 2012. *Governing Africa's Changing Societies: Dynamics of Reform.* Boulder, CO: Lynne Rienner publishers.

Masquelier, Adeline. 2009. *Women and Islamic revival in a West African town.* Bloomington, IN: Indiana U Press.

N'Diaye, Boubacar. 2009. "To Mid-Wife—and Abort—a Democracy: Mauritania's Transition from Military Rule, 2005-2008." *Journal of Modern African Studies*, 47(1), 129–152.

Ould Ahmed Salem, Zekeria. 1999. "La démocratisation en Mauritanie: une illusion postcoloniale." *Politique africaine, 75*, 131–146.

Peiffer, Caryn and Pierre Englebert. 2012. "Extraversion, Vulnerability to Donors, and Political Liberalization in Africa." *African Affairs, 111*(444), 355–378.

Reynolds, Andrew and Timothy D. Sisk. 1998. "Elections and Electoral Systems: Implications for Conflict Management." In *Elections and Conflict Management in Africa*, eds. Timothy Sisk and Andrew Reynolds. Washington, DC: United States Institute of Peace Press.

Soares, Benjamin F. 2009. "The Attempt to Reform Family Law in Mali." *Die Welt Islams, 49*, 398–428.

Tayob, Abdulkader. 2007. "Muslim Publics: Contents and Discontents." *Journal for Islamic Studies, 27*, Thematic Issue: "Islam and African Muslim Publics," 1–15.

van Vliet, Martin. 2014. "Weak Legislatures, Failing MPs, and the Collapse of Democracy in Mali." *African Affairs, 113*(450), 45–66.

Villalón, Leonardo A. 1994. "Democratizing a (Quasi) Democracy: The Senegalese Elections of 1993." *African Affairs, 93*(371), 163–193.

Villalón, Leonardo A. 1996. "The Moral and the Political in African Democratization: The *code de la famille* in Niger's Troubled Transition." *Democratization, 3*(2), 41–68.

Villalón, Leonardo A. 2010. "From Argument to Negotiation: Constructing Democracies in Muslim West Africa." *Comparative Politics, 42*(4), 375–393.

Villalón, Leonardo A. 2011. "Senegal: Assessing Risks to Stability." In *The Stress-Testing African States Project*. Washington, DC: Center for Strategic and International Studies.

Villalón, Leonardo A. and Mamadou Bodian. 2020 (forthcoming). "Education, Citizenship, and National Identity in the Sahel." In *The Oxford Handbook of the African Sahel*, ed. Leonardo A. Villalón. Oxford: Oxford University Press.

Villalón, Leonardo A. and Phillip A. Huxtable, eds. 1998. *The African State at a Critical Juncture: Between Disintegration and Reconfiguration*. Boulder, CO: Lynne Rienner Publishers.

Villalón, Leonardo A. and Abdourahmane Idrissa. 2005a. "Repetitive Breakdowns and a Decade of Experimentation: Institutional Choices and Unstable Democracy in Niger." In *The Fate of Africa's Democratic Experiments: Elites and Institutions in Comparative Perspective*, eds. Leonardo A. Villalón and Peter VonDoepp. Bloomington, IN: Indiana University Press, 27–48.

Villalón, Leonardo A. and Abdourahmane Idrissa. 2005b. "The Tribulations of a Successful Transition: Institutional Dynamics and Elite Rivalry in Mali." In *The Fate of Africa's Democratic Experiments: Elites and Institutions in Comparative Perspective*, eds. Leonardo A. Villalón and Peter vonDoepp. Bloomington, IN: Indiana University Press, 49–74.

Villalón, Leonardo A. and Peter VonDoepp, eds. 2005. *The Fate of Africa's Democratic Experiments: Elites and Institutions in Comparative Perspective*. Indiana University Press.

Whitehouse, Bruce. 2017. "Political Participation and Mobilization after Mali's 2012 Coup." *African Studies Review, 60*(1), 15–35.

Chapter 2

Controlled Democratization, Institutional Reforms, and Political (In)Stability in Mauritania

Zekeria Ould Ahmed Salem

The series of political crises, coups, and aborted democratic "transitions" that have marked Mauritania since the 1990s cannot be explained as a direct consequence of the institutional reforms undertaken in the context of democratization. Rather, these phenomena must be understood in relation to the complex postcolonial trajectory of the country, in which tensions rooted in military, political, ethnic, generational, ideological, geopolitical, and even economic or international dynamics have played a role. My objective in this chapter is to demonstrate this proposition, stressing in particular that the struggles between various actors (army factions, political movements, elites and social groups, and others) over political change and control of state power have themselves been central in shaping the political substance of the "democratic" debates over state institutions. In the Mauritanian case, the various institutional dynamics that have characterized the country were initiated by military regimes that claimed to be democratizing. These regimes then struck alliances with broad sectors of the civilian elite to create coalitions that have been attempting to impose their political agenda on society and on other political actors, generally too weak to mobilize the internal or international support needed to form a meaningful opposition. In this context, reforms of the state tend to be instrumentalized by competing military, social, political, and even institutional forces. Studying the political dynamics that arise from attempts to build, maintain, reform, or destroy the country's institutions during periods of "democratization," then, may help us to better understand the consequences of such pluralist moments on the resilience of the state, and its rootedness in society.

From this perspective, I propose to construct an analytical narrative of Mauritania's institutional and political experience over some two decades—specifically from 1991 to 2014—in order to explore the ways in which a subtle interplay of alliances and oppositions developed between political, social, economic, and military forces, in view of controlling the institutions, powers, and resources of the state. In so doing, I will emphasize the profiles of the actors involved, as well as the significance, modes, and effects of the different institutional choices that were made. I will also stress, however, that even though "democratic reforms" have been the tree that has hidden the forest of fundamental political relationships on the ground, they have nevertheless had some effects—if often ambiguous and paradoxical ones—on the nature of the state and on its institutions.

This has taken place in a context in which "democratization" has emerged, rather ironically, as the benchmark reference for all debates and discussions on political institutions taking place in the country.

AN UNSTABLE COUNTRY?

The "third wave of democratization" reached Mauritania in the early 1990s in a historical context familiar to students of African politics.[1] But the experience that subsequently unfolded is the continuation of an earlier history of institutional instability, to which I now briefly turn. A "frontier-country" (Ould Ahmed Salem 2004)—both Arab and African, multiethnic, straddling the West African Sahel and the Maghreb—Mauritania was ruled by President Mokhtar Ould Daddah, following independence from France in 1960 until July 10, 1978, when a successful putsch against the "Founding President" ushered in the era of coups d'état. The Comité Militaire de Salut National (CMSN) that then took power at the time was quickly beset by a series of crises and eventually deposed its leader, Colonel Moustapha Ould Mohamed Saleck, who was replaced in 1980 by a group of officers headed by Mohamed Mahmoud Ould Ahmed Louly. The following year, Ould Ahmed Louly in turn made way for Colonel Mohamed Khouna Ould Haidalla, who ruled the country with an iron fist until his own fall, on December 12, 1984, in a coup organized by Colonel Maaouya Ould Sid'Ahmed Taya, who was to hold power for some two decades.

On April 15, 1991, Ould Taya bowed to the international and national pressures generated by the third wave, and agreed to establish a multiparty system with universal suffrage. But rather than producing change, this allowed Ould Taya to become the first Mauritanian president to be formally elected after a competitive election, in 1992. Through the subsequent decade, Mauritania went on to experience a sham democracy, with the president being reelected twice (in 1997 and 2003) under highly controversial circumstances. On August 3, 2005, a coup engineered by Colonel Ely Ould Mohammed

Vall finally put an end to Ould Taya's reign and ushered in a new period of democratic transition that lasted eighteen months, culminating in the election of former cabinet minister and retired government official Sidi Ould Cheikh Abdallahi, in March 2007. Civilian rule, however, was to be short-lived. On August 6, 2008, General Mohammed Ould Abdel Aziz seized power with the support of the parliamentary opposition and installed the Haut Conseil d'Etat militaire (HCE), with the promise of a return to a "true" civilian and democratic government. In late 2008, the HCE organized a gathering of notables, government officials, and politicians in proceedings referred to as the "Estates General of Democracy" (*États généraux de la démocratie*) and succeeded in launching an electoral process that was to culminate in a presidential election on June 6, 2009. The process ground to a halt, however, thanks to the mobilization of opponents of the coup, international pressure, and threats of a boycott from most political parties. An agreement for a "transition" was eventually signed in Dakar in May 2009, under the aegis of the international community and, on July 18 of the same year, a presidential election finally took place.

Although very competitive, the election was nevertheless won by the coup leader and then ex-general, Mohammed Ould Abdel Aziz. Ould Abdel Aziz even succeeded in getting reelected for a second five-year term in June 2014, in an election that was deemed free and fair by international observers, but that was boycotted and denounced by the main opposition parties.

In such an apparently chaotic context, the question of the reform of institutions and of the resulting impact on the capacity to withstand political shocks is far from straightforward, given that the processes of democratization are so often undercut. And yet, the era opened by the advent of political pluralism in 1991 has, haphazardly, created a new institutional landscape and a new "grammar" for power relations, where reference to democracy has become imperative. The "democratic process" has reconfigured state institutions in a new legal and formal framework that affects the behavior of political actors, even in the wake of a coup. The different stages of "democratization, Mauritanian style" are illustrative of this paradox.

FROM CONTROLLED DEMOCRATIZATION TO THE RESTORATION OF AUTHORITARIAN RULE

Mauritania underwent crucial social, institutional, and political changes under Colonel Ould Taya's twenty-year rule (1984–2005). The period may be divided into two segments: one (from 1984 to 1999) is marked by the consolidation of Ould Taya's power—chiefly through the mechanism of "democratization"—and another (2000–2005), which witnessed the decline

and abrupt fall of his regime. Democratization, launched in 1991 following the adoption (via referendum) of a pluralist constitution, established the
institutions and practices of democracy in the country: elections were held,
a parliament installed, the number of media sources multiplied. But this process was intertwined with a restoration of authoritarian rule and a series of
political crises. In this climate, institutions were created and destroyed in the
rather remarkable ways to which I now turn via a reconstruction of the key
episodes of this trajectory.

Democracy to the Rescue of Authoritarian Rule?

Following a pattern observed elsewhere,[2] Ould Taya's regime used the transition to democracy to build its own legitimacy and to solve the multifaceted
crisis it confronted in the early 1990s. This was all the more easily done given
that the government had already put in place a system of "local democracy,"
as the policy was called. In this process, municipal elections had been held
in 1986 and 1990, but in a strictly controlled process; only "independent"
lists were allowed to compete, and political parties were thus kept out of the
picture. The number of participating lists was limited, and freedom of the
press was nonexistent. However, some groups of people were able to speak
out, even if indirectly, on local and to some extent national affairs. It is in
this period that the future political leaders of the country started to mobilize
their own power bases.

This experience in "local democracy" was used by the regime to justify its
assertion that the democratic reforms undertaken later were only a continuation of an initiative it had already started, quite independently and well before
internal and international pressures for democratization swept over Africa.
The second municipal elections of 1990 were particularly important in this
regard, given that they came shortly before the "third wave" democratization
process that Mauritania was to undertake starting in April 1991. There had
been, to be sure, internal calls for political pluralism by intellectuals, union
leaders, and youth leaders in the form of collective letters,[3] but these initiatives were little known in the country or outside. And so, contrary to what
happened in other African countries, popular pressures were insignificant in
the Mauritanian democratic process. On the other hand, international pressure clearly played a significant role in this small, poor, and aid-dependent
country.

In June 1990, at the much-discussed Franco-African summit held in La
Baule, France, French President François Mitterrand made a surprisingly
strong case for democracy in Africa. This apparent shift in the African policy
of the former colonial master came in a context where the Mauritanian
regime was facing numerous internal and international problems for which a

modicum of political opening seemed to present a solution. In the late 1980s, Mauritania was caught in a severe external crisis with Senegal, complicated by an equally severe ethnic crisis in the country itself. A growing protest movement by "Negro-Mauritanians" (as members of the minority ethnic groups of the Haalpularen, Soninke, and Wolof referred to their collective identity) denounced the hegemony of the Arab-speaking majority (some 70 percent of the population). In 1986, the *Force de Libération Africaine de Mauritanie* movement was set up and was later accused by the regime of having attempted a coup the following year (Ciavolella 2010). When violence erupted in April 1989 in Senegal and Mauritania—with people in each country targeting nationals of the other country—the governments of the two countries jointly organized the repatriation of their citizens. The Mauritanian state seized the opportunity and expelled a large number of people of Haalpularen ethnicity—about eighty thousand people—into Senegal and, to a lesser extent, Mali. Moreover, in 1990, somewhere between 180 and 300 Black Negro-Mauritanian soldiers were shot to death in Mauritanian army barracks (Marchesin 1992; Jourde 2002). This humanitarian stain on the regime, which human rights organization had begun to publicize to the outside world, became a direct and personal threat to Ould Taya's legitimacy. Further adding pressure to the regime, a foreign policy characterized, in the words of Pazzanita, by an all-out "quest for external protection" had led the regime into the arms of Saddam Hussein's Iraq, including during and after its invasion of Kuwait (Pazzanita 1992). As a result, Arab donors, the main financial supporters of the Mauritanian state, withdrew from the country in 1990, as did its Western and international partners—including the European Union, France, the IMF, and the World Bank—increasingly distrustful of a more and more isolated regime.

It was in this dangerous climate that, in April 1991, Ould Taya announced that Mauritania would undertake to democratize. In July, a new constitution was adopted in a referendum with 97 percent of the vote. The military ruling body, the CMSN, decreed the establishment of freedom of the press and of association. But, given that democratization had not been forced on the military rulers by the populace, the regime also kept a tight hand on the process. Neither the new constitution nor the electoral law was subjected to a mechanism of political dialogue with other political or social actors. The regime rejected the call for a "national conference" put forward by some activists, and refused to install an independent electoral commission or even to put in place guarantees for transparency. Nevertheless, opposition parties were legally recognized, the most important one at this point being the *Union des Forces Démocratiques* (UFD). The first competitive presidential election was held on January 24, 1992. Having resigned from the military to stand as a civilian, President Ould Taya was elected with over 63 percent of the vote, while Ahmed Ould Daddah (a brother of the country's first president) received only 33 percent of the vote, leading him to denounce the results as "fraudulent." The ensuing legislative elections, organized in March, were boycotted by the opposition, leaving all seats in parliament to be taken over by the government-created *Parti Républicain, Démocratique et Social.*

Democratization thus served only to provide some legitimacy to a nondemocratic regime. Institutional reforms were either illusory from their inception, or rendered meaningless afterwards. Even the political context remained inherently authoritarian: rigid control was maintained over the judiciary, parliament (the National Assembly and the Senate) remained subordinate to the executive, the written media was heavily censored, and the audiovisual media remained under state monopoly. The instrumentalization of the new institutions was made strikingly obvious when the newly elected National Assembly, fully packed with members of the ruling party, passed an amnesty for the killing of Negro-Mauritanian troops in the 1989–1990 period. Thus, not only did democratization appear as a ploy to buttress Ould Taya's position, but it also led to whitewashing the army's accountability for its alleged crimes.

The strategy was so insolently successful that the authorities seemed simply unable to resist provoking the opposition, and thus decided that the second presidential election of the "democratic" era would be held on a highly symbolic date, December 12, 1997. This was the anniversary of Ould Taya's 1984 coup, and the choice of date signaled that the president intended to start his new term in smug triumphalism and confidence in his position. It helped that the United States and France had by now decided that Ould Taya was reputable. During a state visit to the country in 1997, just a few days before the election, French president Jacques Chirac referred to Ould Taya as "wise" (*sage*). The international financial institutions (World Bank and IMF) now worked with his government in supportive ways. The regime was thus offered a clear opportunity to launch into a full-blown restoration of authoritarian rule, and to turn its back on institutional reform (Ould Ahmed Salem 1999).

A Post-Democratic Turn?

In this way, Ould Taya managed to deflect the international pressures of the late 1980s and early 1990 through a process of sham democratization. Institutions installed in the name of democracy were only empty shells. The municipal councils, the constitutional council, parliament, and the civil service had no room for maneuver and blindly followed government instructions. The process of restoring authoritarian rule, which was paradoxically stimulated by the country's "democratic stabilization," gained new momentum with Ould Taya's predictable reelection in the December 1997 elections. At that point, the opposition was harassed or otherwise gutted through cooptation and the corruption of its leaders by the regime. Opposition figures who joined the regime—very numerous after 1992—censured their former allies, and those who did not fought each other. Despite the creation of a common opposition umbrella, the *Front des Partis d'Opposition*, the multiplication of divergent currents underlined the inexorable decomposition of the opposition. Thus, for instance, the UFD, the main opposition party in 1992, splintered within five years into no less than ten dissident formations. The regime also worked directly against the opposition. Leaders were arrested, parties were banned, with the case in point being the abolition by decree of Ahmed Ould Daddah's UFD in June 2000 and of Messaoud Ould Boulkheir's *Action pour le Changement* in 2002. Nor could civil society provide an outlet for forces for change. In that period, the national order of attorneys, *l'Ordre National des Avocats*, was one of the rare independent associations and hence an object of constant harassment by the regime (Ould Ahmed Salem 2005).

Given the lack of transparency, the opposition boycotted the presidential election of 1997, and the legislative and municipal consultations subsequently held in 2001 were an obvious travesty: despite their very visible and evident popularity, opposition parties won only one Senate seat in 1994, one National Assembly seat in 1996, and some ten municipalities in 2001.

This situation was also reflected in the country's political economy. As Ould Taya's government was "democratizing" in this singular fashion, the rents from structural adjustment and aid created opportunities for corruption and for the privatization of public companies and the financial sector. On the other hand, the regime was more careful in its handling of non-institutional political forces, including factions and key figures in the military, groups in business circles, and certain technocratic elites. Selective recruitments into the political personnel of the ruling party, often on the basis of tribal affiliations, became commonplace. Actors in the private sector directly funded electoral campaigns in exchange for public contracts. The regime aimed at creating social adherence to the idea that, under its aegis, everyone would have their share of the national cake, as the saying went. The unofficial discourse was that Western-style institutions were not good at maintaining "true distributive justice," which would draw all regions, tribes, ethnic groups, and coteries into the realm of power, each in its own turn. Frequent cabinet reshuffles, as well as new appointments at the top of "juicy"[4] public companies and services, were supposed to broadcast, somewhat insidiously, the notion that ballots were not the only routes to equality and justice. In this way, demands for democracy could be discredited and made to look less important than other, more informal governance practices that were based on tribalism and ethnic ties, and were kept alive through clientelism and corruption (Ould Ahmed Salem 2000). The submission of elites, both civilian and military, to Ould Taya, was thus constructed in this way. Democratization as an avenue for the demilitarization of power also played into Ould Taya's hand by producing a weakening of the army, with the exception of the presidential protection unit, the *Bataillon de Sécurité Présidentielle* (BASEP).

At the turn of the 2000s, the military was in crisis. The younger officers and the rank and file were marginalized in a context where the security apparatus was impoverished and starved of material and of funds. And yet it was this very policy that was to lead some factions in the army to look out for any sign of weakness in the regime and try to bring back into fashion the era of coups and military takeovers, especially given the rampant corruption in the country and the growing climate of insecurity throughout the Sahel region. Eventually, the winds blowing in that direction were to have their effect, and a new series of coups began in June 2003.

Before addressing this critical period, let us note that, over the period that was coming to an end, democratization had not really weakened institutions and had even allowed the regime to gain a firmer grip on the state's apparatus. And even if the president's personal power was preponderant, institutional decorum, electoral routine, and nominally democratic judicial channels actually led to greater state control of populations and resources. But the control was largely superficial, and the power struggles within the system built by Ould Taya—both in the political personnel and in the military—ended up getting the better of his regime. These factors, in fact, played a greater role in his downfall than did the efforts of disgruntled army officers, or those of the organizations and opposition figures spawned by the democratization process.

THE RETURN OF COUPS AND NEW ATTEMPTS AT DEMOCRATIZATION

The attempted coup of June 8, 2003, engineered by a group of officers colorfully dubbed "the Horsemen of Change" (*Les Cavaliers du Changement*), sorely tested the Ould Taya regime, and, while unsuccessful, it did initiate the process that led to the dictator's undoing.[5] The bloody attempt—which left fifteen dead—did not topple the regime, but it revealed to those in power that their system was fragile and suffered from a lack of legitimacy. It was clearly impossible to change Ould Taya's power by way of the ballot, as was confirmed by his "victory" with 85 percent of the vote in November 2003. That electoral consultation took place in a very tense political climate, and electoral fraud was more evident than ever.

The divide between the regime and public opinion was worsened by corruption, clientelism, and the growth of inequality (N'Diaye 2001), and foreign policy had become a cause of popular anger among the passionately pro-Palestinian population following the establishment of diplomatic ties with Israel in 1999. The aborted coups and the ill-defined threat of more of the same to come, the multiple trials of opposition figures including moderate Islamists, and the imprisonment of candidates before the presidential election of November 2003 all indicated that the regime had entered an era of chronic instability. The attack, in June 2005, on the far-northern military barrack of Lemgheity by an Algerian terrorist group—the Salafist Group for Preaching and Combat (GSPC), which was later to become Al-Qaeda in the Islamic Maghreb (AQIM)—stunned the country and had a significant impact in the military circles closest to the president. The attack resulted in sixteen deaths among the troops and created a panic throughout the security apparatus. It seems to have contributed to hastening the preparation of the coup that was masterminded, and eventually carried out on 3 August 2005, by the presidential security unit (BASEP), led by Colonel Mohamed Ould Abdel Aziz, and in collaboration with Colonel Ely Ould Mohamed Vall, general director of the highest police agency, the *Sûreté de l'Etat*. Vall was appointed president of a newly created *Comité Militaire pour la Justice et la Démocratie* (CMJD), which proclaimed its complete break with the "nondemocratic" situation that had prevailed until then. This new historical phase provides a clear illustration of the fundamental politics of creating and destroying institutions in Mauritania.

A Democratic Coup: The So-called "Exemplary" Transition of 2005–2007

Paradoxically, the 2005 CMJD coup opened a new era of institutional reform in view of relaunching a democracy, which, according to the coup makers, had thus far been "blocked." The new rulers' discourse was in fact radically new; having managed to carry out a bloodless takeover of power, they declared that they would hand over power to democratically elected civilians during a two-year process which they would content themselves with overseeing. Strikingly, the junta did in fact engage in a process of re-democratization and radical institutional reforms, but events that followed were to quickly put the new institutions to the test.

The CMJD's announced plans for the transition to democracy would last less than two years, and was to include the organization of new legislative and presidential elections. The members of the military council in power, as well as those of the civilian government they had put in place, were to be barred from standing as candidates. The transition included a dialogue with the political class and civil society. An interim "constitutional charter" adopted by the regime suspended the parliament elected in October 2001, but kept in place other institutions, including the High Council of the Judiciary, the Supreme Court, the High Islamic Council and the Court of Auditors. Even the Constitutional Council was preserved in view of possible consultation for guidance on constitutional issues. These various moves served to signal the will to arrange a rapid return to constitutional legality.

A political process was also set in motion to create the conditions for a successful democratization agenda. All political prisoners were released and three inter-ministerial committees were put in charge, respectively, of the "democratic transition process," "justice," and "good governance." These committees were to submit three written reports to public conferences known as National Dialogue Days (*Journées Nationales de Concertation*, JNC) that were held over three days in October 2005, in a very open fashion. These reports were the object of heated but largely constructive debates among nearly six hundred participants representing all political parties, NGOs, civil society organizations, the media, and other important sections of the populace. These JNC events were the very first structured opportunity in the country's history for free exchange of ideas between various political and social forces. After this de-facto "national conference," a formal agreement signed by all participants reflected a national consensus over various crucial issues: the electoral timetable, constitutional reforms, structural reforms required for the establishment of the rule of law, reforms of the judicial system, and the establishment of an independent electoral commission. The members of the commission were also appointed following a negotiated consensus between the political parties and civil society organizations. In the ensuing months, a population census was undertaken for electoral purposes. The transition program proceeded so smoothly and successfully that the government actually decided to reduce the initially planned transition period by four months, to nineteen months rather than two years.

Moreover, in order to defuse possible frustrations among future opposition groups, a law was passed creating a formal body to represent the democratic opposition, the *Institution de l'Opposition Démocratique*, funded by the state and to be headed by the future leader of the legally recognized parliamentary opposition. More importantly, the junta seemed intent on responding to demands for the expansion of rights, regardless of the origins of those asking for them. This led to the creation of novel institutions, including a media supervisory body, *Haute Autorité de la Presse et de l'Audiovisuel*, a human rights defense agency, *Commission Nationale des Droits de l'Homme*, and an elections monitoring institution, the *Observatoire Indépendant des Elections*. Freedom of the press experienced an unprecedented improvement during the period; no newspaper was censored in the period, a policy that proved to have an enduring legacy. Other measures attempted to promote good governance, such as the creation of a financial crime inspectorate, the *Inspection Générale d'Etat*, which quickly became feared even among civil servants quite skilled at abusing the system. It is also this zeal for institutional reforms that accounts for the state's adherence to the Extractive Industries Transparency Initiative, an important move in a country with a large mining sector that was just then starting oil production.

In the end, this transition program was strictly implemented, against all expectations. Following a referendum, a more liberal constitution was adopted, which, for instance, included a limit of two six-year terms for the presidency. A proportional representational system was adopted for the legislative elections and numerous new parties were authorized, with the exception of Islamist formations—since the constitution excluded parties based on ethnicity and religion. Islamist politicians, however, were able to compete through independent candidacies during the legislative and municipal elections of March 2006. According to all participants, those elections had been free and fair (Soares 2006). The presidential election followed a year later and, after a second-round runoff, anointed as president Sidi Mohamed Ould Cheikh Abdallahi, an independent candidate supported by some factions in the army and by a section of the former opposition to Ould Taya's regime.

All observers, national and international, warmly greeted the transparency, credibility, and technical efficiency of the series of elections. After the presidential election, Ahmed Ould Daddah, the historic leader of the UFD and principal loser in the race, even hastened to congratulate his rival, and this gesture—a rare one in the African and Arab worlds—prompted talks of "a miracle" from the international media and observers (Hamilton 2007; Zisenwine 2007).

This seemingly impeccable trajectory, however, had a hidden side. Many wondered from the beginning of the process whether Mauritania had in fact undergone a process based on "justice and democracy" or "just another coup d'état" (N'Diaye 2006). During the transition, some members of the CMJD, led by Colonel Ould Abdel Aziz, secretly worked to influence the electoral process and the entire political reconfiguration of the country, with effects that would soon prove decisive. Indeed, this hidden and unrecognized aspect of the transition was to affect Mauritania's democratic trajectory through a rather swift return of the army to power. The scenario thus provides an appropriate opportunity to study the resilience of institutions established via a democratic transition, as we shall see later.

The Hidden Face of the Miracle of a True-False Democratic Renewal

During the course of the 2005–2007 transition, a polemic had erupted over the partiality of some of the junta's members and the psychological pressure they might have exerted on some opinion leaders in favor of allowing "independent candidacies" for the legislative elections of 2006. The political parties had complained that independent (nonpartisan) candidacies had not been forbidden by law. But the colonels, led by Ould Abdel Aziz, had worked behind the scenes first to encourage independent candidacies and then to ensure the victory of Sidi Ould Cheikh Abdellahi. Presented in his campaign slogans as "the president who reassures," Abdellahi seemed to offer the military and the political establishment a guaranty of continuity against the more radical change that a victory by Ahmed Ould Daddah would have represented. It was rumored that the members of the CMJD held that they would never have overthrown their erstwhile master and protector Ould Taya only to deliver power to the very opposition groups that they had long fought, and which would be tempted in revenge to engage in a witch hunt that could potentially strike the military top brass. That fear seemed all the more justified because, under Ould Taya, the main administrative, military, and economic forces that controlled the state had consistently assisted in the harassment of the opposition and their allies. In the post-coup period, the opposition had tried to reassure the CMJD leaders over what they intended to do once elected, but they were clearly not successful.

The clandestine activism of Ould Abdel Aziz and his civilian and military friends ensured the victory of independent candidates and former members of Ould Taya's presidential majority in the parliamentary elections of November–December 2006. The presidential election would subsequently help to unite these heterogeneous but dominant forces in the future parliament, which would come to work in collaboration against the parties of the former opposition. As early as January 2007, the association of independent candidates, the *Rassemblement National des Indépendants*, and the parties of the former majority met and put in place a coalition that came out on top in elected positions, under the name *al-Mithaq* (The Pact). Al-Mithaq specified from the outset that its goal was to win a majority in the National Assembly in order to provide the necessary support for the future president; it did indeed take fifty-three out of the ninety-five seats in the new parliament. This "majority" quickly backed the "independent candidate" in the upcoming presidential elections, Sidi Ould Cheikh Abdellahi, and thus helped ensure the support of the most influential members of the political and economic class of the country, easily running ahead of the other twenty candidates, who lacked such support.

Yet, in spite of this, the results of the first round of the presidential election, on March 11, 2007, were not decisive, and it was immediately clear that the second round would not be an easy win for either of the main competitors (see table 2.1).[6]

Although disadvantaged by the great number of candidacies from the opposition, Ould Daddah hoped to profit from a vote transfer from his

Table 2.1   **First Round of Presidential Election, March 11, 2007**

Candidate	Party	Results (%)
Sidi Ould Cheikh Abdallahi	Independent	24.79
A. Ould Daddah	*Rassemblement des Forces Démocratiques* (RFD)	20.68
Zine Ould Zeidane	Independent	15.27
Messaoud Ould Boulkheir	*Alliance Populaire Progressiste* (APP)	9.8
Ibrahima Mokhtar Sarr	*Alliance pour le Justice et la Démocratie* (AJD)	7.94
Saleh Ould Hanenna	*Parti Hatem*	7.65
Mohamed Ould Maouloud	*UFP*	4.08

political allies in the second round. But in the end, only the three last losing candidates—totaling a modest 17 percent of all votes in case of a full transfer—called on their followers to support him. The former governor of the Central Bank from 2004 to 2006, Zeine Ould Zeidane, who came in third with 15 percent of the vote, and Messaoud Ould Boulkhair, fourth with almost 10 percent of the vote, formally agreed to back Sidi Ould Cheikh Abdellahi in the second round. As a result Ould Cheikh Abdellahi won unequivocally, with 52.85 percent of the vote.

Immediately following his election, President Abdellahi implemented the deal with Ould Zeidane and Ould Boulkhair, which had been signed between the two electoral rounds, and which had simple but consequential stipulations: Ould Zeidane had demanded to be appointed prime minister, while Ould Boulkheir, already a deputy, had requested four key ministerial positions and—more importantly—that Sidi Ould Cheikh Abdellahi instruct the parliamentary majority to elect Ould Boulkheir as chairman (presiding officer) of the National Assembly. The Mauritanian parliament came thus to be headed by the leader of one of its smaller parties, and four cabinet positions were filled by Messaoud Ould Boulkheir's followers. By thus providing an important role in his system to Messaoud Ould Boulkheir, a historic leader of the Haratines (Arabic-speaking former slaves) and an inflexible and uncompromising opponent of Ould Taya, as well as a stern critic of the CMJD during the transition period, the new head of state secured a huge symbolic victory and undermined the traditional opposition, led by Ould Daddah.

Yet, the implementation of these second-round agreements was strongly resented by members of the parliamentary majority, who felt slighted by their lack of representation in the new government. The opposition itself was also disappointed, given the fact that it held almost 48 percent of the seats in the legislature and had hoped to be included in a broad-based, inclusive government (*gouvernement d'ouverture*), which the opposition had argued would have been well-advised at that exceptional and difficult period in the country's history. Far from fading, this initial disagreement would eventually negatively affect the functioning of the new political system, to the point of producing a dramatic and brutal upending of the new Mauritanian "democratic miracle."

Life and Death of a Frail Little Democracy

Subsequent political developments confirmed—sometimes violently—that the democratic regime put in place at the end of the "CMJD transition" did not produce legitimate institutions. Some members of the opposition even termed the new political dispensation "illegitimate." The new president's candidacy had been at the minimum "assisted" by Colonel Ould Abdel Aziz, an influential member of the CMJD; Prime Minister Zeine Ould Zeidane had come in third in the ballot (15 percent), very far behind the man who had arrived in second place. Messaoud Ould Boulkheir, the leader of the *Alliance Populaire Progressiste* (APP), was elected president of the National Assembly even though his party had only five deputies, including him. He had arrived in this position thanks to the new government's arm-twisting of the deputies from the majority. The newly elected president formed a government open only to two groups: first, the members of his own campaign staff, and second, the representatives of his second-round allies. It was clear that the country was being governed by a motley assortment of people who had been brought together only following a series of compromises and electoral deals, and this fact had as a consequence their very fragmented hold on state power. The creation of a new party in early 2008, the National Pact for Democracy and Development (PNDD-ADIL), which intended to unify the president's support base, did not succeed in curbing the growing challenges from within his own camp. But, more importantly, the president was, in the end, a victim of the informal help he had received from a section of the old political establishment, and especially from certain military officers.

Right after his election, Ould Cheikh Abdellahi had entrusted his personal security and the direction of the army staff to Colonel Mohamed Ould Abdel Aziz and to his faithful associate, Colonel Mohamed Ould Ghazouani, both of whom he had freshly promoted to the rank of general. In this way, he had given them unchallenged authority within the military, an institution in which they each had so far held only modest positions. The new generals quickly set about to extend their powers, and to remind Ould Cheikh Abdellahi of the debt he owed them. This deep and central misunderstanding was to produce the crisis which, step by step, would lead to the demise of this frail little democracy (Foster 2010).

The new head of state soon roused the hostility of his parliamentary majority and his backers in the army. These two poles, supported—oddly enough—by unlucky rival Ahmed Ould Daddah, ended up forming a strange alliance in order to create difficulties for the country's "first-ever democratically elected president," as Ould Cheikh Abdellahi was proclaimed by his supporters. In this way, these groups orchestrated an instrumentalization of state institutions and perpetuated complex constitutional and legal debates. Barely a year into his election, and given a lack of rapid economic and social results which could have translated into popular support, Ould Cheikh Abdallahi's position was considerably weakened. On a purely political level, he did indeed begin to implement some of his key promises, including organizing the return of the Negro-Mauritanians who had been deported to Senegal in 1989, and adopting an antislavery law. And even though all of the candidates had pledged to take such measures during the presidential campaign, it does not appear that conservative Mauritanians, and especially those from the dominant Arab-Berber community, appreciated these political gestures. Some among them were even vocally critical about the fact that Ould Cheikh Abdellahi had apologized in the name of the state for the injustices suffered by Negro-Mauritanian minorities under Ould Taya.

In this context, army generals and those who were disappointed in the new dispensation—including many among the new deputies—came together to try to destabilize the government. Even some of the parties that had been close to him began to call for the resignation of the government and even of the president, whom they accused of corruption and nepotism. A looming institutional crisis began to take shape. In this context, a group of twenty-five deputies and twenty-three senators resigned from the newly created presidential party, the PNDD-ADIL, asserting their intention to set up a different political formation. The group, which had ties with a number of military officers covertly led by General Ould Abdel Aziz, grew steadily and even managed to get Ahmed Ould Daddah's RFD party involved in its maneuvering. The latter was only too happy to create difficulties for a regime, which, from his point of view, had robbed the country of a much-needed political change.

In May 2008, the dismissal of Prime Minister Ould Zeidane and his cabinet and the formation of a new government headed by Yahya Ould Ahmed al-Waghf marked a new stage in the impending crisis. The move was supposed to expand the ruling majority to newer opposition parties. While Ahmed Ould Daddah's RFD declined to enter the new cabinet, two Islamists from the Tawassoul party agreed to participate, together with the *Union des Forces du Progrès* (UFP), which was awarded three ministries. But this government was also marked by the comeback of barons of the Ould Taya regime, including numerous former cabinet ministers. These various appointments only further angered the deputies of the majority, who were not consulted and who thus decided to move to a new gear in their activism against the president.

Accordingly, on June 30, 2008, thirty-nine deputies from what was still known as the "presidential majority" put forth a motion of no confidence. In the face of the pressure thus brought to bear on his government, the head of state threatened, during a formal speech, to dissolve the National Assembly. At this point, the generals led by Ould Abdel Aziz and the representatives of the opposition no longer made any secret of their goal to find a way to put a "constitutional" end to Ould Cheikh Abdallahi's presidency. Yet no one expected the decision the president would make in the early hours of 6 August 2008: the issuance of a decree removing General Mohamed Ould Abdel Aziz from his position as the head of presidential security, and General Mohamed Ould Ghazouani from his tenure as army chief of staff. As soon as the national radio broke the news, the dismissed generals unceremoniously seized power and arrested the "most legitimate president in the country's history," in the terminology of his followers. The generals proceeded to suspend the constitution and install a *Haut Conseil Militaire d'État* under the chairmanship of General Ould Abdel Aziz, the newly designated head of state (Ciavolella 2009).

The new strongman claimed that he only wished to defend democracy against the derailment of the goals of the transition that had taken place under Ould Cheikh Abdellahi. Despite support from a majority of deputies to the National Assembly as well as a portion of the opposition and civil society, the coup was condemned by the international community and in national opinion. This new stage in Mauritania's evolution is important for the argument of this chapter not only because it triggered—for the first time—significant popular and political resistance to a coup in the country but also because it led to unprecedented debates on constitutional procedures for resolving the crisis, on the legitimacy of institutions, and on the legitimacy and stability of the state itself.

BACK TO SQUARE ONE: PUTSCHES, STATE FRAGILITY, AND INSTITUTIONAL DEBATES

The new junta eventually received the support of both chambers of parliament. It also got the backing of the main opposition party, the RFD, led by Ould Daddah, who declared that he "understood" the reasons for the coup. Other key sectors of society, as well as key economic and intellectual elites, followed suit. The coup thus quickly became a fait accompli, and the return of Sidi Ould Cheikh Abdellahi to power was deemed impossible—and unacceptable—by the junta. Unofficial accusations blamed the former president for having entered into open conflict with the very parliamentary majority that had carried him to power, as well as for having distanced himself from the high-ranking officers who had promoted democracy in Mauritania and personally supported his candidacy to the presidency. The failings for which he was blamed were said to reflect the desperate moves of a leader who had failed at governing the country. The toppled head of state was said to have disregarded the rules of democratic governance and to have created a system of corruption, leaving economic development and the country's security in shambles. The junta thus denied that it had carried out a coup, but rather that it had merely proceeded to introduce a "rectification," and it declared that it was ready to restart the democratic process which had been compromised by the former president. The new government similarly explained that the events in Mauritania did not amount to a "coup d'état" but were only an "institutional crisis" that thus only required a constitutional settlement. As a matter of fact, General Ould Abdel Aziz pointed out that no other constitutional institution had been suspended. As General Aziz maintained, only the presidency had become vacant and was to be filled as soon as possible, through democratic means.

The coup was, of course, immediately condemned by the international community. The United States, for one, recalled its ambassador. Ould Cheikh Abdellahi's followers quickly organized a democracy defense group, the *Front National de Défense de la Démocratie* (FNDD), under the leadership of the Chairman of the National Assembly Messaoud Ould Boulkheir. They launched a variety of anti-coup activities, mostly demonstrations, sometimes riotous, calling for the restoration of democracy, the reinstatement of the deposed president, and the return of the army to their barracks. While the junta rejected these demands, it rarely repressed the demonstrations, and when it did, it went about it halfheartedly. Daily life carried on as usual during this unusual, indeed odd, political interlude. Neither freedom of movement nor of expression were curtailed, and public services functioned normally. Even on the day of the coup, people went about their business as if nothing was happening, including in the area around the presidential palace. The international community was robust in its response, with France's condemnation somewhat more measured than that of the United States. In conformity with the provisions in its charter that reject "non-constitutional regime changes," the African Union duly suspended Mauritania and established a "goodwill" mission tasked with bringing the country back to constitutional normalcy.

In the face of this political stalemate, there were numerous proposals in the country for a way out of the crisis. The junta itself proposed the convening of an "Estates General of Democracy," as early as September, and in which all political and social forces in the country would convene and decide upon a new transition agenda. The idea was rejected not only by the FNDD but also by Ould Daddah's RFD, which had eventually joined that alliance after breaking with the junta. Despite these objections, the military rulers nevertheless went ahead and unilaterally organized the "Estates General of Democracy." During its sessions, various parties and groups talked of their respective support (or lack of opposition) to the coup. The most important result of these discussions—which were given broad media attention—was the adoption of a timetable for the presidential election, to be held on June 6, 2009.

But, Ould Boulkheir, the main organizer of FNDD and president of the National Assembly, made a counter-proposition. In his view, while a new presidential election needed to be held, it should be preceded by a reinstatement of Sidi Ould Cheikh Abdellahi as president, with the stipulation that he could not be a candidate, but would supervise the electoral consultation. The proposal was seen as a major concession by someone who had been such a fierce opponent of the coup, and it had the advantage of seeing the deposed head of state as part of the solution, not the problem, in the ongoing political crisis. In these conditions, even to his closest allies it no longer appeared that the continuation of the president's term was an absolute requirement. But Ould Cheikh Abdallahi, who was released in November 2008 and enjoyed the support of international partners, categorically rejected this proposal put forth by his friends, demanding a reversal of the coup and his own reinstatement. These steps, in his view, were a prerequisite for entering into any dialogue with the junta and its backers.

The junta, on the other hand, was intent on legitimizing the regime of Ould Abdel Aziz through a presidential election. As such, the leader of the coup resigned from the army and declared his candidacy in the unilaterally scheduled election, with several other puppet candidates rounded up to act as foils. A full and formal electoral campaign was launched, including several tours of the country to engineer consent and sway the population. Eventually, however, the campaign was suspended thanks to an international mediation effort spearheaded by Senegal and France, and in May 2009, all of the actors in the Mauritanian crisis gathered for talks in Dakar.

Toward a Resolution of the Constitutional Crisis?

On June 2, 2009, the three main poles of Mauritania's political life—the FNDD supporters of Abdellahi, Ould Daddah's RFD party, and the HCE military junta—signed a rather original kind of political agreement, whereby President Sidi Ould Cheikh Abdellahi was to temporarily resume power in the course of a formal ceremony, at which he would then announce his resignation in view of contributing to the resolution of the country's institutional crisis. With the deposed president's agreement to this "sacrifice," it thus became possible to organize a succession that, even if forced, would still be constitutional. In this way, the presidency was declared formally "vacant," and the position was filled by the Chairman of the Senate in accordance with constitution provisions for such a situation. A transitional government that included all parties that had been represented in the Dakar negotiations was put in place, under the same prime minister, appointed a year earlier by the coup leaders. This caretaker government was charged with running the country during the weeks leading up to the presidential election, scheduled to take place on July 18. Contrary to expectations, the Dakar agreement also permitted Ould Abdel Aziz's candidacy, provided only that the general resign from the army. An electoral commission staffed with the representatives of the participating parties was also established.

The two-month transition was uneventful. However, it soon became clear, thanks to both the presence of a prime minister he had appointed and, more importantly, to the unstinting support of the army and other security forces, where he had placed faithful friends, that Ould Abdel Aziz remained the real power holder during that period. It came as no surprise that despite the presence of eighteen candidates—including Ely Ould Mohamed Vall, the leader of the first transition, in 2007—by then ex-general Mohamed Ould Abdel Aziz won the election on July 18, 2009, prevailing in the first round with 53 percent of the vote.

The former coup maker, having removed the "first-ever democratically elected president" (with his erstwhile support, to boot) thus became the legally elected president of the Islamic Republic of Mauritania. The country thus reverted to "constitutional normalcy," in the words of the African Union. But if this highly unlikely scenario had in fact played out, it was owing to a number of internal and external political factors that merit noting. Indeed, if the international community (the African Union, the European Union, and France) had sponsored this rather odd resolution, it was in part because they very much wanted to reestablish a strong and stable power system in the country, given a regional context where the terrorism of AQIM seemed to be taking hold. In December 2006, five members of a family of French tourists were murdered in Mauritania, and a few months later, in February 2007, a French nightclub in downtown Nouakchott was attacked by men armed with automatic weapons. Mohamed Ould Abdel Aziz exploited this situation to present himself as the strong leader that this small country needed to fight terrorism, noting that Ould Cheikh Abdallahi had in fact authorized an Islamist party, Tawassoul, and had shown himself to be "ineffective" in the struggle against radicalism (Ould Ahmed Salem 2013). General Aziz and his colleagues in the HCE thus managed to impose, at the international level, the notion that they were the best guaranty against state collapse in Mauritania.

The propaganda was so successful that the new regime in Nouakchott could allow itself to take risky international initiatives that were popular at home, such as breaking diplomatic relations with Israel, whose ambassador was expelled from the country. This act allowed Ould Abdel Aziz to present himself as a nationalist leader in the eyes of most Mauritanians, themselves largely supportive of the Palestinian cause. Moreover, during his first year at the helm of the state following his coup, the new president presented himself as the "president of the poor," whose only wish was to "fight corruption" and ensure economic justice. He thus took a series of measures that were broadly welcomed on the street: reinforcement of security and safety conditions, subsidies for primary commodities, "emergency plans" for underprivileged neighborhoods in urban areas, building of roads, aggressive initiatives against the mismanagement of public funds, and more. This strikingly new discourse for Mauritania, and his tireless energy in undertaking actions to secure popular support, proved highly effective (Ciavolella 2009; Foster 2010).

These same factors had helped Ould Abdel Aziz not only to obtain favorable terms in the Dakar agreement but also to turn all of the provisions of the agreement to his own advantage. His clear victory in the election of July 18, 2009, left those who opposed the coup in an awkward position, and allowed him to legitimate his actions in the eyes of the international community. This, however, did not end the institutional debates in the country, but only created new bases for engaging in them, as subsequent events were to show.

A New Military Democracy: Mauritania under Abdel Aziz

Paradoxically, the "constitutional" success of Ould Abdel Aziz's coup placed the question of the continuation of institutional reforms in Mauritania center stage. Throughout the coup period, and even after a political settlement had been reached, political actors had continued with passionate debates about the shape of political institutions and the means of strengthening democracy. This situation was certainly the result of the combined effects of the democratization struggles of 2005–2007 and of the relatively open political struggles that had characterized the rule of Ould Cheikh Abdallahi.

After a short period of hesitation, the coup opponents conceded the newfound legitimacy of the former coup maker. The main opposition parties, the APP of Messaoud Ould Boulkheir and the RFD of Ahmed Ould Daddah, accepted that the election was free and fair, while the Islamists of the Tawassoul party (Thurston 2012), who had been among the more strident members of the FNDD, even joined forces with the new president's party, the Union Pour la République (UPR), for the senatorial elections of November 2009. Very soon thereafter, the opposition parties called for the implementation of the provisions in the Dakar agreement that related to dialogue. They pointed in particular to clauses that recommended political partnerships in the exercise of power, early legislative elections, and other similar provisions intended to strengthen national unity, reconciliation, and stability. The government and the opposition, however, did not interpret these rather vague articles of the Dakar agreement in the same way. For Ould Abdel Aziz, the people had chosen their rulers in a democratic manner that had been accepted by everyone. His regime, therefore, was under no obligation to partner with its opponents to run the country. The fundamental law of the country, in his view, was the constitution, not an agreement intended only to put an end to a circumstantial political gridlock.

Opposition parties, on the other hand, presented the provisions for dialogue in the Dakar agreement as the second component of a two-part political settlement that needed to be implemented for the new regime to be fully legitimate. This divergence of views led to a heated debate that dominated much of Mauritanian political life and structured political relationships through the end of 2011. Eventually, President Abdel Aziz agreed to organize an official dialogue process between the party he had created (UPR) and the opposition, in view of adopting institutional reforms concerning the electoral code, the status of the military, the strengthening of democracy, gender equality, and other issues. But a section of the opposition—including UFP, Tawassoul, RFD and the small *Hatem* party—demanded certain prerequisites before any discussion with the government. They argued that dialogue was only possible if the regime showed its "goodwill" by recruiting people from the opposition into top public offices, taking immediate steps to liberalize the press, and agreeing that the president himself, and not just officials from his party, would take part in debates.

President Abdel Aziz rejected this, retorting that a dialogue such as the one envisioned was not a personal matter, but rather an institutional process. And moreover, from his point of view, the prerequisite measures formulated by opposition parties had to be thought of as potential outcomes of dialogue, and not something that must precede it. In the end, another section of the opposition, including the APP led by Messaoud Ould Boukheir, still at the helm of the National Assembly, agreed to take part in the dialogue process. They were joined by the *Alliance pour la Justice et la Démocratie*, led by Ibrahima Mokhtar Sarr (the losing candidate in the presidential elections of 2007 and of 2009), by the Arab nationalist party, *Sawab*, and by the *Wiam* party, recently founded by a former Ould Taya cabinet minister, Boydiel Ould Houmeid.

Thus, in late November 2011, the process was formally launched and while non-inclusive, it was also presented as an open and frank dialogue "without taboos." Despite being boycotted by the main parliamentary opposition, this dialogue yielded an agreement that substantially modified the institutions and legal texts of the country through a wide-ranging set of key measures. These included: a change in the constitution acknowledging the country's cultural diversity and recognizing ethnic minority languages, the adoption of new constitutional clauses intended to uproot the traditional practice of slavery—now defined as a "crime against humanity"—an increase in the number of members of the Constitutional Council appointed by the chairmen of the

National Assembly and of the Senate, a reform in the composition and duties of the High Council of the Judiciary, increased access to the public media by the opposition, the liberalization of audiovisual media, the preservation of the institution of a formal gathering of opposition parties, *Opposition démocratique*, with a leader who henceforth had to be an elected official (such as a mayor, deputy, or senator) instead of merely a party boss, access to all information of financial, economic, or social significance for the opposition (with the exception of classified data), the establishment of a permanent Independent National Electoral Commission (CENI) in lieu of the temporary body that had been in existence up to that point, an increase in the numbers of deputies—climbing from 95 to 145, with the goal of better representing the country's regions—the banning of the practice whereby politicians would change their party allegiance after having been elected (*nomadisme politique*), and the oversight of parliamentary work by outside organizations. Importantly, the dialogue also led to an agreement to pass a law that would ban military personnel from engaging in political activities, and to adopt a constitutional amendment forbidding coups d'état (although with a clause specifying that the perpetrators of previous coups could not be prosecuted). A monitoring committee was subsequently put in place to oversee the implementation of this broad agreement.

The conditions under which the negotiations were held did not appear favorable to the effective implementation of the agreement that had been reached. Those in the opposition who had boycotted the process dismissed the agreement as a "worthless outcome," since in their opinion the president would be unable to implement it. It is noteworthy that these debates were taking place as the Arab Spring was in full swing, notably in North Africa, and the more radical opponents of Abdel Aziz were hoping to take advantage of this context. They had, for instance, launched a campaign with the catchphrase "Aziz get lost!" (*Aziz dégage!*), echoing the successful Tunisian call for Ben Ali to relinquish power (*Ben Ali dégage!*). But Ould Abdel Aziz chose not to use repression against the demonstrations, strikes, and other actions intended to destabilize his government through 2012 and 2013. He contented himself instead with declaring that the Arab Spring posed no threat to him since he had been in power for only two years, and that Mauritania was governed by the rule of law, of which he was the defender.

Despite this tense context, the agreement that was reached during the dialogue process with the moderate opposition was in fact applied. Between 2011 and 2013, the constitution was amended, the media fully liberalized, and a permanent electoral commission established. But the government rejected the call—from the RFD and the UFP—for a new set of discussions in which they would now be willing to take part, a refusal which added to the tense political climate that would continue into 2013 and 2014.

By calling for the president's departure in a series of public events and demonstrations throughout 2012, the opposition contributed to plunging the country back into a crisis of confidence between opposition and government. The liberalization of the mass media (including radio and television), the consolidation of freedom of expression and of the press, and the growing stability of the country, all failed to prevent a radicalization of the opposition. While the *Aziz dégage!* campaign was not successful in its main goal, it still clearly played a strong role in the postponement of the legislative elections that had been initially scheduled for November 2012. The government claimed, however, that the delay was due only to technical procedures intended to ensure completion of a civil registry operation underway, laying the groundwork for the upcoming election. The very fact of the delay was used by the government to underline its earnestness in all matters of safety, security, and institutional stability.

A serious and unexpected incident, however, soon rekindled the debate on institutional problems. On October 13, 2012, President Abdel Aziz suffered a gunshot wound while traveling in the desert. This was officially presented as an error, an instance of "friendly fire" in which an army officer mistakenly aimed at the president's car. The president was secretly flown to France for medical care, and while there, he remained completely silent on the specifics of what had happened and on the state of his health. The opposition seized the opportunity and vigorously proclaimed the need, under such circumstances, to declare the presidency vacant and to launch a new transition process. Though rather clever, the maneuver failed miserably. All indications are that the regime enjoyed real stability and was supported by institutions that continued to operate despite the widespread concern of the ruling elites and the populace. One might also attribute this outcome to the army's loyalty to Abdel Aziz. On November 24, 2012, the president made a triumphal return to Mauritania, with large crowds welcoming his arrival at Nouakchott's airport.

Initially rather flustered and discredited, the opposition soon resumed its aggressive stance of protest and contestation. Throughout 2013, the opposition tried to gain a foothold in power by demanding the installation of a transitional government mandated to "solve" what they continued to label the country's "political crisis." In response, Abdel Aziz persistently repeated that there was no institutional crisis in the country at all, and that the only path to power was through the ballot box. In the context of this "dialogue of the deaf," legislative and municipal elections were held in November 2013. The so-called radical opposition, grouped as the *Coalition de l'Opposition Démocratique* (COD), boycotted the polls, while the "moderate opposition," assembled as the *Coalition pour une Alternance Pacifique*, agreed to participate. In the end, the presidential UPR and its allies won an absolute majority in the National Assembly, and the June 2014 presidential election, which took place under similar conditions, easily gave Abdel Aziz a second (and officially final) term, with 85 percent of the vote.

One might have thought that the coup of August 6, 2008, would put a definitive end to Mauritania's democratization process. In fact, this has not proven to be really or entirely the case. The Dakar agreement and its implementation actually kept the democratic debate alive, despite the fact that it also allowed the regime produced by the coup to gain legitimacy through the ballot box. Open debate, freedom of the media—now accessible to the opposition—and institutional reforms did not seem to weaken the new government. In fact, these changes seem to have even provided it with new political resources. Rather, the relationship between ruling party and opposition seems instead to have spurred further discussion on legitimacy, the rule of law, institutions and their control, and the expansion of individual liberties.

The end result is a very active political life in Mauritania, with an opposition that is extremely dynamic, which leads the government to feel compelled to justify its policy choices, to play by institutional rules, and to abide by democratic norms of conduct. Besides the social and political claims occasionally put forward by the opposition, the entire society seems to take to the streets from time to time, and demonstrations in front of the presidential palace have become something of a tradition in the country. The president claims that this situation is "evidence of a healthy democracy" and should never be repressed, though the limits of this tolerance are unclear. At the same time, this situation puts significant stress on the social and political fault lines in Mauritania. The regional context of terrorism in the Sahel further threatens the country's stability and may endanger the Mauritanian democratic process and its rather chaotic management. Internally, larger social problems may add to the political cacophony, possibly worsening the structural fractures of Mauritanian society, or putting them to the test. Such social questions are becoming ever more pressing, especially with regard to the status of the large community of people of slave origin—the Haratines—or of resource-sharing between the Arabic-speaking and the Black African ethnic groups. Far from being relegated to the background, these issues appear to piggyback on a social context that tends to be shaped by them. Even if Mauritania's democratization has not markedly weakened nor strengthened institutions, it also does not seem to have achieved normalcy, and it remains dependent on larger political and social processes.

CONCLUSION

Democratization is a historical sequence that does not appear to have direct and exclusive effects on state consolidation, given that it is only one component in a cluster of very diverse political factors and dynamics. The state in Mauritania was neither strengthened nor weakened by the political debates and institutional reforms undertaken in the framework of democratization, rather, it was simply reconfigured. The stability of institutions remains contingent on non-institutional factors and, in particular, on very complex political processes. Democratization is not the key factor in the strength or weakness of institutions, since the politics of establishing or reforming institutions in the name of political pluralism played no direct role in strengthening or weakening the state.

I have attempted to demonstrate this through an account of the postcolonial twists and turns of institution formation in Mauritania. In this sense, we have seen that it was during the second stage of military rule, in the late 1990s, that the democratic imperative increasingly gained ground. A silent and latent crisis led the ruling regime to carry out a kind of easing of authoritarianism rather than to undertake a formal and genuine democratization process, and this was driven not by an erosion of the regime's legitimacy, but rather by the effort to quell both external and internal threats to its survival. The process of "controlled democratization" helped the regime to maintain itself by other means, and to strengthen its power over state institutions. In the process, change from above, generally through a coup that is then most often stamped as "democratic," has become a constant in Mauritanian political life.

In such a context, the relative importance of debates on institutions and the democratic agenda in the public sphere can be seen as a potent cover for the perpetuation of authoritarian practice. The 2005–2007 transition and the aftermath of the 2008 coup demonstrate this point well. These episodes show that the institutional dimension of political reform did not depend solely on democratization dynamics, but was very much contingent on the objective political conditions in which the democratic opening and the establishment of pluralism took place. In this view, state institutions have neither been really weak, nor particularly strong. On the other hand, ruling regimes have always maintained a high degree of control over society, public order, and institutions themselves. In other words, institutions were never strong in their own right, but were effective to the extent that they were successfully instrumentalized by regimes that were often authoritarian in outlook. That is why resistance to the numerous coups that have occurred in the country has been exceptional and, on the whole, limited to the experience of 2008–2009.

Yet, I do not wish to suggest that institutions were always mere playthings of power-driven actors. Institutions based on the principles of representative democracy were, and remain, effective constraints on the actions of these actors, since they impart structure and organization to regimes. For instance, if freedom of association and freedom of speech have seen quite stunning growth in Mauritania in the troubled 2005–2008 period, it has been due to the fact that, despite being coup makers, the new leaders were intent on appropriating the label of democracy, and its attendant reforms. Precisely because they wanted to instrumentalize institutions, they needed to take them seriously. At this juncture, it therefore appears that the political future of state building and institutional consolidation in Mauritania has come to depend on an answer to the question of knowing just how far this ambiguous strategy can work, and in particular whether it can withstand the growing pressure of social actors who are increasingly aware of their rights and of the real implications of democratization, without weakening its institutions. Such an answer will not come from the institutions themselves, but rather from the emerging power struggles between political and social actors, and the extent of resources that each will have at their disposal at a given historical moment.

NOTES

1. The phrase is of course Huntington's (1991). For African discussions, see Bratton and van de Walle (1997) and Villalón and Von Doepp (2005).
2. See the chapters on Burkina Faso and Chad in this volume.
3. The so-called *Lettre des 25 personnalités* and the *Lettres des 125 cadres*, see Pazzanita (1992).
4. Strikingly, the term "juicy" (*juteux*), which was initially used to designate those Ministerial departments endowed with significant financial resources, was to become a widespread euphemism in the local press.
5. The coup instigators fled the country and established a rebel movement in exile, before attempting another coup in August 2004 in which they were quickly arrested and imprisoned.
6. As in other Francophone Sahelian countries, presidential elections require an absolute majority for a first-round win; in the event that no candidate gets over 50 percent of the vote, a second round is required between the top two.

REFERENCES

Bratton, Michael and Nicholas Van de Walle. 1997. *Democratic Experiments in Africa: Regime Transitions in Comparative Perspective*. Cambridge: Cambridge University Press.
Ciavolella, Riccardo and Marion Fresia. 2009. "Entre démocratisation et coups d'État." *Politique africaine* 114(2): 5–23.
Ciavolella, Riccardo. 2010. *Les Peuls et l'Etat en Mauritanie. Une anthropologie des marges*. Paris: Karthala.
Foster, Noel. 2010. *Mauritania: The Struggle for Democracy*. Boulder: First Forum Press.

Hamilton, Richard. 2007. "Profile: Mauritania's New Leader." *BBC News,* March 26. Accessed June 3, 2015. http://news.bbc.co.uk/2/hi/africa/6496441.stm.

Huntington, Samuel P. 1993. *The Third Wave: Democratization in the Late Twentieth Century.* Norman: University of Oklahoma Press.

Jourde, Cédric. 2002. "Dramas of Ethnic Elites Accommodation: The Authoritarian Restoration in Mauritania." PhD diss., University of Wisconsin–Madison.

Marchesin, Philippe. 1992. *Tribus, ethnies et pouvoir en Mauritanie.* Paris: Karthala.

N'Diaye, Boubacar. 2001. "Mauritania's Stalled Democratization." *Journal of Democracy* 12(3): 88–95.

N'Diaye, Boubacar. 2006. "Mauritania, August 2005: Justice and Democracy, or Just Another Coup?" *African Affairs* 105(420): 421–441.

Ould Ahmed Salem, Zekeria. 1999. "La démocratisation en Mauritanie: une illusion postcoloniale." *Politique africaine* 75: 131–146.

Ould Ahmed Salem, Zekeria. 2000. "Prêcher dans le désert: l'univers du Cheikh Sidi Yahya et l'évolution de l'islamisme mauritanien." *Islam et sociétés au sud du Sahara* 14–15: 5–40.

Ould Ahmed Salem, Zekeria. 2004. *Les trajectoires d'un État frontière. Espaces, évolution politique et transformations sociales en Mauritanie.* Dakar: Codesria.

Ould Ahmed Salem, Zekeria. 2013. *Prêcher dans le désert. Islam politique et changement social en Mauritanie.* Paris: Karthala.

Pazzanita, Anthony G. 1992. "Mauritania's Foreign Policy: The Search for Protection." *The Journal of Modern African Studies* 30(2): 281–304.

Soares, Benjamin F. 2006. "Islam in Mali in the Neoliberal Era." *African Affairs* 105(418): 77–95.

Thurston, Alexander. 2012. *Mauritania's Islamists.* Carnegie Endowment for International Peace. March: 1–24.

Villalón, Leonardo A. and Peter VonDoepp, eds. 2005. *The Fate of Africa's Democratic Experiments: Elites and Institutions.* Bloomington: Indiana University Press.

Zisenwine, Daniel. 2007. "Mauritania's Democratic Transition: A Regional Model for Political Reform?" *Journal of North African Studies* 12(4): 481–499.

Chapter 3

Constitutional Revisions, Democracy, and the State in Senegal

Ismaïla Madior Fall

A rare case among African countries, not only has Senegal never experienced a military coup, but it also embarked on an ongoing experiment with multiparty democracy much earlier than any of its neighbors. Going against the single-party trend in Africa, Senegalese opposition political parties were explicitly legalized in the mid-1970s, and participated in the contested elections of 1978. Strikingly, competitive elections have been organized on a regular and uninterrupted cycle since then. In March 2000, Senegalese democracy passed a crucial developmental milestone when political power changed hands via the ballot box for the first time. Twelve years later, the robust health of Senegalese democracy was to be confirmed by a second successful turnover of power, as another incumbent president was defeated at the polls. Its pioneering role in the development of democracy in Africa and the achievement of three peaceful transfers of political power have frequently earned Senegal flattering labels as an "exceptional case" and a "showcase for democracy" or, more recently, as a "model for the region," in the words of then-U.S. secretary of state Hillary Clinton during a speech delivered in Dakar in 2012.[1] While the reality of Senegal's democratic progress is undeniable, a full appraisal does require some nuancing of these glowing assessments, as this chapter undertakes to demonstrate via an analysis of the politics of constitutional revision in the country.

Since independence in 1960, constitutional revision has been part and parcel not only of democratization but also of the state-building process in Senegal. Despite frequent constitutional reforms, the political regime has remained stable (Sy 2009; Fall 2009). Senegalese constitutional instability has not posed any serious challenge to the normal operation of state institutions and—unlike in many other African countries—the frequent reforms have not been accompanied by political instability. Babacar Kanté, an early student of the phenomenon, described Senegal as an "instance of political continuity and constitutional instability" (1989, 145). To be sure, the Senegalese have distinguished themselves at manipulating their constitution for some rather unorthodox purposes, notably as what might be called a "therapeutic" treatment for political crisis (Kanté 1989, 158). This was in fact one of the secrets behind Senegal's long-standing reputation as a model democracy in Africa (Moudjib 1978), an assessment that some observers have consequently preferred to qualify with labels such as "semi-democracy" or "quasi-democracy" (Coulon 1990; Villalón 1994; see also Coulon 1992; Copans 2000).

When longtime opposition leader Abdoulaye Wade defeated the twenty-year incumbent President Abdou Diouf in 2000, the transition in power was quickly followed by the adoption of a completely new constitution, with great fanfare, on January 22, 2001 (Sy 2005). This new constitution was heralded as a definitive text that would remedy the various perceived shortcomings that had led to constant change.[2] And yet, rather quickly, the practice of frequent constitutional revision was revived, calling into question the vaunted "maturity" of Senegalese democracy, and suggesting potential dangers ahead. Within a few years, the very document that had been put forward as a final resolution to the country's earlier institutional problems, and that was intended to provide a stable legal foundation, was itself revised no fewer than fifteen times. The continued—and indeed accelerated—recurrence of constitutional revisions during President Abdoulaye Wade's two terms in office (from 2000 to 2012), and the consequences of this dynamic for both democracy and the state in Senegal is thus a complex topic in need of critical examination.

As a starting point, such an analysis requires that we note the conventional distinction (among Francophone constitutional law specialists) between "formal" and "material" constitutions (*constitution formelle* and *constitution matérielle*), and between "rigid" and "flexible" ones (*constitution rigide* and *constitution souple*). In Senegal, a choice had been made in favor of a rigid constitution, with its corollary requirement that constitutional revisions have to be made through a different and more challenging process than that leading to the adoption of ordinary laws. The empirical record, however, shows that the legal constraints put in place—intended to protect the permanence and stability of the constitution—have proven inefficient or, at the least, non-dissuasive. Throughout Senegalese history, the various governments that have succeeded each other at the helm of the state have undertaken often disruptive and opportunistic modifications of the constitution. From a purely quantitative viewpoint, Senegal would probably rank as a record holder in terms of frequency of resorting to constitutional revision, earning the country a reputation of constitutional instability that was actually significantly enhanced after the accession of Abdoulaye Wade to power in 2000.

What critical factors and political conditions have motivated this pattern of frequent constitutional revision in Senegal? Two dimensions of the problem can be highlighted to emphasize the particularity of the Senegalese pattern—and therefore its interest. First, the processes of revision itself, which should normally be defined by a routine set of actions that are clearly specified in the constitution, have instead turned out to be flexible and malleable, and thus to be easily amenable to unorthodox manipulations. Second, an analysis of the objectives, the logic, and the stakes of specific constitutional revisions, and their relationship to the dynamics of democratization (Gazibo 1998; Morlino 2001), reveals paradoxes and ambiguities in which, in terms of entrenching democracy, the best rubs shoulders with the worst: revisions appear to sometimes strengthen (consolidate) the democratization of the political regime, and at other times, to weaken (deconsolidate) it.

From a procedural point of view, given the provision for revision specified in Article 103 of the 2001 constitution, and in its general orientation, the Senegalese constitution appears in every way to be a rigid one. Analysis of the actual practices of constitutional change, however, indicates an ease and malleability of the procedures of revision made possible by a series of legal provisions, and further magnified by nonlegal (political) considerations. An example of that malleability is in the risks of fraud that result from the use of the technique of referendum to introduce certain revisions.

On a more substantive level, the analysis of the content of revisions points to the need to make a distinction between revisions that either consolidate or deconsolidate democracy (Fall 2012). In the first case, the revision is more or less consensual, and, at the very least, noncontroversial. Substantially progressive, it improves the working of institutions and/or signals progress in the practice of democracy and the rule of law. The second type of revision is regressive and controversial. Its real motivations have very little to do with care for institutional development, democratic rationality, or progress in the rule of law.

One could object that this distinction between consolidating and deconsolidating constitutional revisions lacks objectivity. First, the promoters of any given revision will naturally tend to reject the critique that their proposed amendment has any deconsolidating character, and this would, in any case, never be apparent in the official rationale for a revision. Second, there are cases of revision that combine both consolidating and deconsolidating elements. For analytical reasons, I choose to avoid the creation of intermediary categories and instead consider that, with respect to criteria for democratization,[3] a dualistic perspective—in which revisions are considered either consolidating or deconsolidating—entails a better, more elegant approach. In each case, all that is required is to parse the clues embedded in the general nature of the new provisions. If that general nature seems, on the whole, to

be promoting democracy, then the new law belongs in the category of consolidating measures; and if, on the contrary, the envisioned reform appears
substantially regressive, it falls into the category of deconsolidating revision. It is to be noted, in any case, that such deconsolidating revisions, even
when they are rejected by public opinion, face no significant obstacles (certainly not that of constitutional review) since the relevant institutions would
generally deem that they lack the legal authority to assess these revisions.

In this study, then, I subject constitutional revision in Senegal to critical
analysis through the observation of two central features: procedural malleability, and substantial ambivalence.

THE MALLEABILITY OF PROCEDURES FOR REVISION

Senegal's constitution stipulates the procedure for revision in a single article,
and the specificity of that procedure allows us to classify it as a "rigid constitution." Nevertheless, there is a fair level of malleability in the actual practice
of revision, resulting from a combination of factors which together create
incentives that tempt actors to the fraudulent use of referendums.

A Mixture of Explanatory Factors

Constitutional revision is readily undertaken in Senegal. This observation is
justified first from the constitutional provisions themselves, but also from a
set of factors rooted in the actual workings of the political system. The malleability of the procedure is above all an outcome of the legal norms, but it is
also intensified by factors that lay beyond the legal framework.

The legal procedure is framed in a standard formula regularly found in the
constitutions of Francophone African countries, appearing as Article 103 of
the Senegalese constitution of January 22, 2001:

> The power to initiate a revision lies concurrently with the president of the
> Republic and the deputies. The prime minister may propose a revision of the
> Constitution to the president of the Republic. The bill or proposition of revision
> of the Constitution is adopted in accordance with the procedure stipulated in
> Article 71. The revision is finalized after having been approved in a referendum.
> However, the bill (or proposition) is not subject to a referendum if the president
> of the Republic decides to submit it for approval to the National Assembly. In
> that case, the bill or the proposition is approved only when it receives a three-
> fifths majority vote in the National Assembly.[4]

The procedure for constitutional revision underlines the political and
institutional preeminence of the president of the Republic, a characteristic

of the type of presidentialism which Senegal has adopted since 1963 (Hesseling 1985). While the law puts the president and the deputies on an equal footing in terms of the power to initiate revisions, in practice there has been a near-exclusive domination of the process by the former. This is to be expected, since the president of the Republic defines and leads the nation's policy, which includes constitutional policy. The monopoly the president has acquired over initiating constitutional legislation is only one component of his control over legislation in general. Nevertheless, the deputies are authorized to submit a bill of constitutional revision, a point that merits some discussion. First, the law does not specify whether this is an individual or collective power of deputies, and what has tended to happen is that deputies have acted on an individual basis. But the status of deputy in fact leaves them little room to maneuver to initiate legislation and, as a result, since 1960, there have been very few constitutional reforms initiated by deputies. On the contrary, there have been many more revision bills fielded by the government than by deputies in the legislature, which again highlights the president's near-monopoly on revision prerogatives. This is a consequence of the ways in which primacy of the presidency marks the workings of Senegal's political institutions (Aivo 2007, 515). Thus, out of thirty-eight constitutional revisions in fact implemented between 1960 and 2009, only five originated in the legislature. Moreover, an examination of the motivations behind these rare deputy-fielded bills shows that they were actually inspired by the power of the executive.

All high-impact revisions that affect the state of democracy and the rule of law—or the balance of the regime—are in fact pushed through by the president of the Republic. Conversely, minor revisions—especially if they are somewhat controversial—may be entrusted to deputies. The final approval of the revision could happen either as a result of a referendum or at the National Assembly, as is stated in Article 103 of the constitution. The wording of the article suggests that the norm for the approval of a constitutional revision is intended to be by referendum, but leaves open the option that the president could choose to go through the National Assembly, which leaves the final political decision on the process in presidential hands. As it turns out, it is the exceptional process—legislative approval—that has consistently been the preferred method of validation, rather than the expected norm—referendum approval. Only in the case of a revision affecting presidential terms of office is a referendum mandatory. In all other cases, convenience and the political certainty of passing the revision have de facto made the legislative method of approval the normal way. In the period 1960–2009, only one revision—in February 1970—was made through a referendum.

The procedure for revision specified in Senegal's constitution thus appears easy to implement, especially given certain characteristics of Senegalese

political practice. Prominent among these is the most common configuration of party representation in parliament, with an overwhelmingly dominant
majority. This fact is primarily a consequence of the electoral or voting
system for legislative elections. Until 2016, Senegal's 150 deputies were
elected, for five years, by direct universal suffrage in a mixed electoral system: ninety deputies were elected through a first-past-the-post list system
(in the forty-five *départements*) and the sixty remaining seats elected via a
national proportional representation system.[5] In general, candidates in these
elections are members of political parties (or of coalition of parties), the only
forms of organization that have demonstrated their capacity to actually win
representation.[6]

The mixed nature of the voting system for legislative elections has two
consequences: on the one hand, the first-past-the-post simple majority system governing the election of deputies at the *département* level allows the
one party with the broadest national base—or, increasingly, a coalition of
parties—to easily achieve a majority in parliament. On the other hand, the
election of sixty deputies in a proportional voting system guarantees representation in the National Assembly even for the smaller parties. While
mixed in principle, the distribution of parliamentary seats produced by
this voting system greatly favors the emergence of a strong majority party.
Thus, a party that earns less than (but close to) 50 percent of the vote—as
was the case in 1998 and 2001—can easily translate that into an enhanced
majority of over 60 percent of seats, which is all that is needed to revise
the constitution. Thus, for example, in the legislative elections of 1998, the
Socialist Party (PS) earned 93 seats out of 140 with 616,847 votes, against
its main rival, the Senegalese Democratic Party (PDS), which obtained only
23 seats with 470,270 votes. With a difference of just 146,547 votes, the PS
thus secured a crushing majority in parliament—notwithstanding the fact
that the combined total number of votes received by all the other seventeen
party lists (811,847) well exceeded the total won by the PS. There were
similar results in the legislative elections of 2001 following the presidential
transition. The "*Sopi*" coalition[7] supporting Abdoulaye Wade won almost
75 percent of the seats (89 out of 120) with less than 50 percent of the vote
(931,617 out of 1,878,846). Here, too, the lists that opposed the coalition
collectively received more votes, but secured only the thirty-one remaining
seats, slightly more than 25 percent. In the legislative elections of 2007, the
parliamentary dominance of Abdoulaye Wade's ruling PDS party (131 seats
out of 150) was even further magnified by a boycott from the more important
opposition parties.

Such results—in particular those of 1998 and 2001—very clearly show that
parliamentary representation is rarely an accurate reflection of the real power
balance in the political arena. A conventionally bipartisan party system,

along with the voting system used in the parliamentary ballot, promotes the dominance of a party (or a coalition of parties), and gives a simple qualified majority a means of constitutional revision. The combined effects of the voting system for legislative elections (first-past-the-post for the majority of deputies) dramatically increase the chances that the presidential party can dominate the legislature, and that this majority would obediently back his initiatives. In this context, then, the ease with which Senegal's constitution has historically been modified is unsurprising. The executive faces no procedural concerns when initiating such a process, and one could suggest that the key factor behind parliamentary acquiescence to revisions that occur as a matter of course is the abuse of majority rule (Open Society Initiative for West Africa 2010, 8). To the extent that the voting system largely determines the outcomes of an election, a reform of this process might be needed to improve balance and stability in Senegal's struggling democracy (Dahl 2001, 125). At any rate, one outcome of the present dispensation is that, in contrast to what happens elsewhere (where projects of constitutional revision quite frequently die in the legislature) Senegal's National Assembly has never rejected one since independence, and parliamentary opposition has never been strong enough to block a project supported by the majority.

THE TEMPTATION TO FRAUD:
REFERENDUM AND THE REVISION PROCESS

The tendency to revise the constitution is so established in Senegal that the rules defining the process may be instrumentalized or flouted through actions that amount to fraud. In the first instance, we might speak of a fraudulent use of referenda, and in the second instance, a fraudulent evasion of that same procedure.

The Fraudulent Use of Referendum

The historic political transition following the elections of 2000 was at first seen as incomplete in Senegal, since the democratic replacement of one president by another was not immediately accompanied by a parallel change in the legislative majority. Given changes introduced in the early 1990s, the next legislative elections after the presidential election of 2000 were not due until three years later.[8] Thus, Senegal entered an unprecedented situation of "cohabitation"—a president and a parliamentary majority from two different parties. The president could not dissolve the National Assembly to seek new elections and a more favorable majority, since the law gave him that right only if the National Assembly tried to censure the government. In such

a context, it was not easy for him to implement the constitutional reforms
he had pledged during the campaign, and there was little chance that his
political adversaries would help him push them through in the legislature.
Any revision that would have to go through that route would be precarious,
since it would be perceived to threaten the interest of those who were in
the position to either "pass" it—in case of a parliamentary process of revision—or "adopt" it, in case of a referendum. Given the evident political risks
and the juridical impasse, the president chose to forego the revision process
altogether, and instead to propose a new constitution, to be prepared by an
appointed commission placed under his close supervision.

—When the new constitution was ready, the president used Article 46 of
the abrogated one to adopt it without going through the National Assembly.
Wade argued that that article gave him leeway to adopt new laws, upon a
proposition from the prime minister and after consultation with the presidents
of the National Assembly and of the Constitutional Council. It was not clear,
however, that by "new laws," the article meant to include a new constitution.
Most specialists would disagree that a bill could carry the burden of a full
constitutional text, and Senegal's constitutional traditions did not support
such an interpretive leap. As critics pointed out: How could it be possible
for an article in a constitution to terminate the same constitution? This was
plainly illogical, they argued; a constitution cannot incorporate a mechanism
for its own demise, nor provide the weapons for its own destruction. The truth
of the matter is that, in this respect, the constitutional replacement process of
2000 was made possible for political reasons in the wake of Wade's election,
and without a basis in legal procedures.

In fact, an analysis of the rationale of the commission that had reformed
Senegal's constitution in 1963 shows that Article 46 had been written for
use in case of "particularly important issues" (*questions particulièrement
importantes*) (Hesseling 1985, 43). The idea was to shield the procedure in
Article 46 from measures taken to revise the constitution, or any plebiscitary
measures that could do damage to democracy. As a matter of fact, Article
46 had never been used to revise the constitution, let alone to submit a new
constitution for the approval of the people. An argument was advanced that
the procedure was valid since a notice from the Constitutional Council had
endorsed it[9] but this was unconvincing to many for at least two reasons: first,
the notice from the council was only a legal opinion that could not authorize,
forbid, nor provide any cover for an irregularity; second, the notice appeared
to go beyond the jurisdiction of the council, which would normally be limited
to providing legal advice for a referendum on an ordinary bill, not a constitutional text. By contrast the action was taken as if the constitution and the law
are one and the same. Thus, in response to a letter from the president dated 3
November 2000, the council wrote that

> given that Article 46 of the Constitution states that the President of the Republic may, upon a proposition from the prime minister, and after consultation with the president of the Assemblies and a notice from the Constitutional Council, present any bill in a referendum . . . [and] that the President of the Republic holds, through that constitutional statement, the right to initiate a referendum without distinction as to whether the object is an ordinary law or a constitutional text,

the referendum was within the line of due process.[10]

In the dominant interpretations of Francophone jurisprudence, the procedure specified in Article 46 of the constitution of 1963 could not be used even for a minor constitutional revision, let alone the full adoption of a new constitution (Liet-Veaux 1943, 116–151; see also Ouedraogo 2001, 111). This was the case because the process for constitutional revision was specifically provided for in an article (89), under the title, "On Revision." The interpretation used to justify the adoption of the new constitution was thus strongly criticized among jurists, leading the well-known Senegalese constitutionalist El Hadj Mbodj to describe it as "constitutional fraud." "The method used," he wrote, "hijacked the procedure in a way that threatens the very foundations of the rule of law, which demands that the state, as it is subject to law, must correctly interpret and apply the letter and the spirit of legal norms, avoiding setting precedents or customs that would undermine the bases of democracy" (Mbodj 2007). Given the political context and lack of any clear directives from the writers of the constitution, a procedure intended for an ordinary legislative referendum was used for a full revision of the constitution. This misappropriation of the legal procedure was, a few years later, followed by another politically motivated action in the opposite direction, when a referendum was sidestepped in an instance when it was legally required.

Fraudulent Evasion of a Referendum

The issue of both the length and number of presidential terms is a major political debate in Africa. It is very often the main point of contention in constitutional debates and reform movements (Cabanis and Martin 2007, 349). In spite of its reputation as a democracy, Senegal is not an exception to this; presidential terms have been the object of several revisions concerning both the length of the term and the number of terms allowed. In reaction to past events, the constitution of 2001 included several important innovations, notably the introduction of a set of clauses intended to shield presidential terms from attempts at revision. To discourage these, revision was made contingent on a referendum, itself a politically heavy and onerous procedure. The choice of this method is rooted in Senegal's political history. The idea, clearly, was to stabilize the presidential term to a period of time that corresponds to modern democratic norms. In the past, the length of the prescribed presidential term in the constitution had been quite unstable (Gautron and Rougevin-Baville 1977, 62): seven years between 1960 and 1963, four years between 1963 and 1967, five years between 1967 and 1992 and then changed to seven years between 1992 and 2001.[11] After the change of government in 2000, the enthusiasm for democratic norms at the time led to a consensus that the presidential term in Senegal should be decisively limited to five years, corresponding to the general practice in other Franco-phone African countries. It was high time, many argued, to do away with the longer terms that had been much decried, and finally abandoned, in France as well as in many African countries. The five-year term appeared ideally modern: neither too long, like the seven-year term, nor too short, like the four-year term of the U.S. presidency. Moreover, the same Article 27 of the new constitution limited a president to two consecutive terms. Given the history of this debate in Senegal, where term limits had been adopted and rescinded several times,[12] the writers of the 2001 constitution included a clause whereby any change related to the number of presidential terms had to be effected through a referendum.

Given the essential objective of giving legal stability to presidential term limits, it seemed very clear that it was not legally possible to interpret Article 27 in a way that would avoid the requirement of a referendum. Nevertheless, following his reelection in 2007 and in an increasingly tense political climate, the Wade regime proposed a rather stretched interpretation of the term limit clause, arguing that it applied to the limit of two terms but not to the five-year term length. This interpretation was highly criticized, and in fact two prominent members of the committee that had written the constitution, Babacar Gueye and Demba Sy, publicly denounced it and argued that there was absolutely no ambiguity in the clause and that the article could only be changed via referendum.[13] Nevertheless, the government of Abdoulaye Wade, relying on its strong parliamentary majority, pushed through the constitutional revision to reinstate the old seven-year term in October 2008.[14]

THE AMBIVALENT CONTENT OF REVISIONS

The politics of constitutional revision in Senegal are complex and ambiguous. There are times when revisions are widely accepted by a range of political actors and by public opinion, as they are seen to add value to democracy. These are what I term "consolidating revisions." At other times, however, revision has been used self-servingly by political actors with the power to impose them, and have thus threatened the progress of politics and democratic consolidation. These are what I will deem "de-consolidating revisions."

Consolidating Revisions

Democratization in Senegal's political system has often occurred through a demand and response mechanism, whereby governments revised the constitution to accommodate shifts and aspirations within the system. When that has happened, the rule of law and democracy have become further entrenched, and the functioning of institutions has been enhanced (Sy 2009).

A Deepening of Democracy

In theory, constitutional revisions aim to improve the practice of democracy. In Senegal, political liberalization and democratic openings did in fact flow from a series of constitutional revisions. Thus, political pluralism was introduced and further strengthened by successive revisions promoted by Presidents Léopold Sédar Senghor and Abdou Diouf in the 1970s and 1980s. In 1975, after years of single-party rule, Senghor pushed through a constitutional bill that recognized the existence of three modern "ideological currents," each of which was mandated to correspond to a political party: The "democratic socialist" ideology was adopted by Senghor's own *Parti Socialiste* (PS); the "liberal democratic" position was allocated to the *Parti Démocratique Sénégalais* (PDS) of future president Abdoulaye Wade; and the "Marxist-Leninist or Communist," label was assumed by a third, smaller party, the *Parti Africain de l'Independence* (PAI) (Fatton 1987). Whatever the real reasons behind the reform, it was a crucial step in starting a process leading to the development of multiparty democracy in Senegal—an exception in sub-Saharan Africa at the time. New political voices were heard and elections became competitive, with the prominent participation of leaders from opposition parties (Tine 2002). This first revision was followed by an additional revision, in December 1978, that recognized a fourth party, representative of conservatism (Gounelle 1981, 44).

There were further consolidating revisions under President Abdou Diouf, who assumed office in 1981 following the resignation of President Senghor (Diop and Diouf 1990). The most famous of these was the implementation of a complete multiparty system in May 1981, following a revision that removed the cap on the number of authorized parties, and abandoned the notion of prescribed "ideological currents" (Nzouankeu 1981, 323). This revision signaled the political willingness of the ruling party to accept opposition—including the fact that opposition parties would seek to conquer state power instead of merely "contributing" to it. In the exhilarating era that followed this opening, the number of recognized political parties quickly grew from four to fourteen, genuinely opening up the political arena to competition for power (Sylla 1987, 231).

A decade later Diouf was also to oversee and promote another major consolidating revision, in October 1991. This was the outcome of an extensive period of political dialogue and negotiation that was triggered by the heated disputes that followed the presidential and legislative elections of 1988 (Young and Kanté 1992). To avert a similar crisis for the upcoming 1993 elections, Diouf appointed a commission to propose a new electoral code. All political parties were involved in writing the code, and the reforms were consensually adopted by the National Assembly.[15] Among other things, they lowered the voting age to eighteen, reintroduced presidential term limits, and required an absolute majority for the election of the president, obliging a second round run-off if no candidate received over 50 percent in the first round. These reforms undoubtedly entailed major democratic progress for Senegal, and were widely hailed as such. Unfortunately, however, they did not prevent the results of the presidential and legislative elections of 1993 from being bitterly disputed when the incumbent president and his party were declared the victors (Villalón 1994). Even if the revision had qualitatively improved the nature of the electoral system in Senegal, it did not—nor could it—eradicate an entrenched culture of fraud nor the extraordinary advantages of incumbency in this context (Cruise O'Brien et al. 2002, 110). Senegal was still a few years away from a level of transparency that could "normalize" its democratic electoral processes.

Under President Wade, consolidating reforms were to become less frequent, and indeed a few years after his election, Wade initiated revisions that could hardly be considered to contribute to the progress of democracy. Nevertheless, Wade's tenure included several consolidating revisions to note (Sy 2009, 171). First, Wade promulgated the new constitution of 2001 itself, which ensured new rights and freedoms, and restored some of the consensual democratic gains of the early 1990s that had been eroded by controversial constitutional revisions in 1998. In November 2006, a bill was introduced to extend voting rights to members of the military and paramilitary, who had previously been barred from voting. The move appeared suspicious to some, and lent itself to some controversy, but in fact can be considered a genuine consolidating revision in terms of expansion of democracy. This revision also points to the fact that Wade's consolidating revisions all belong in the category of what might be called the "social constitution," as opposed to the "political constitution," to use the classical distinction made by Maurice Hauriou. Thus, through measures which have produced what Stéphane Bolle has labeled a "feminization of the constitution,"[16] Wade modified several articles so as to promote equal access of women and men to elected offices and to nominated positions at both national and local levels (Sindjoun 2009, 430). Styling himself as a "militant for the cause of women," or "the gender advocate," Wade thus laid the constitutional foundations for gender equity in politics, leading to significant changes in Senegal's public life, first in the legislative elections of 2012, and then in the local elections of 2014.

Another revision under Wade's tenure that should be considered consolidating, of a more "international" nature, was adopted in August 2008. It introduced the legal categories of the crime of genocide, and of crimes against humanity, both undertaken in view of the then-pending trial of the former president of Chad, Hissène Habré.

Improvements in the Functioning of Institutions

Most of the revisions that scholars view as consolidating of democracy are essentially technical in nature, and they aim to improve the functioning of institutions. Senegal's original constitution was modified as early as 1961, barely a year after independence. In November 1961, a revision conferred on the president the right to dissolve the legislature. This was done to offset the legislature's right of censure, and thus avert the emergence of a regime dominated by the National Assembly. This was the only real revision of Senegal's first constitution. A year later, in December 1962, the country found itself in the grips of an extremely serious political crisis that pitted President Senghor against the president of the council, Mamadou Dia (Hesseling 1985). Events progressed rapidly, and Dia was eventually removed and imprisoned, where he was to remain until 1974. In the wake of the crisis, Senghor managed to pass a bill proposing a new constitution to be adopted via a referendum. Importantly, the new text—the constitution of March 7, 1963—established an entirely new political regime, one which designated the president of the Republic as the sole head of the executive branch. This revision, however, was not initially designed as a permanent change to the Senegalese system, but was rather adopted in emergency conditions and intended to solve the immediate crisis and shore up Senghor's leadership, in a context where he had to confront the sound constitutional arguments of his main rival. The right to dissolution was reintroduced in the constitution by a revision in June 1967, with the provision that when it was used, the president must also resign, and new presidential and legislative elections must be organized (Gautron 1967, 5).

But, the most important Senghor-era reform that targeted the functioning of institutions was the one adopted in 1970. In light of its thoroughness, some scholars, such as Seydou Madani Sy, consider it to have changed the constitution entirely (Sy 2009, 81). That revision had many motivations, including reacting to the great social crisis of May 1968; the need to protect the head of the state by providing him with a political fuse (that is, a prime minister); President Senghor's desire to eventually end his political career and therefore to manage his own succession; and the quest for a political system that would truly work for Senegal as he understood it. Therefore, the law that was passed in February 1970 was a full overhaul of the constitution, and it introduced some remarkable innovations, namely: presidential term limits (two five-year terms), "parliamentarization" of the presidential regime with the creation of a government headed by a prime minister, restoration of some reciprocity between the executive and the legislative powers, with the accountability of the government to parliament, along with the executive right to dissolve parliament.

The reform was ultimately to give definitive shape to the institutional architecture of Senegal's political system, although it was called into question just thirteen years later. In 1983, in a bid to assert his own power and to prove that he was not merely Senghor's handpicked heir, President Diouf completely reversed these reforms by ending the semi-presidential system put in place in 1970 and re-instituting a presidential regime (Nzouankeu 1981, 323). This was to be a short-lived measure, however, and in April 1991 the new consensual revisions reinstated the Senghorian-style reformed constitution, complete with a prime minister and mixed parliamentary and presidential features. Diouf's reformist zeal would also extend to the administration of justice, which had up to that point been shielded from the unending constitutional twists and turns. Highly specialized courts were created in the name of an efficient differentiation of the justice system: a Constitutional Council to be in charge of constitutional review of laws and international agreements as well as of electoral litigation, a Council of State that was to be in charge of judicial review and advising on public administration, and as in France, a *Cour de Cassation* for appeals. This series of judicial reforms was completed—under Diouf—with a final revision establishing the General Accounting Office, in January 1999.

Wade also promoted and oversaw a judicial reform nine years later by creating, in August 2008, a Supreme Court which replaced the *Cour de Cassation* and the Council of State and combined their responsibilities. One objective of Wade's reform was to rationalize the system—that is, to end Diouf-era specialization, thought to be too costly both financially and in terms of staff and personnel.

In sum, one can conclude that in Senegal, constitutional revisions over the years have largely also used to ensure a better functioning of state institutions in ways that generally improved the quality of Senegalese democracy. Early modifications accelerated the country's embrace of democracy, and successive revisions had the effect of entrenching democratization. Between 1960 to 2015, out of thirty-eight constitutional revisions a majority (twenty-three) could be considered to have contributed to consolidating democracy, many through improving the functioning of state institutions. Unfortunately, however, this progress was uneven, and at times weakened or even reversed by the significant number of what might be considered "deconsolidating revisions."

Deconsolidating Revisions

The first identifiable sign of deconsolidating revisions is that they are controversial, since the governmental majority that initiates them does not try to reach a consensus with other political forces. The process is typically carried out unilaterally, ignoring both the denunciation of opposition parties and public protest. To analyze them, it is important to also examine the passivity that judges charged with constitutional review often display in this regard.

Deconsolidating constitutional revisions also display, in the way they are implemented as well as in their content, at least two underlying logics or motivations: one based on the desire to hold on to power, and the other inspired by a desire to settle scores. Both of these agendas obviously damage the credibility of the law and its supporting institutions. The desire to hold onto power is behind numerous constitutional revisions throughout the political history of Senegal. More constitutionally prudent than his successors, President Senghor was the author of only one revision by which he aimed to maintain his hold on power: the elimination of presidential term limits in 1970, along with the introduction of a succession clause that was eventually to enable a transfer of power to Abdou Diouf upon Senghor's mid-term resignation in December 1980. These constitutional maneuverings were defended as part of the necessity of ensuring the "continuity of power" in a fledgling state, an argument that found some justification (Chéramy 1976, 19). However, given that the political regime provided for succession through universal suffrage in case the president's office became vacant, this was criticized by many and might well be considered a deconsolidating revision. Thus, even though it was praised as a "fine instance in which an African head of state organized his succession" in a way that "led to a quiet transition in Senegal" (Kanté 1989, 158), the revision represented a serious departure from the democratic norm of allowing the people to choose their leaders.

In the same vein, after eighteen years in office, and faced with the real threat of a loss at the polls, Abdou Diouf gave in to the temptation to try to rework the constitution to ensure his hold on power. In October 1998, he thus proposed a revision bill that put an end to the principle of the so-called *quart bloquant*, that is, the rule that in addition to the majority a candidate needed to receive the vote of one-fourth of registered voters to get elected in the first round of a presidential ballot. The bill also removed the two-term limit for the presidency, despite the fact that this was one of the consensual compromises of the debates in 1991 that were considered as "democratic gains," and were in principle irrevocable. The move was justly interpreted—both by the opposition and by public opinion—as calling into question the founding rules of the game of Senegal's renovated democracy, and something that established the bases for a potential "president for life" (Guèye 2009, 18). With the same

motivation of guaranteeing his hold on power, Diouf promoted a law that created a Senate in March 1998, of which he would name a significant number
of members. The new chamber allowed him to expand his clientelistic base
in preparation for future electoral confrontations.

Tellingly, an analysis of the ultimate effects of Diouf's manipulative revisions of 1998 reveals an interesting and important paradox. Although in
form and process the revisions were clearly deconsolidating constitutional
measures, their real effect in terms of the political mobilization and subsequent events which followed could be said to have been one of promoting a
consolidation of democracy. That is, they did not prevent Senegal's political system from in fact achieving—between 1998 and 2000—qualitative
progress toward genuine democracy, culminating in Diouf's defeat and an
unprecedented electoral transition of power in the elections of April 2000.

The elections of 2000 were certainly historic in that they resulted in a
change of the head of state, but they did not create a new political culture.
The new president in fact quickly adopted the established political practices
of his predecessors. Thus, in the same way that Diouf had created the Senate
as a means of providing sinecures to his political allies, Wade established a
Conseil de la république pour les affaires économiques et sociales (Council
of the Republic for Economic and Social Affairs), later replaced by the *Conseil économique et social* (Economic and Social Council). Having initially
been abolished in the constitution of 2001, the Senate itself was resurrected
in February 2007, provoking very negative denunciations as "one institution
too many" (*l'institution de trop*), "a sinecure for public retirees" (*une siné-
cure pour retraités publics*), and "a political launchpad" (*un tremplin politique*) (Hesseling 2010). These revisions must be considered deconsolidating
in large part due to the very polemical context in which they were pushed
through, and owing also to the bad reputation that the institutions they created immediately incurred in public opinion. Such institutions may well at
times serve as valuable appendages of a modern state, but the nonconsensual
manner in which they were implemented deprived them of the legitimacy that
would have made them useful.

The desire to maintain power was also evident in a decision to extend the
tenure of the National Assembly deputies who had been elected in 2001. In
this perspective, the major Wade-era deconsolidating revision was indeed the
extension of the length of the terms of deputies combined with successive
postponements of the legislative elections,[17] justified by spurious arguments.
Since Wade had been elected to a seven-year term in 2000, and deputies to a
five-year term in 2001, the extension of their mandate was justified in terms
of realigning presidential and legislative elections, so as to save on financial costs. In fact, in the context of Wade's declining popularity, there were
real fears that elections might produce an opposition-dominated National

Assembly. By disturbing electoral timetables, these revisions thus had a deconsolidating effect on the electoral process and, ultimately, on democracy. They helped those in power to shape the electoral process to their advantage at the cost of introducing a crisis of confidence in the electoral game between protagonists. This ultimately led to a contested and difficult electoral process in 2007, when Wade's victory in the presidential election was strongly disputed and the legislative elections were widely boycotted.

These examples suggest that in Senegal's political context, constitutional law is seen more as a "resource" than as an "obligation" (Sindjoun 2009, 579), that is, something used by those in power to stay in power rather than to control the exercise of power. This was clearly a recurring pattern throughout the country's first three presidential reigns and is not absent from the context of the current fourth president. Fifteen out of thirty-eight constitutional revisions to 2015 were clearly of a deconsolidating nature. It is true that all three presidents did contribute, in some ways, to the consolidation of democracy in the country, but they also contributed—to different degrees—to slowing the process and at times to its weakening.

It may be useful to comparatively assess the impact of successive presidents in terms of the impact of their respective approaches to the constitution, and for what it reveals about their place in the politics of democratization in Senegal. A simple statistical distribution of the two types of revision over time shows that the frequency of deconsolidating revisions has increased as Senegal's political system has aged. Senghor introduced eight constitutional revisions, of which only one—the establishment of a constitutional order of succession in 1976—can be deemed deconsolidating (and indeed this should be nuanced, as discussed below). Of Diouf's fourteen revisions, four were of a deconsolidating character. Finally, Wade holds the record for revisions, with a total of fifteen modifications of the constitution (including the wholesale change of the constitution itself in 2001), and out of which ten were clearly of the deconsolidating type.

Unquestionably, Wade pushed through the highest number of deconsolidating reforms. Wade consistently professed his commitment to a democratic order and justified his actions in democratic terms, but in his actions, he did at times seem to show a preference for a kind of enlightened despotism. His hold on power was never stable, and the all-too-easy resort to constitutional changes as a way to "fix" difficult political situations was a reflection of the inherent fragility of his political position (Fall 2006, 75).[18] By contrast, Senghor, a man of letters steeped in a Hellenistic worldview, found the law suspicious and believed, along with the Ancient Greeks, that the less a country legislated, the happier it would be. In his twenty-year tenure as president (the same length as Diouf's tenure and longer than Wade's), he made a remarkably moderate use of constitutional revision. Diouf in turn was essentially a civil servant with a high degree of respect for the rule of law, which he saw as a corset to which one must generally adjust, except when the law constrained governance or threatened an official not yet ready to leave an office (Tirera 2006). Wade, on the other hand, was a lawyer who thought that the law should serve his cause. He developed an almost playful rapport with the law, which he saw as a flexible entity that he could endeavor to manipulate as he saw fit in order to justify actions that served his needs.

The current head of state, Macky Sall, began his term with a cautious approach to revisions, initially reluctant to tinker with the constitution. In September 2012, he did initiate one constitution revision, in response to public demands and following his campaign promises, by eliminating the unpopular institution of the Senate in September 2012.[19] Then in 2016, after significant debate about his campaign promises to undo some of Wade's revisions, he initiated a referendum on fifteen constitutional amendments, including a reduction of the presidential term limit from seven years to five. Although some in the opposition criticized the timing and some aspects of the referendum, many of the proposed changes were widely seen as progressive and responding to popular demands. They included the limitation on the age of presidential candidates to seventy-five, the legalization of independent candidacies in all elections, and constitutional recognition of the official status of a "leader of the opposition," named by the largest opposition party. A council of local governments, the *Haut conseil des collectivités territoriales*, was also created to promote local governance and development.

The high incidence of constitutional revisions has inevitably engendered chronic instability. A fixture of Senegal's political history, the practice has varied quantitatively in accordance with political eras and with the head of state. Thus, between 1960 and 1962, the first constitution of Senegal underwent two revisions—one per year, as that constitution was replaced in 1963. From 1963 to 2001, the country's second constitution was revised nineteen times, an average of once every other year, but with moments of hyperactivity: four revisions in 1991, followed by three the following year. After 2000, the revision habitus reached new heights. The constitution of 2001 had already undergone fifteen revisions by 2012, that is, an average of one revision every five months, with a few peaks of activity. In 2007, there were four revisions, followed by seven revisions in 2008, the most revisions in one year up to that point. The overall trend shows that constitutional instability is on the rise and makes Senegal somewhat of an exception even in Africa. As Jean-Louis Atangana Amougou concluded after a survey of political systems in Europe and Africa, "with the exception of Senegal, Africa's constitutions know no more revisions than those of other countries in the world" (2007, 598).

In this respect, Senegal is clearly an outlier and its "sins" are both quantitative and qualitative; revisions have been far too frequent and their content has not always reflected a democratic rationale. This damaging characteristic of Senegal's constitutional revisions is worsened by the fact that they are sometimes used to settle scores among political actors. Babacar Kanté once observed, regarding the revisions of the constitution of 1963, that they had "often been . . . the final word in conflicts and other subjective concerns, despite the reasons and motivations publicly advanced" (Kanté 1989, 154). One example of this feature of constitutional revisions in Senegal is the changes that have been introduced, under both Diouf and Wade, in the position of president of the National Assembly. Diouf thus changed the constitution to shorten the term of that office specifically for the purpose of removing Habib Thiam from that position.[20] A similar motivation was evident some twenty years later, when Macky Sall was evicted from the same office through a constitutional revision proposed by Wade. The term of office of the chairman became subject to annual renewal via the legislature's internal rules and regulations rather than being constitutionally prescribed to five years, and the deputies were empowered to remove a sitting president of the Assembly—all measures that led in due course to the fall of Macky Sall from the position. Similarly, it was solely for the purpose of removing Mbaye Jacques Diop from the chairmanship of the Council of the Republic for Economic and Social Affairs that a constitutional revision scrapped the institution altogether, replacing it with the newly minted Economic and Social Council.[21]

In light of these examples that show that a constitution can be used as a weapon to destroy or impair the political career of an individual (Thiam 2007, 150), one must still agree with Kanté's observation, made almost thirty years ago, that, "in Senegal, there is no hesitation in modifying the fundamental charter [constitution] to someone's advantage or disadvantage" Kanté (1989, 156).

In the end, given the political realities of presidential party dominance of the legislature, deconsolidating revisions in Senegal have always received the unconditional support of a parliamentary majority. Despite their controversial nature, they have generally been passed in a context where a collective defense of the constitution from the ranks of public opinion is unable to block the changes, and in which the judiciary has attempted no regulation of such excesses. An important exception to this rule, perhaps signaling a new phase in Senegal's political development, occurred on June 23, 2011, when massive popular demonstrations in front of the National Assembly led President Wade to withdraw a proposed revision that would have allowed a candidate to win the presidency in the first round of voting with only 25 percent of the vote, without need for a runoff election (Sy 2012).

Finally, the role of the judiciary remains a point of significant contention in the debate on constitutional revisions in Senegal. When deconsolidating revisions that undermine democratic principles are introduced, some political actors call for judicial action to provide a check on such politically motivated changes. In fact, however, and following the example of French jurisprudence,[22] Senegal's judiciary has tended to renounce any right to review revision bills for conformity with the constitution. In a ruling in June 2003, the Constitutional Council stated that it had no power to pronounce itself on any case beyond those that had been specifically assigned to it in the constitution, and that the constitution did not confer on it any role in the review of constitutional revisions (Fall 2008, 372). This jurisprudential policy that claims that constitutional laws are beyond the purview of judicial decisions (*l'injusticiabilité des lois constitutionnelles*) (Favoreu 2003, 792) has been consistently maintained by Senegal's constitutional judges.[23]

In this context, then, the politics of democratization in Senegal present a fascinating and paradoxical puzzle. The country has distinguished itself in the region and beyond for its exceptionally frequent reliance on constitutional revisions, and these revisions have frequently been "deconsolidating" in the sense of being driven by clearly political motives rather than by a search for deepened or improved democratic procedures. Yet the country has also witnessed the development of what is clearly one of the most democratic regimes in the region, having twice seen incumbent presidents defeated at the ballot box and peacefully relinquish power. In the Sahelian region marked by crisis and diminished state power, Senegal also shows every indication of maintaining a resilient and capable state. What to make of this paradox? One can only hypothesize that the intense politics of constitutional debates and institutional reforms in Senegal have, ultimately, been factors reinforcing both the capacity of the state and the consolidation of democratic institutions.

NOTES

1. Clinton declared that if anyone doubted that democracy could prosper in Africa, they should come to Senegal, adding that Americans admire Senegal as one of few African countries to have never known a military coup d'état. She ended the speech by thanking Senegal for being a model. Her speech is discussed in Arsène Flavien Bationo, "Macky Sall et les nouveaux enjeux géopolitiques du Sénégal", available at: http://lestratege.info/maky-sall-et-les-nouveaux-enjeux-geopolitiques-du-senegal/.

2. The decade leading up to the 2000 transition had been marked by turbulent contestation and negotiations between government and opposition over existing democratic institutions. The new constitution was touted as a reflection of a new political maturity that would end such institutional debates.

3. See Jérôme Lafargue (1996, 18) for an excellent definition:

> By democratization, I mean therefore the process which, in the long run, leads one to observe, in a combination, the existence of demands for democracy, a formal debate on the need to reform the political system, an effective reform of the system, the organizing of multi-party elections, freedom of political expression, and the internalization, by the governed, of the various rituals of democracy.

4.
L'initiative de la révision de la Constitution appartient concurremment au Président de la République et aux députés. Le Premier ministre peut proposer au Président de la République une révision de la Constitution. Le projet ou la proposition de révision de la Constitution est adopté selon la procédure de l'article 71. La révision est définitive après avoir été approuvée par référendum. Toutefois, le projet ou la proposition n'est pas présenté au référendum lorsque le Président de la République décide de le soumettre à l'Assemblée nationale. Dans ce cas, le projet ou la proposition n'est approuvé que s'il réunit la majorité des trois cinquièmes (3/5) des suffrages exprimés.

5. In January 2016, MPs adopted a law that increased the total number of seats from 150 to 165. Henceforth, sixty deputies will be elected on a national list according to a proportional system. The rest will be directly elected based on a first-past-the-post list system: ninety seats by multi-member constituencies in Senegal's forty-five *départements* and fifteen seats determined by eight constituencies representing the diaspora. This allocation of seats first came into effect during the July 30, 2017, legislative elections.

6. Independent candidacies remain possible, as per the constitution and the electoral code.

7. "Change" (*sopi* in the original Wolof) was the slogan of Abdoulaye Wade's campaign and became the name of the coalition that supported him in the second round of the 2000 presidential elections and the legislative elections that followed.

8. Until 1993, presidential and legislative elections in Senegal were held on a regular five-year schedule. Part of the negotiated reforms of the early 1990s, however, included an extension of the presidential term to seven years. Legislative elections were thus held in 1998, giving a strong majority to the ruling PS party, while the historical presidential election in which PS president Abdou Diouf was defeated took place in 2000.

9. Conseil Constitutionnel, Décision n 3/2000 du 9 novembre 2000.

10. Conseil Constitutionnel, Décision n 3/2000 du 9 novembre 2000.

11. These constitutional changes were mostly short-lived, however, and it is important to note that in fact from 1958 to 1993 presidential elections were regularly held on a five-year cycle.

12. Such was the case with the limitation placed on the Constitution in 1970 that was later revoked in 1976, then reinstated in 1992, and again annulled in 1998.

13. Sy went on record to call the revision a fraud against the constitution in a televised show, in October 2008.

14. This change would again become an issue under Macky Sall's presidency. Sall, who was elected in 2012 under the seven-year provision, had campaigned on the promise that he would again reduce the presidential term from seven to five years.

However, in February 2016, he sought the advice of the Constitutional Council—Senegal's highest body for the interpretation of the Constitution. The Court ruled that President Sall had taken the oath of office to serve for seven years as elected, and that he therefore could not shorten his current term. In a referendum on fifteen constitutional amendments on March 20, however, this change was approved by 63 percent of voters. This provision, however, went into effect only at next presidential election in 2019.

15. Loi 92-15 et 92-16 du 7 février 1992 portant code électoral.

16. See "Quand Wade fait réviser sa Constitution," blog post at *La Constitution en Afrique*, available at: www.la-constitution-en-afrique.org. June 8, 2008.

17. Loi constitutionnelle n° 2007-21 du 19 février 2007 modifiant la loi n° 2006-11 du 20 janvier 2006 prorogeant le mandat des députés élus à l'issue des élections du 29 avril 2001.

18. See also A-L. Coulibaly (2003, 23).

19. Loi constitutionnelle n°2012-16 du 28 septembre portant révision de la Constitution.

20. Loi n° 84-38 du 24 mars 1984 abrogeant et remplaçant le 1° de l'article 51 de la Constitution.

21. Loi constitutionnelle n° 2008-31 du 07 août 2008 portant suppression du Conseil de la République pour les Affaires économiques et sociales et à son remplacement par le Conseil Economique et Social (Loi constitutionnelle n° 2008-32 du 07 août 2008).

22. Décision n° 92-312 DC du 2 septembre 1992, relative au traité de Maastricht.

23. See, for example, the court rulings on the challenges to the constitutional revisions changing the tenure of the National Assembly, or the proposed creation of the post of Vice President: *Décision 92/2005 Affaire n° 3/C/2005 Prorogation du mandat des députés (18 janvier 2006, Décision n° 2/C/2009 du 18 juin 2009* sur la loi constitutionnelle n° 2009-22 du 19 juin 2009 instituant un poste de vice président de la république).

REFERENCES

Aivo, J. Frédéric. 2007. *Le président de la République en Afrique noire francophone: genèse, mutations et avenir de la fonction*. Paris: L'Harmattan.

Atangana Amougou, Jean-Louis. 2007. "Les révisions constitutionnelles dans le nouveau constitutionnalisme africain." *Politeia* 7: 583–622.

Cabanis, André and M. Louis Martin. 2007. "La pérennisation du Chef de l'État: l'enjeu actuel pour les constitutions d'Afrique francophone." In *Mélanges en l'honneur de Slobodan Milacic, Démocratie et liberté: tension, dialogue, confrontation*, edited by Philippe Claret et al., 349–380. Brussels: Bruylant.

Chéramy, Bruno. 1976. "Une révision constitutionnelle au Sénégal." *Éthiopiques: revue négro-africaine de littérature et de philosophie* 7:113–121.

Cruise O'Brien, Donal, Momar-Coumba Diop and Mamadou Diouf. 2002. "Léopold Sédar Senghor, Abdou Diouf, Abdoulaye Wade, et après?" In *La construction de l'État au Sénégal,* edited by Donal Cruise O'Brien et al. Paris: Karthala.

Copans, Jean. 2000. "La tradition démocratique au Sénégal. Histoire d'un mythe." In *Démocraties d'ailleurs: démocraties et démocratisation hors de l'occident*, edited by Christophe Jaffrelot. Paris: Karthala.

Coulibaly, Abdou Latif. 2003. *Wade, un opposant au pouvoir. L'alternance piégée.* Dakar: Les Editions Sentinelles.

Coulon, Christian. 1990. "Senegal: The Development and Fragility of a Semidemocracy." In *Politics in Developing Countries*, edited by Larry Diamond, Juan Linz and Seymour Martin Lipset. Boulder: Lynne Rienner Publishers.

Coulon, Christian. 1992. "Avant-propos: La démocratie sénégalaise: bilan d'une expérience." *Politique africaine* 45: 3–8.

Dahl, A. Robert. 2001. *De la démocratie.* Paris: Nouveaux Horizons.

Diop, Momar-Coumba and Mamadou Diouf. 1990. *Le Sénégal sous Abdou Diouf: état et société.* Paris: Kharthala.

Fall, Alioune Badara. 2006. "La démocratie sénégalaise à l'épreuve de l'alternance." *Afrilex* 5: 3–63. http://afrilex.u-bordeaux4.fr/sites/afrilex/IMG/pdf/05dossfall. pdf.

Fall, Ismaïla Madior. 2008. *Les décisions et avis du conseil constitutionnel du Sénégal.* Dakar: Centre de Recherche, d'Etude et de Documentation sur les Institutions et les Législations Africaines.

Fall, Ismaïla Madior. 2009. *Evolution constitutionnelle du Sénégal: de la veille de l'Indépendance aux élections de 2007.* Paris: Karthala, 2009.

Fall, Ismaïla Madior. 2012. *Les révisions constitutionnelles au Sénégal. Révisions consolidantes et révisions déconsolidantes de la démocratie sénégalaise.* Dakar: Centre de Recherche, d'Etude et de Documentation sur les Institutions et les Législations Africaines.

Fatton, Robert. 1987. *The Making of a Liberal Democracy: Senegal's Passive Revolution, 1975–1985.* Boulder: Lynne Rienner Publishers.

Favoreu, Louis. 2003. "L'injusticiabilité des lois constitutionnelles." *Revue française de droit administratif* 4: 792–795.

Gautron, Jean-Claude. 1967. "La Révision constitutionnelle du 20 juin 1967 au Sénégal." *Revue sénégalaise de droit* 2: 5–21.

Gautron, Jean-Claude and Michel Rougevin-Baville. 1977. *Droit public du Sénégal.* Dakar: Centre de Recherche, d'Etude et de Documentation sur les Institutions et les Législations Africaines.

Gazibo, Mamoudou. 1998. "La problématique de la consolidation démocratique: les trajectoires comparées du Bénin et du Niger." PhD diss., Institut d'Etudes Politiques, Bordeaux.

Gounelle, Max. 1981. "Les effets pervers du multipartisme constitutionnellement limité." *Penant* 91: 44–52.

Guèye, Babacar. 2009. "La démocratie en Afrique: succès et résistances." *Pouvoirs* 129: 5–26.

Hesseling, Gerti. 1985. *Histoire politique du Sénégal: institutions, droit et société.* Paris: Karthala.

Hesseling, Gerti. 2010. "Le Sénat au Sénégal: une attraction secondaire." *Afrilex* 6: 1–27. http://afrilex.ubordeaux4.fr/sites/afrilex/IMG/pdf/Le_Senat_au_Senegal _une_attraction_secondaire.pdf.

Kanté, Babacar. 1989. "Le Sénégal: un exemple de continuité politique et d'instabilité constitutionnelle." *Revue juridique, politique et économique du Maroc* 22: 145–160.

Lafargue, Jérôme. 1996. *Contestations démocratiques en Afrique: sociologie de la protestation au Kenya et en Zambie*. Paris: Karthala.

Liet-Veaux, Georges. 1943. "La fraude à la Constitution: essai d'une analyse juridique des révolutions communautaires récentes: Italie, Allemagne, France." *Revue du droit et de science politique en France et à l'Étranger* 2: 116–151.

Mbodj, El Hadj. 2007. Preface to *Textes constitutionnels du Sénégal de 1959 à 2007* (réunis et commentés par Ismaïla Madior Fall). Dakar: Centre de Recherche, d'Etude et de Documentation sur les Institutions et les Législations Africaines.

Morlino, Leonardo. 2001. "Consolidation démocratique: La théorie de l'ancrage." *Revue internationale de politique comparée* 8(2): 245–267.

Moudjib, Djinadou. 1978. "Sénégal: un iceberg démocratique." *Afrique Nouvelle* 1945.

Nzouankeu, Jacques-Mariel. 1981. "La consolidation et le renforcement de la démocratie au Sénégal: la révision constitutionnelle du 6 mai 1981 et le multi-partisme illimité." *Revue des Institutions Politiques et Administratives du Sénégal* 2: 323–384.

Open Society Initiative for West Africa, Centre pour la Gouvernance démocratique. (2010). *Constitutionnalisme et Révisions constitutionnelles en Afrique: le cas du Bénin, du Burkina Faso et du Sénégal*. Unpublished report.

Ouedraogo, M. Séni. 2011. "La lutte contre la fraude à la constitution en Afrique Noire francophone." PhD diss., Université Montesquieu–Bordeaux IV.

Sindjoun, Luc. 2009. *Les grandes décisions de la justice constitutionnelle africaine: droit constitutionnel jurisprudentiel et politiques constitutionnelles au prisme des systèmes politiques africains*. Brussels: Bruylant.

Sy, Alpha Amadou. 2012. *Le 23 Juin au Sénégal (Ou la Souveraineté Reconquise)*. Paris: L'Harmattan.

Sy, Seydou Madani. 2005. "L'alternance politique au Sénégal." In *La Constitution et les valeurs: Mélanges en l'honneur de Dmitri Georges Lavroff*, 593–609. Paris: Dalloz-Sirey.

Sy, Seydou Madani. 2009. *Les régimes politiques sénégalais de l'indépendance à l'alternance politique, 1960–2008*. Paris: Karthala.

Sylla, Salifou. 1987. "Les leçons des élections sénégalaises du 27 février 1983." *Annales Africaines* 1983–1984–1985: 229–265.

Thiam, Assane. 2007. "Une Constitution, ça se révise! Relativisme constitutionnel et État de droit au Sénégal." *Politique africaine* 108: 150.

Tine, Antoine. 2002. "De l'un et du multiple, vice-versa: partis politiques et démocra-tisation au Sénégal de Senghor à Diouf: contribution à une critique de l'imaginaire de la pluralisation politique." PhD diss., Institut d'Etudes Politiques, Paris.

Tirera, Lamine. 2006. *Abdou Diouf: Biographie politique et style de gouvernement*. Paris: L'Harmattan.

Villalón, Leonardo A. 1994. "Democratizing a (Quasi) Democracy: The Senegalese Elections of 1993." *African Affairs* 93(371): 163–193.

Young, Crawford and Babacar Kanté. 1992. "Governance, Democracy, and the 1988 Senegalese Elections." In *Governance and Politics in Africa*. ed. Goran Hyden and Michael Bratton. Boulder: Lynne Rienner.

Chapter 4

Stress-testing Democratic Institutions in Mali

The Political Elite and the Breakdown of the State

Moumouni Soumano

Extolled for twenty years as a striking example of a consolidating democracy—with a successful democratic transition and one unproblematic political transition via elections to showcase its success—the limits of the Malian democratic process were brutally exposed by the coup of March 22, 2012. As Siméant and Traoré (2012) noted shortly after the coup:

> Just a few months ago, Mali was one of the real donor darlings of the international aid community. . . . They praised the existence of democratic institutions in the country, the absence of ethnic politics, and the fact that one of the major actors of the transition of 1991, Captain Amadou Toumani Touré (ATT), who had turned over power to civilians in 1992, had been elected president in 2002 and reelected in 2007, yet had not sought to change the constitution to allow himself a third term, unlike some of his neighboring peers.

In this context, the coup glaringly revealed a host of underlying problems that lay beneath Mali's apparent success. The collapse of what proved to be a house of cards exposed not only the breakdown of the army chain of command, the weakness of the defense and security systems, and the folding of state authority, but also more mundane (yet crucial) issues such as the grave shortcomings of public services in water and health, the decay of the educational system, and the simple physical absence of the state in certain parts of the country. As Malian prime minister Moussa Mara told the French weekly *L'Express*, speaking of the democratic period that had ended in March 2012, "our institutions were based on something worse than quicksand, owing to corruption, the decay of civic consciousness, and the ineffectiveness of unfit leaders."[1]

This political reality, well understood by the Malian population, can be explained as the result of a gradual deterioration of political and economic governance over the course of an extended political process that, in many ways, failed to reconcile the institutional practice of democracy with Mali's social and economic realities, which in turn eroded the power of the state. The institutional shift from a constitutional one-party regime (1979–1991) to a multiparty system based on the separation of powers and the rule of law was not accompanied by a parallel shift in terms of a sense of accountability in the political class, and the key players of the new era did not undertake to depersonalize institutions or to make them more democratic. Rather the process was stonewalled by political actors who put a premium on acquiring and keeping power, rather than on contributing to building institutions. This approach ultimately calcified the party system, subjecting it to intense fragmentation, with the results that parliament could barely perform its task of controlling government action, that judicial authority caved in to the executive, and that corruption grew rampant.

While this chapter cannot fully take stock of Mali's institutional and political reforms following the democratic transition of March 1991, I will attempt nonetheless to understand and show how the behavior of key actors in Mali's democratic process failed to create favorable conditions for the emergence of democratic institutions,[2] including a state that is able to shoulder its sovereign responsibilities, while maintaining a facade of democratic progress. I do not attempt an overall evaluation of the outcomes of this process, important though they are. Rather, my analysis will focus on the ways in which the single-minded logic of acquiring and keeping power—which has defined the behavior of Mali's political elite—contributed to the breakdown of the state and to the army's intrusion into the political arena, clear indications of the extent of the collapse. In this regard, I will first show how the actors and circumstances of the 1991 National Conference introduced flaws in the drafting of the constitution that established the political and legal framework for the new democratic state. I will then illustrate the dilemmas and shortcomings in democratic practice that resulted from that constitution, by analyzing the behavior of the elite that was tasked with giving substance to the constitutionally prescribed institutions, including the state apparatus. I then turn to an examination of the practice of "political consensus, *à la Malienne*" before concluding with a discussion of the national defense and security policy (or, rather, its absence), which dealt the final blow to the collapse of the state with the coup of March 22, 2012.

An explanation for this situation can be traced back further to the development of a political system scarred by eight years of *de facto* single-party rule under Modibio Keita's *Union Soudanaise/Rassemblement Démocratique Africain* (US/RDA), followed by twenty-three years of a constitutional single-party and monolithic regime that restricted political and public freedoms. Under both systems, there was little separation of powers, and any political disagreement—or search for alternatives—was violently repressed on ideological grounds (under US/RDA), or charges justified in the name of state security (under the single-party system) (Diarra 2010). In 1991, a popular uprising, triggering a military intervention to end the widely unpopular regime, led to a transition process and eventually to a constitutional referendum in January 1992 which initiated multiparty politics (see Villalón and Idrissa). These dramatic events, in theory, ushered in a new form of governance, but it proved to be one which did not seriously take into account the legacy of the former regimes, under which the majority of the Malian population had been excluded from political participation and, more generally, from a voice in public affairs. The democratization process of 1991–1992 produced a groundswell of enthusiasm fed by hopes that the new regime would not only guarantee political freedoms and political participation but also create conditions for economic progress. Such hopes and expectations, however, proved short-lived. The contradictions—student unrest, political disputes around elections, concerns about the multiplication of political parties—that surfaced within the three first years of the new democratic era (1992–1995) raised serious questions as to the meaning and objectives of the process. As a consequence, the country quickly witnessed the profound disenchantment of the populace with the promise of democracy, a fact reflected in plummeting voter turnout rates in elections, usually fluctuating between 23 and 27 percent.

To be sure, the democratic process was inherently extremely difficult, as it involved the rapid hasty adoption of a full-blown multiparty system and the various freedoms of a liberal regime, in the context of a difficult and weak economy. The process was therefore bound to be difficult and complicated. In retrospect, however, it appears that the process was also clearly marred by the fact that political will was geared less toward solving such problems, and more toward securing and maintaining power. This much was already apparent in the process for adopting a new constitution.

CONSTITUTIONAL MIMICRY AND
A SCRAMBLE FOR POWER

The tendency—observed in many African countries—of constantly attempting to revise the constitution to secure the power of incumbents has been notably absent in Mali,[3] where any constitutional revision would require a national political process and a referendum. Article 118 of the democratic constitution of the Malian Third Republic adopted in 1992 requires the concurrent agreement of the president and the parliament to initiate any attempt at reform—a not uncommon stipulation in the constitutions of Francophone Africa. In the case of Mali, however, the clause further stipulates that the revision bill must be approved by a two-thirds majority of the National Assembly *and* can subsequently become valid only after having been approved by the people in a national referendum. This convoluted procedure has the advantage of shielding the constitution from opportunistic modifications, but it may also be problematic when there is a need for institutional change to adapt to political evolution and important new dynamics. The constitution was adopted following a referendum in 1992. It shares many similarities with the French constitution of 1958—and was criticized by Malian academics as a pale copy of that document—and it is also marked by the conditions under which it was drafted, which were far from the serene deliberative process that would have been most conducive to efficient outcomes (Wing 2013).

The Constraints of Mimicry

Mali thus adopted the core idea of a liberal-democratic political system based on the principle of separation of powers and highly influenced by the French colonial legacy. Yet the institutional configuration failed to take into account the specifically Malian conceptions of power and authority, resulting in an entanglement of powers whereby the executive operates like a locomotive pulling the legislature and the judiciary in the direction of its choosing. This has led to many anomalies that stem from an incoherent implementation of the legal framework of democratic practice.

This issue was, to some extent, a consequence of the adoption of a variant of the so-called semi-presidential regime established by the French constitution of 1958, which ensures the omnipotence of the president by enabling him to appoint a prime minister and a government as well as the members of some other institutions (such as the Supreme Court), giving him the power to dissolve parliament, and making him commander in chief of the army, as well as president of the high council of the judiciary. The president wields such powers without the possibility of interference from any other official body. Under the successive terms of Presidents Alpha Oumar Konaré (1992–2002) and Amadou Toumani Touré (2002–2012), this presidential supremacy appeared as a form of subtle autocracy, which favored political sclerosis through the ascent of an electorally anointed monarch who was in control of all the important issues of the day. In the political sphere, whenever a decision needed to be made, this fact of presidential power was reflected in rhetorical questions such as "What does the head of the state think of this issue?" or set phrases such as, "in conformity with the will of the President of the Republic." As one deputy confided to the author in an interview, when a bill came up in the National Assembly, many of his peer representatives were more interested in knowing the position of the president than in understanding the content of the bill.

This logic of the personalization of power, rooted in the dominant practices and the political culture of the authoritarian regimes since independence in 1960, constitutes a clear stumbling block for democratization. The leadership of the democratic movement of the 1990s not only failed to break with this logic, but in fact very soon fell back on it as a political weapon that justified actions that served their purposes. Thus the school system was shut down through the invalidation of a school year (*année blanche*) from 1994 to 1995, political opponents were arrested or economically marginalized in 1996, elections were held without an electoral roll in April 1997, leading to their invalidation by the Constitutional Court, and other abuses were committed via the control of state powers and resources. These and similar actions created a mystified aura around "the powers that be," causing damage to processes of accountability central to democracy and reinforcing the notion that informal and personal relationships are more important in the political game than are rules and principles. Such actions also dashed hopes that democracy might represent a clean break in political governance, one that could instead redirect political energy to debates on core values, substantive policies, and blueprints for society.

By uncritically importing the French constitution, the framers of Mali's democratic institutions paid no attention to the country's own social and political parameters, such as the legacy of an abusive executive power or the decisive role of community leaders in both the selection of rulers and the decision-making process. In this context, the National Assembly was thus unable to hold in check a drift toward presidentialism. This was especially the case given that the president holds a proverbial constitutional sword of Damocles over the heads of the nation's representatives in the form of his power to dissolve parliament. The same is true for the judiciary, which is also constrained by social and political imperatives that have put the lie to its formal independence.

Given these conditions, opposition is seen as a form of betrayal of the power-holder, who is endowed with the means to cast aside the offender. In this, there is a marked change relative to the situation before 1991–1992, but also a continuity of sorts. Before 1992, opponents were easily made victims of physical violence or arbitrary imprisonment, whereas after 1992, subtler forms of violence—based on the control of the levers of the state—emerged. These included, for instance, economic marginalization. In an underdeveloped economy such as Mali's, the state is the central purveyor of economic opportunities and access to capital, either through public contracts or official positions. To be cut off from such channels of economic activity can have devastating impacts on the prospects and livelihood of ambitious individuals. As such, the latter know to hold their tongue and acquiesce even to what they may feel are egregious abuses from those in power.

There are also specific technical points that may create intractable problems given the importance of the presidency in Mali's political life, and the country's realities more generally. This much was revealed in the aftermath of the coup led by a previously unknown army captain named Amadou Haya Sanogo in March 2012 (Whitehouse 2012). Article 36 of the constitution states that when the position of president becomes vacant before the end of the term of the incumbent, his powers are assumed by the president of the National Assembly for the period during which elections are organized to replace him. That period, however, cannot exceed forty days after the vacancy has been declared.

This is a difficult clause. By barring the notion that another official—such as a vice president—could complete the term, it requires the hurried organization of elections, providing only forty days for the entire process. But given the material, logistical, and financial limitations that characterize Mali, a forty-day electoral process is impractical, indeed impossible. This reality was repeatedly highlighted in the experiences of presidential elections in 2002, 2007, and 2013, during which delays incurred by the organizing institution and the Constitutional Court (which was charged with proclaiming results) left no time for campaigning in the second round of the election. In the case of a presidential vacancy, these electoral laws have no contingency plans for when such delays occur. Electoral expert Babou Traoré has noted that not only did the constitution fail to address this specific issue, but it also worsened it by giving only very limited powers to the interim head of state, which can lead to institutional gridlock.[4]

This flaw in the constitution was the source of the legal-institutional imbroglio that exacerbated the political crisis that followed the Sanogo coup of March 2012. Following the formal resignation of the overthrown president Amadou Toumani Touré (arranged by the Economic Community of West African States—ECOWAS),[5] the president of the National Assembly was not in a position to organize elections in the tense security situation, which saw heavily armed jihadist militias expanding their occupation of the national territory. Thus, after the constitutionally stipulated forty-day time limit had expired, the legitimacy and legality of the interim president's position became an issue. Political challenges to his tenure culminated on May 21, 2012, when rowdy demonstrators invaded his residence and assaulted him physically, protesting the extension of his status as interim president, which had been decided by ECOWAS. The shocking event not only crystallized the heated debate on the legitimacy of institutions at that point, but also had the effect of preventing the formation of a national consensus on confronting the crisis. In the end, the constitution was ignored by the acceptance of an ECOWAS proposal, which—with the agreement of the coup makers—simply declared that the end of the interim period would be at the organization of new elections. The forty-day time limit was thus simply ignored.

The constitution also provided for a very restrictive electoral system. While most politicians initially wanted a proportional representation system for parliamentary elections, in fact it prescribed a two-round, first-past-the-post list system, a system which poorly represented the country's varied currents of opinion. Thus, when all opposition parties reached an agreement to shift to proportional voting for parliamentary elections in 1996, the ruling *Alliance pour la Démocratie au Mali* (ADEMA) party relied on its supermajority in the parliament to impose a mixed system instead. The Constitutional Court, however, invalidated this change of the electoral procedure, deeming it an unconstitutional change. As a result, parties have taken to setting up common lists on the basis of their known areas of influence. This voting system is further maladjusted to the Malian context in that the electoral district system follows the administrative one. Electoral districts are not based on population counts, but rather on communes. In each district, the number of deputies varies by a proportion of one representative for every 60,000 residents. In this context, the two-round, first-past-the-post list system assigns all seats in the district to the list that eventually wins an absolute majority, even if this is only in the second round. As a result, a large share of voters are underrepresented in parliament, especially if one considers in addition the low voter turnouts (between 20 and 27 percent) and the practices of vote buying. The very democratic legitimacy of the National Assembly can thus be questioned, and this fact might also explain why its decisions are sometimes startlingly out of tune with society, such as in the case of the family code bill that was adopted with a solid majority in parliament in 2009, only to be rejected by a massive citizen mobilization, and then heavily amended (Soares 2009).

Haste and Confusion: The Effects of the Scramble for Power

The inconsistencies and incoherence noted above can partly be explained by the weight of what was at stake in the drafting of the constitution in 1992. This was done in a context of euphoria, restlessness, and rash intrigue, following the rapid loss and reshuffling of political power. The tense climate bred distrust between the leaders of the prodemocracy movement and the military men who had dislodged the authoritarian president Moussa Traoré. The ambiance is well described by Aly Cissé (2006):

During the struggle launched in the street by the social forces that were against the ruling power, public opinion was accepting of the following notion: any form of struggle—peaceful or violent, organized or spontaneous—was welcome as long as it served to push the regime to the brink and helped to open up the political arena. . . . There was as much praise given to the courage of the cadres of [the pro-democracy associations] CNID and ADEMA—who took part in the general march of 30 December 1990—as to the recklessness of the students who indiscriminately plundered and burned public buildings and the private residences of regime notables.

The national conference which followed was organized to ensure the greater participation of the Malian citizenry, and was intended to heal the wounds of the nation. As such, all of the country's social and occupational groups were invited to provide their input in setting national priorities, and to offer new perspectives for governance. The slogans of the period—such as the straightforward "out with the old, in with the new" (*on ne veut plus de l'ancien, mais du nouveau*), or slogans in local languages, such as the Bambara "cleaning thoroughly" (*kokadjè*)—all illustrate the national mood of the time. There were clearly strong popular aspirations for renewal, especially for an end to the corruption and financial malfeasance of the former government.

Beyond the search for a new political order, there were also fears related to the length of the conference, notably that it could indefinitely prolong the transition period—initially scheduled to last nine months. This was worrisome, especially in the ambiance of mistrust that characterized relations within the newly emerging political class as well as between the new politicians and the military. Given these fears, it was decided that the conference would be held over a very short period of time, approximately two weeks (from July 29, to August 12, 1991), during which time about one thousand people, representing all layers of Mali's society, were to participate in drawing up a new constitution.[6] The crowded sessions and the short timespan became themselves a source of pressure, which did not bode well for the careful execution of the complicated technical process of drafting a full new constitution.

For the civilian players, twenty-three years of a single-party regime run by the military had been a tough experience. But there was the desire within elements of the army to maintain power, even though it was unlikely at that point that the population would accept it. An episode in June–July 1991 revealed the tensions within the army when, on the eve of the opening of the national conference, two military men from the interim *Comité de Transition pour le Salut Public* (CTSP)[7] were arrested under charges of corruption committed during the previous regime, and were replaced. More worryingly, the acting Minister for Territorial Administration, Major Diabira Lamine, a close friend of the president of the CTSP, was arrested on July 14, 1991, under charges of conspiring against the CTSP to restore military rule. The news of this attempted coup immediately prompted huge popular demonstrations, organized by the leaders of the democratic movement, in which soldiers and civilians shouted slogans such "eye to eye, feet in the barracks" (*les yeux dans les yeux, les pieds dans les camps*), calling on the military to finish the transition and return to their barracks. The end of the transition period thus became a key priority in itself, and elections—which were set to close the process—became a matter of some urgency. The national conference thus came to be seen as a leash on which it was better not to tug too much—in the form of endless debates—lest it wake the sleeping beast, a sentiment only strengthened by the fact that the conference was presided over by the leader of the junta himself, Amadou Toumani Touré.

On the other hand, the military leaders feared that their mandate would be called into question by the conference participants, who themselves drew legitimacy from the fact that they represented the citizenry. In particular, the political actors who represented the new parties sought to consolidate an automatic majority by means of which they could shape the outcome of the conference. At the same time, there was a rapid multiplication of new political parties and other groups, which itself created new problems. As was noted by Monique Bertrand (quoted in Lange 1999), within three months of the promulgation of the right to create new parties, their numbers grew from one to forty-five, underlining the "very real risk of seeing political life getting bogged down by personal feuds and precarious coalitions." This explosion in the number of political parties clearly aimed to position those who founded them in roles that would allow them to have a say in the scramble for power.

All these elements—tension and mistrust as well as the context of a scramble for power—increased the fragility of the process. As far as institution building was concerned, a wide but ultimately superficial consensus was sought to avoid confronting difficult issues that arose from the social and political context of the country. This was marked, for instance, by crucial questions such as the nature of the political regime, the voting system, and the funding of political parties.

Several conference participants originally wanted a parliamentary regime, in which the head of the state would be chosen by the National Assembly. However, the influence of invited "technical experts" such as the French jurist Robert Badinter,[8] along with a segment of the Malian political class quashed this idea, arguing notably that a parliamentary regime was prone to instability. While there was some truth to that perspective, it is also the case that a semi-presidential regime posed the risk of a slide into presidentialism (i.e., the excess of presidential authority), and given the country's authoritarian past, a more substantial debate at the national conference might have presented an occasion for considering constitutional solutions to this potential problem.

The contentious issue of the funding of political parties was also summarily set aside by a large majority of participants, who argued that parties should not receive public funding because they were "merely free political associations."[9] This notion, which misunderstood the role of political parties, revealed just how much the workings of democracy—and its relations to a state that would protect its principles—were unclear to many of the participants in the conference. Indeed, by 1996, experience had convinced Malian leaders that there had to be some level of public funding for parties in the Malian context, and a major resolution of the conference was thus discarded.

Despite this situation, the constitution of 1992 nonetheless represented progress in the institutionalization of democracy in Mali, both through the development of a strong form of constitutionalism, and also in the safeguards provided for the operation of the new regime. The participatory process through which the constitution was drafted helped to make people feel its importance in the legal structures of the country. And the diversity of social and professional groups implicated in the process[10] partly explains why the conference ultimately adopted a rigid constitutional framework, one which makes amendments difficult by requiring consultation of the populace for any important change of an institutional or legal nature.

In addition, the constitution included not only provisions for the freedoms and institutions of a liberal democracy, but it also guaranteed administrative decentralization and set up an autonomous Constitutional Court, endowed with the powers of constitutional review and of adjudicating electoral disputes. In the past, these powers had belonged to a section of the Supreme Court. The autonomy of the Constitutional Court empowered it to eventually issue several landmark decisions that have provided useful safeguards in electoral matters, and which have undoubtedly helped to maintain some hope for the democratic process in Mali. Lastly, the constitution limits the president to two consecutive terms. There have been feeble attempts to revisit this issue, but given its sensitivity in popular sentiment and the safeguards included in the constitution itself, they were unsuccessful.

The procedural rigidities of Mali's constitution reflect the trepidations of its citizens, and the widespread reluctance to accept institutions able to adapt to the fluctuations inherent in politics, given the painful past experience of single-party rule, and the popular fear of the confiscation of power. And yet, the institutions created by this constitution have consistently been subordinated to the power of the executive and manipulated to align with presidential priorities. This reality has been manifest in a variety of ways: the appointment of prime ministers without a majority in the National Assembly (first in 1992–1993, then again from 2001 to 2014); the corresponding weakness of the National Assembly and its failure to play its key role of exercising control over the government; the many institutional abuses that piled up at election times; and the so-called "political consensus" form of governance that emerged after 2002 as parties all bent themselves to presidential will. These and other issues originated from the political class's focus on acquiring power for themselves, with little concern for the effects of their actions on the political regime, nor, ultimately, the fate of the Malian people. The management of elections further highlights this problem.

THE OPPORTUNISTIC INSTRUMENTALIZATION OF ELECTIONS

In the process of constructing Malian democracy, the organization of elections has clearly been the most problematic point of contention, and although it has also been the object of the greatest number of attempts at institutional reform, no satisfactory outcome emerged in over twenty years of experimentation. The consequences of this for the relationships between voters and elected officials, as well as with the state itself, are of critical importance. In particular, as we shall see below, the nature of the agencies in charge of the various parts of the electoral process has remained unclear, and all political actors seem to generally accept fraud in a logic of "the end justifies the means," an approach that has consistently alienated voters in Mali.

What Institutions for Electoral Management?

Over twenty-two years of democratization, Mali has proven unable to institutionalize a reliable institution capable of organizing free and fair elections. Reflecting popular skepticism, the major challenge in the founding elections of the democratic period—referendum, legislative, and presidential—organized in 1992 to end the transition period, was the declining turnout rate, as striking illustrated in the table 4.1.

These early polls were organized by the state administration itself, which provided the benefits of experience and the ability to reach all corners of

Table 4.1   1992 Elections in Mali

		Turnout (%)
January 12	Referendum	43.5
January 19	Municipal	32.1
February 23	First round legislatives	22.3
March 8	Second round legislatives	20.5
April 12	First round presidential	23.6
April 26	Second round presidential	20.9

Source: Ministry of the Interior.

the national territory. But trust quickly eroded between the opposition and the majority party that had emerged from the 1992 elections, and by 1993, opposition parties had begun to loudly question the neutrality of the administration in electoral matters. The political troubles and social unrest that began on the eve of elections in 1996 persisted into the following year in the form of a heated dispute over the electoral lists, finally leading to the creation of an independent body, the *Commission Electorale Nationale Indépendante* (CENI), in January 1997 (Fakoly 2004; Fay 1995). It should be noted that the adoption of this institution was identical to measures taken in most other neighboring Francophone countries experimenting with democracy, and it represented a break from the French-inspired tradition of having the state administration run elections. Loada (2007) correctly underlines that, in each of these cases, it was a coalition of opposition parties and civil society that led the charge against a model that had long been marred by partisanship and corruption, and pushed to create this new institution.

The new CENI included representatives from the ruling majority party, the opposition, and from civil society. Originally intended to organize both the legislative and presidential elections of 1997, it ultimately did not provide the definitive solution to the legitimacy of the electoral process that had been hoped for. In the absence of a viable electoral list, the CENI declared itself unable to organize elections by March 9 (the date required by the constitution), and President Konaré consequently accepted its decision and dissolved the National Assembly on March 3, 1997. This move allowed the president to sidestep a constitutional crisis, by pushing through the organization of elections by April 13, that is within the longer time limit prescribed by the constitution for elections to be organized following a legislative dissolution.

The result, however, was a total fiasco and a large-scale waste of limited resources due to the chaotic organization of the polling. In response, the opposition parties quit the CENI in anger and challenged the outcome of the elections at the Constitutional Court. The court sided with the opposition and annulled all results, pointing out that "no electoral list was presented to the court to enable it to declare that the first round of the legislative elections of April 13, 1997 was valid and reliable." Despite this severe blow to the electoral process, President Konaré ordered that the presidential elections take place as planned on May 11, 1997, that is before new legislative elections could be organized. All the leaders of the opposition parties boycotted the process, with the exception of the president of a small political party, a merchant who later admitted to having accepted payment to stand as the sole other candidate, so as to "save the presidential election and the country" by providing a veneer of legitimacy to the election. In this context, Konaré's inauguration to a new term on June 8, 1997, was tarnished by mass protest demonstrations and the arrest of five opposition leaders. By forcing the continuation of the electoral process, ostensibly so that the provisions on time limits would be respected, Konaré actually imposed a more significant unconstitutional process by inverting the order of the two elections: the legislative and the presidential. Building on the weight of his presidential "victory" *before* the parliamentary elections, Konaré thus ensured his party a parliamentary majority given the tendency to align with the executive to attempt to benefit from the privileges and advantages he can grant. Despite its much-vaunted democratic transition, then, the deeply flawed first elections that followed already indicated troubling limitations to Mali's democratization process (Villalón and Idrissa 2005).

This failure, however, was not that of the CENI. Rather, the broader Malian political class had proven to be irresponsible in its handling of the electoral process, in a context in which lack of preparation (with regard to the voting registry and time constraints) was itself turned into a point of contention between opposition leaders—clamoring for a postponement of the election—and the incumbent, who saw an opportunity to cling to power. A measure of instability thus crept into the country's emerging democratic politics, especially given the boycott of the presidential election, just five years after the transition. In an effort to reestablish a consensus, a national political forum was convened in January 1999 and—having brought together politicians from both government and opposition along with civil society and religious leaders—submitted a proposal whereby part of the CENI's duties, including logistics and oversight of elections, would be transferred to the Ministry of Territorial Administration. The CENI would be confined to the roles of supervision and monitoring. This agreement was in fact implemented at the next elections in 2002, and since then the running of elections has been shared by a combination of institutions and special bodies: Material organization of elections has been in the hands of the Ministry of Territorial Administration; the voting registry is managed by the *Délégation Générale aux Elections*; access to public media is monitored by the *Comité National de l'Egal Accès aux Médias d'Etat*; the validation of interim results proclaimed by the Ministry is the responsibility of the Constitutional Court; and the supervision of the whole process by the CENI (Baudais and Sborgi 2008).

The CENI includes delegates from the majority party, the opposition, and civil society. As opposed to some others in the region, it is not a permanent body, but rather only one that is mobilized during electoral periods. This obviously means that institutionally it cannot develop its own human capital and experience—something counterproductive, given Mali's financial limitations and lack of human resources. In this context, the shared method of organizing elections has been a subject of debate in Mali, and for reasons of transparency and efficiency, many actors have argued for a single-body system for elections management. Imperfections are part of any learning process and can be useful if they lead to self-scrutiny and reform. But the organization of elections in Mali has taken instead the form of successive disposable experiments, in that after each election a new formula is developed, and no one takes stock of what went awry in the previous one.

Such conditions are not conducive to democratic institutional development and strengthening. For instance, despite demands from the opposition, the work of the CENI has never been audited. Moreover, the very fact that elections were so poorly managed, when there was a timeline of five years leading up to them, suggests political incentives for the continuation of flawed elections. This key factor may be explained by the mistrust between political actors, who were all aware that all actors were prepared to engage in fraud and corruption in order to win, since the acquisition of power was their end goal. An electoral institution that works in a professional and transparent fashion may be an obstacle to outside manipulation of the process, and for this very reason, there was no desire to develop one. For instance, despite the central role of the Ministry of Territorial Administration in the organization of elections—sometimes as the central agency for doing so—it did not establish a department specifically devoted to electoral matters. The reactivation of a host of temporary governmental and technical bodies, on the eve of elections, not only significantly increases costs but it also multiplies and scatters decision-making centers so that confusion easily results from problems of coordination. This is compounded by the fact that there is also no permanent staff in charge of running the various sequences of the process, and therefore no accumulation of experience or skills.

Elections Mired in Fraud and Corruption

Beyond the immediate political stakes of elections and the multiplication of political parties,[11] a culture of fraud and corruption among actors whose priority is acquiring power above all else has represented a major obstacle to the strengthening of democratic institutions via the electoral process. Given that elections are framed primarily and simply as the gateway to power, they also act as a focus for all actions—including illicit ones—that could advance individual ambitions. As Marie-France Lange has noted about Malian democracy, "The quest for power, henceforth bound to the electoral process, increasingly depends on clientelism and confirms the fact that elections are won by fraud and bribery" (1999). Disgusted by this situation, the then-president of the Constitutional Court, Salif Kanouté, issued a stinging critique of political actors after having proclaimed the results of the legislative elections of 2007: "Reading all of these applications," he noted, "one can see the material and moral face of voting in this country. It is the epitome of fraud. Above all, I fail to understand how those who are tasked with the duty of protecting the national interest inside polling stations are the same ones who falsify numbers, who invert numbers." Similarly, the lawyer Mountaga Tall, president of the *Congrès National d'Initiative Démocratique-Faso Yiriwa Ton* (CNID-FYT), and a former member of parliament, elaborated on this theme during a public debate in January 2010:

> All voices of authority—political parties, independent candidates, the media, the Constitutional Court, even the head of the state—have denounced the unreliability of our electoral system. Fraud, bribery, large-scale corruption, have become commonplace. An election in Mali today is nothing but an equation of financial means, complicities in the administration and a mastery of electoral techniques, combined with a good dose of cynicism. In this cocktail, the personal qualities of the candidate and the program he defends are of only marginal importance.[12]

Yet, even though politicians and other national leaders regularly deplore this situation, there is a popular sentiment—noted by Bagayoko and Tessougue (2011)—that fraud is itself "an integral part of politics," and that as a result it still goes unpunished; legal sanctions for fraud, themselves very comprehensive, are ignored.

In this context, it is not surprising that Mali's electoral woes are also tied to the thorny issue of the relationship of its citizens with democratic politics, marked by low turnout rates and confusion over the role citizens must play in building a working electoral process. As Lange has further noted, "if Malian society as a whole was outraged by the inability of the government to organize the elections of 1997, one may wonder if the citizens themselves have become aware of the fact that it was their own personal practices which, taken together, had led to the confusion" (1999). Ultimately, efforts to reform the process via institutional solutions have not been sufficient, given the embedded popular sentiment about elections; elections are often depicted as a market opportunity where voters can organize to sell their support. Thus, in an interview during the 2007 elections, one community leader summed up this common practice and its motivations by saying that "elections are our way of getting money from lying politicians because after they are elected, they forget us." A corresponding logic thus develops among politicians, who feel that since they "paid" to get voted in, they do not owe anyone anything. This deep-rooted culture of mistrust creates a wide gap between citizens and their representatives and helps to explain the extremely high levels of parliamentary turnover: 70 percent in 2007, and over 90 percent in 2013.

A key problem lies in the fact that the organization of Malian elections has relied heavily on international donors, who tend to focus their attention on the electoral period rather than on a continuous engagement to try to build the popular legitimacy of election process. Partly in reaction to this, successive governments have developed a wait-and-see attitude between elections, and have started to mobilize resources only as the run-up to elections begins, hoping to secure the support of donors. A journalist in the daily *Les Echos* remarked that "the general elections of 2013 will cost either forty-four or fifty billion CFA francs, depending on the type of registry decided upon. The national budget has earmarked twenty-five billion for that purpose. The rest of the funding has to be found elsewhere" (February 6, 2013). At root, the lack of a credible electoral institution is a stain on the legitimacy of the Malian electoral process, and the result has been that rather than strengthening state institutions, consecutive elections as they have been organized in Mali gradually eroded public confidence in the institutions of democracy and in the capacity of the state itself.

A POLITICAL CONSENSUS: MAINTAIN
POWER ABOVE ALL ELSE

The so-called consensual management of political power in Mali that characterized the regime of President Amadou Toumani Touré in the period from 2002 to 2012 might, on the surface, find some cultural justifications in old local practices of governance. These include the famous *arbre à palabres* (*toguna* in Bambara), the tree or shelter under which civil debates are conducted in many villages, or the *soud baba*, literally "the paternal home," with a similar purpose. These are both frequently evoked as places of dialogue and exchange on community affairs, where decision-making emerges consensually from the consideration of diverse perspectives. People are consulted, respond according to their views and interests, and a solution takes shape. The chief will then approve it, though his role is more that of a facilitator rather than someone who holds specific powers and privileges.

Transferring this traditional governance practice to the fundamentally different context of the new democratic politics was tempting—given its cultural resonance—but also tricky. In particular, the nature of power in these modern state conditions was not necessarily conducive to the framing of this type of social consensus. Unlike the chief who presides over debates in traditional spaces of exchange, the president of the republic holds extensive powers and privileges—including those of appointment and dismissal—and thus sits at the top of a hierarchical system. Yet on the other hand, he is also more vulnerable because he needs support to lend legitimacy to his choices, and he is in power for a fixed period of time, which very naturally feeds the ambitions of his subordinates. As a result, "consensus" in this context really means the quest for a compromise over power, decision-making, and political action. If the tribulations of the electoral process in the first decade of Mali's democratic experiment did little to build institutional strength and legitimacy, the second decade under Amadou Toumani Touré dug a deep divide between a political class marked by cronyism in the name of "consensus" and the Malian citizenry.

Concretely, the result over the tenure of Toumani Touré's rule was a weakening of all other centers of institutional power in favor of the presidency. The "debate" within traditional consensus formation—without which there is in fact no consensus—was overlooked, while general deference to the president/chief's word was expected. To be sure, the *toguna* process aims at smoothing out contradictions, while the democratic process is based on the statutory admission of contradictions. However, both processes have normative underpinnings that emphasize the value of multiple voices, expressed either collegially (*toguna*) or through constructing a balance of powers (democracy). Such normative underpinnings were absent from the system invented in 2002. Instead, this new consensus rested on a logic of "sharing of the national cake" (Sow 2008).

It certainly did not present a common political project that would have resulted from the synthesis of clearly defined party programs. Lange writes that "after the failure of the checks and balances that could have become a guarantee of political integrity, there rapidly emerged a claim for everyone's right to corruption." The consensus was also not representative of the combined interests of the people. Rather, the objective was to gain and keep power for the political class through a sort of "nonaggression pact" and a promise of unswerving loyalty struck between the president and the political parties that supported him. The consensus also included a de fact "succession pact" with the political leadership, but this fact introduced an element of Machiavellian politics in that the parties supporting President Toumani Touré's policies could also be called to account for them, thereby compromising their chances of seeming to be proponents of an alternate agenda at election time. Clearly, the implicit trade-off for party support served to widen Toumani Touré's power base. An analyst from the Malian daily *Le Flambeau* summed this up, noting:

> Beyond any political and institutional ambitions, the consensus was rather seen as being based on a form of reciprocity whereby support for the ruler was to be compensated by certain advantages such as rewards of ministerial posts in the government, tax exemptions, trade monopolies, a "license for injustice and extensive freedoms." Presented to the world as a model of pluralist democracy, the consensus was actually a tool of political manipulation and public diversion that did not help in the anchoring of democratic principles. (December 11, 2012)

This mode of governance was also reinforced by the fragmentation of the party system, caused by divisions that emerged between individuals rather than between ideas. For instance, Ibrahim Boubakar Keita, who was to be elected president in 2013 after the restoration of elected rule, initially left ADEMA to create the *Rassemblement pour le Mali* (RPM) in 1994, because of friction over party leadership. Similarly, in 2004, opposition leader Soumaïla Cissé left ADEMA and created the new *Union pour la république et la démocratie* (URD), following leadership conflicts about whether a candidate should be put up against incumbent president Toumani Touré. Given these practices, outside observers variously describe many of the country's political parties as "economic interest groups" participating in the "neo-patrimonial system characteristic of the reigning power relations" (Roy 2005), or as "clientele parties with no ideology" (Chauzal 2011). In this context, political opposition is principally concerned with spoils and resources rather than ideas and political projects. While the depiction of the regime as purely clientelistic can be debated, it is clear that the general retreat of opposition parties during the presidential elections of 2002 and 2007 in favor of the officially "independent candidature" of Toumani Touré included a strong element of a logic of "sharing of the pie." If major parties declined to present a candidate, this was as part of a quid pro quo, which clearly had no demonstrable ideological basis. The result of the process was thus only the further weakening of the state by clouding political and institutional responsibilities in a haze of impunity.

COMFORTING POWER BY WEAKENING MILITARY INSTITUTIONS

"The Malian Army disintegrated, ruined by factional strife, state ineptitude, and corruption," wrote two journalists in the French daily *Le Monde* following the collapse of the Malian government (Châtelot and Guibert 2013). The comment reflects a key fact about the fate of the Malian army in the democratic era. In the decades of authoritarian rule, the Malian army did not have better resources or more equipment, and it was plagued by some measure of corruption to be sure, but it was characterized much more by the discipline and professional training expected of a well-ordered military institution. This difference must in large part be attributed to its being much less subjected to politics. Malians, at the time, were reasonably confident in its capacity to fulfill at least the basic tasks of defense and security. They were as a result extremely surprised by the turn of events in 2012, following the combined Tuareg rebellion and the jihadist advances that quickly followed and the coup of March 22, 2012. The rapid and unexpected fall of the main northern towns suddenly revealed the advanced state of deterioration of their national army. In particular, Malians realized to general shock that any meaningful collaboration between the political authorities and the military leadership had been completely eroded, leading to poorly planned initiatives that weakened and divided the army.

A Neglected Army

The military was never a major concern of the political leadership that emerged in the Malian transition to democracy and this neglect was to last for the twenty years of the democratic experiment, from 1992 to 2012. Thus, under both Presidents Konaré and Toumani Touré, no military planning act was ever passed, and there was no identifiable policy for defense and security. As we have seen, the relations between government authorities and the military were marked by distrust: the former were wary of possible coup attempts, while the latter feared being stigmatized by a civilian regime that had emerged from a popular uprising. In such circumstances, collaboration was minimal, and there was no effort made to reform the army in a way that would make it more democratic and prepare it for new security challenges.

For the Malian civilian authorities, especially in the context of the consensus system, the political settlement of conflict and contradictions had demonstrated its merits, and a military contribution to conflict resolution was not seen as likely or desirable. President Konaré (1992–2002) is reported to have said that he was a "man of peace" with no interest in waging war, and despite his military origins, his successor, Toumani Touré, consistently strove to resolve the so-called northern question through a political and regional settlement—perhaps because he was well aware of the stakes as they related to the situation of the military in Mali. Indeed, an analysis of the various agreements signed between the political authorities and the leaders of the Tuareg rebellions raises serious questions about their understanding of the role and value of a military institution. In essence, the government of Mali agreed to militarily withdraw from a portion of the territory and to leave security issues in the hands of paramilitary groups.

This was the result of stipulations in various accords brokered by Algeria in Tamanrasset (1991) and Algiers (2006), as well as in the National Pact of 1992. With no regard for the concept of the sovereign rights and responsibilities pertaining to the state (*la fonction régalienne de l'État*), the northern districts were "demilitarized," bestowing on the regions of Gao, Timbuktu, and Kidal (the latter created as part of the process) an extensive form of autonomy euphemistically called a "special status."[13] This process itself predates the democratic transition. Already, under the authoritarian rule of Moussa Traoré, some "unprecedented" wide-ranging concessions, "at least in West Africa" had been made and these could "only make sense for reasons lying beyond the conflict area" (Klute 1995). In any case, the path of political settlement rather than military confrontation meant that after the Algiers agreement of 2006, 3,000 Tuareg combatants were hurriedly recruited into the army, with a great number of them—around 150—promoted to the rank of officer, to the great frustration of career officers. In 2012, many of these Tuareg recruits deserted and joined the new rebellion.

A Divided Army

The Malian army was divided by factors that resulted from the particular context of the transition to democracy, and also—more paradoxically—from the ways in which political authorities tried to improve relations with the military.

In the heady atmosphere of democratization in 1991–1992, Malian soldiers, like other socio-professional groups, made corporatist demands related to their living and work conditions which were—as for other social groups—extremely poor. A movement led by the rank and file and the noncommissioned officers was organized in an informal manner in 1992, with a head committee and a mandate similar to that of a union. This coordinated movement was an implicit but clear indictment of the higher-ranking officers, who had already been accused of being out of touch with the needs of the troops. In response, the government proposed the passage of a military planning act that would take into account the demands of the troops while also gradually strengthening the capacities of the army. The proposal was shelved as soon as the movement in the army died down. The frustration that had provoked it did not vanish, however, but rather grew into a source of disenchantment and quiet decay within the army. Ignoring this, the Malian government missed a unique opportunity to reform the military.

In fact, as was regularly noted by military insiders,[14] even though the coordination committee of the movement had officially self-dissolved, it survived in a more informal fashion, constituting a network of horizontal solidarity among the rank and file that both weakened the hierarchical chain of command and symbolized the gulf that existed between the common soldier and the officer corps. Further divisions appeared when special advantages were granted to the paratrooper commando, the *Bérets rouges*, who were put in charge of presidential security under President Toumani Touré (2002–2014), himself a former member of that corps.

In the absence of a policy of serious reform of the military, a political "solution" emerged, notably an appointment system shaped chiefly by the need to placate the "recalcitrant ones," and to acquire the support of others. Starting in 2000, high-ranking military officers were named to all ministerial departments, as well as to certain so-called strategic posts, such as the voter registration commission, and the body that supervised the funding of political parties. Military men were also appointed to head the Ministry of Territorial Administration, and some found their way to positions within the presidency. A precedent to this approach may be found in events in 1994, when the gendarmerie students "revolted" and went on a rampage, creating a one-night panic across the city of Bamako. This episode was ended by a political settlement whereby the riotous students, instead of being sanctioned, were appointed to the civil service and assigned to posts in prison administration and civil defense.

Another issue sorely in need of reform was the dubious character of many recruitments and promotions, which favored the sons and relatives of high-ranking officers, including even the son of President Konaré (Fakoly 2004). As Thiénot noted, quoting a resident of Bamako: "the problem is not money, it is unfairness. The officer corps is not in sync with the values of the troops, as nine out of ten officers are sons of officers; they have inherited their positions. They constitute a caste that does not find it easy to inspire the respect of noncommissioned officers, themselves tired of all the string-pulling." (2013, 4) To top it off, generalships were created in droves—more than fifty—for the benefit of high-ranking officers, and at the expense of noncommissioned officers and of the rank and file. These rapid promotions did not correspond to any clear system of merit-based criteria, and, consequently, the level of frustration among the troops increased.

While to be sure there were problems in the military before democratization, it is also clear that the transition to democracy in Mali gradually worsened their institutional articulation within the state. No clear vision of the role of the army was developed, nor an agenda for reforming it elaborated. Actions were taken haphazardly to recruit or train military cadre, with little connection to changing security and defense imperatives. More damningly, the practice of political settlements and related faults marginalized the military, partially for budgetary reasons, but mostly so that they could be subordinated to the political priorities of government leaders—first and foremost to acquire and maintain power.

CONCLUSION

Ironically, and strikingly, the gradual weakening of the Malian state, leading to its collapse in 2012, was the result of the cumulative effects of a series of shortcomings that were triggered by the specific political characteristics of the democratization process itself. In a strange twist, the institutional reforms of the state that were developed and implemented in the name of democratization followed a logic that violated the very values, norms, and principles that justified them. Political actors used popular aspirations for democracy to advance their own interests. The proliferation of these interests, which drove the core dynamics framing governance and the processes of reform in the name of democracy, in fact stifled the institutionalization of democratic institutions.

The level of poverty of the population contributed to making a vision of politics as a social elevator acceptable, but the side effect was the development of a central logic of acquiring power and staying in power, either directly or through various compromises and compacts. This created a bizarre kind of governance practice—virtual in its policies and ephemeral in its results—that was contingent on the flux of personal interests, connections, and intrigues. In the end, issues of the utmost importance, such as the military problem and the security policy, were unlikely to be freely or forcefully debated in public institutions such as the National Assembly. Instead, they were decided in meetings between people who subjugated solutions to their personal interests in the name of consensual politics.

In a sense, it was democracy itself that was not taken seriously. Its institutions were set up but remained lifeless, as is illustrated by the limitations of the electoral process. One can only hope that the tragedy of 2012–2013 and their continued consequences will spur behavioral change among the political elite, at the very least by putting an end to the poisonous system of "consensus"—if not to the underlying social and political reasons for its emergence. Thus, to the surprise of both Malians and the outside world, the peculiar political processes that had characterized the widely hailed democratization of the country had had the perverse effects of weakening the state to the point that it was unable to withstand the shocks of 2012.

Attempting to learn lessons, we might conclude that far from being inevitable, the situation in Mali following 2012 can present an opportunity to return to some fundamentals of the democratic process. This will require redefining the powers and the mandates of key institutions, as well as the nature of the relationships that bind them together so as to create the legal and institutional conditions favorable to the emergence of depersonalized democratic institutions. Most importantly, there is a need to secure the conditions for the emergence of real institutional counter-powers and opposition, of democratic politics as debates and clashes of alternative political programs rather than of consensus. This must be done on the basis of a commitment by political actors to break with the personalization of political practice and to create a new dynamic founded on the centrality of institutions and the respect for their roles, in the image of what Habermas and others have qualified as "constitutional patriotism" (Müller 2006).

NOTES

1. *"Nos institutions reposaient sur des sables plus que mouvants, et rendus tels par la corruption, le recul de toutes les citoyennetés, et les carences d'un leadership qui n'était pas à la hauteur."*

2. By "democratic institutions," I mean both the ones prescribed by the Constitution (the presidency, government, National Assembly, Supreme Court) and the ones that are the result of democratic practice, such as political parties.

3. Examples include Burkina Faso in 1997 and 2014, Senegal in 1998 and 2012, Madagascar in 1998, Guinea in 2001, Tunisia in 2002, Gabon in 2003, Chad in 2004, Togo in 2005, and Niger in 2009.

4. A former secretary general at the ministry of territorial administration, and an electoral expert for the International Foundation for Electoral Systems, Traoré said this in a workshop organized by the *Centre Malien pour le Dialogue Interpartis et la Démocratie*, in January 2013.

5. This formal "resignation" from the position from which he had been overthrown in the coup followed an agreement signed with the junta on April 6, 2012.

6. Thirty-six political parties and 1,070 associations and unions were represented at the conference.

7. This committee, which included representatives from the military and from a variety of associations and unions, had replaced, on March 31, 1991, a purely military body, the *Comité de Réconciliation Nationale* (CRN), which was installed by the participants in the coup of 26 March 1991.

8. Robert Badinter is a French jurist with an expertise in African constitutional processes, who was invited in that capacity to assist in the drafting of Mali's Constitution.

9. This was the expression used by civil society participants to the national conference.

10. Over a thousand associations represented civil servants, rural workers, artisans, the unemployed, and the military; these various groups all had members in the commissions that worked on drafting different aspects of the constitution.

11. There are over 120 registered parties in Mali, even though on average only fourteen win seats in the National Assembly at each election.

12. The text of this speech was available on a Facebook posting at: http://www.tall mountaga.org/pages/La_democratie_malienne_Enjeux_et_Perspectives-2943573.ht ml, under the title "La démocratie malienne : Enjeux et Perspectives."

13. The Tamanrasset agreements state that people in the three northern regions will freely manage their local and regional affairs through representatives working in elected assemblies, and in accordance with a particular status granted by law.

14. In interviews carried out over an extended period by the author.

REFERENCES

Baudais, Virginie and Enrico Sborgi. 2008. "The Presidential and Parliamentary Elections in Mali, April and July 2007." *Electoral Studies* 27(4): 769–773.

Châtelot, Christophe and Nathalie Guibert. 2013. "Une armée malienne tombée en ruines." *Le Monde,* February 5.

Chauzal, Grégory. 2011. "Les règles de l'exception: la régulation (du) politique au Mali et au Niger." PhD diss., Institut d'études politiques de Bordeaux.

Cissé, Ali. 2006. *Mali: une démocratie à refonder*. Paris: L'Harmattan.

Diarra, Abdoulaye. 2010. *Démocratie et droit constitutionnel dans les pays franco-phones d'Afrique noire : cas du mali depuis 1960*. Paris: Karthala.

Fakoly, Doumbi. 2004. *Le Mali sous Alpha Oumar Konaré*. Ivry-sur-Seine: Editions Silex/Nouvelles du Sud.

Fay, Claude. 1995. "La démocratie au Mali, ou le pouvoir en pâture." *Cahiers d'études africaines* 35(137): 19–53.

Hugeux, Vincent. 2014. "Mali: 'Un accord avec les rebelles ne suffira pas à régler la question du terrorisme.'" *L'Express*, October 7. Available at: http://www.lexpress.fr/actualite/monde/afrique/mali-un-accord-avec-les-rebelles-ne-suffira-pas-a-reg ler-la-question-du-terrorisme_1608449.html.

Klute, Georg. 1995. "Hostilités et alliances. Archéologie de la dissidence des Touaregs au Mali." *Cahiers d'études africaines* 35(137): 55–71.

Lange, Marie-France. 1999. "Insoumission civile et défaillance étatique: les contra-dictions du processus démocratique malien." *Autrepart* 10: 117–134.

Le Flambeau. 2012. "'Le consensus à la malienne': De la réciproque au paradoxe." Maliweb.net, December 11. Available at: http://www.maliweb.net/editorial/le-cons ensus-a-la-malienne-de-la-reciproque-au-paradoxe-111038.html.

Loada, Augustin and Luc Ibriga. 2007. *Droit constitutionnel et institutions politiques*. Ouagadougou, Burkina Faso: Faculty of Law and Political Science.

Ministère de L'Administration Territoriale et des Collectivités Locales, Direction Nationale des Collectivites Territoriales. 2010. "Études sur le bilan et les perspec-tives de la décentralisation au Mali." 102 pp. Available at: http://knowledge.ucl ga.org/IMG/pdf/etude_bilan_60fe.pdf.

Müller, Jan-Werner. 2006. "On the Origins of Constitutional Patriotism." *Contempo-rary Political Theory* 5: 278–296.

Roy, Alexis. 2005. "La société civile dans le débat politique au Mali." *Cahiers d'études africaines* 178(2): 573–584.

Siméant, Johanna and Laure Traoré. 2012. *Mali: Le Putsh et le Nord Vus de Bamako*. Sciences Po. Centre de Recherche Internationales, October 2012. Available at: http://www.academia.edu/24770545/Mali_Le_Putsch_et_le_Nord_vus_de_Bama ko_avec_Johanna_Sim%C3%A9ant_.

Soares, Benjamin F. 2009. "The Attempt to Reform Family Law in Mali." *Die Welt des Islams* 49: 398–428.

Sow, Abdoulaye. 2008. *L'état démocratique républicain: la problématique de sa construction au Mali*. Brinon-sur-Sauldre: Grandvaux.

Tessougue, Daniel and Siaka Bagayoko. 2011. "Étude sur la corruption politique dans le processus électoral au Mali." Unpublished report prepared for the United Nations Development Program (UNDP).

Thiénot, Dorothée. 2013. "Mali: Les origines du coup d'État militaire du 22 mars 2012 et l'état actuel de l'armée malienne." Association Cultures et Progrès. Avail-able at: http://www.acp-europa.eu/wp-content/uploads/2014/06/12-Analyse-Ma li-Armée-malienne-fin.pdf.

Villalón, Leonardo A. and Abdourahmane Idrissa. 2005. "The Tribulations of a Suc-cessful Transition: Institutional Dynamics and Elite Rivalry in Mali." In *The Fate of Africa's Democratic Experiments*, edited by Leonardo A. Villalón and Peter VonDoepp. Bloomington: Indiana Univ. Press.

Whitehouse, Bruce. 2012. The Force of Action: Legitimizing the Coup in Bamako, Mali. *Africa Spectrum* 47(2–3): 93–110.

Wing, Susanna D. 2008. *Constructing Democracy in Transitioning Societies of Africa: Constitutionalism and Deliberation in Mali*. New York: Palgrave Macmillan.

Chapter 5

Democratic Struggle and State Building in Burkina Faso

Between Manipulation and Resilience of Institutions

Augustin Loada

At the end of October 2014, Blaise Compaoré, Burkina Faso's head of state for twenty-seven years, fled the country after a popular insurrection toppled his regime. Twenty-three years earlier, in 1991, Compaoré—who had come to power following a brutal coup d'état—had sought to legitimize his power by organizing multiparty elections. He was first elected to the presidency in a contested vote that was boycotted by the opposition, but that nevertheless launched the process that we might refer to as "democratic institutionalization." The core argument of this chapter is that, despite the fact that Compaoré and his regime were not committed to democracy and cared more about their own power than about building democratic institutions, the struggle around these institutions was powerful enough to gradually erect roadblocks to authoritarianism, and indeed eventually to lead to its demise. I will argue that it was not so much any specific political strategy, internal social force, or outside pressure which in the end brought down Compaoré's sham democracy, but rather that the democratic institutions which he had erected to attempt to entrench his power in the end took on a life of their own, and ultimately slipped beyond his control.

I start with a short background of Burkina's political history as it led to the advent of the Compaoré regime, describing the process of democratic institutionalization as it came into being in the context of that regime's efforts at building its legitimacy. I then show how the regime attempted to control and check the process by manipulating key electoral institutions and the system of checks and balances. Next, I examine the ways in which these institutions—flawed as they were—proved more impervious to manipulation than the regime had expected. The "resilience" of democratic institutions will then be analyzed in relation to the actions of political opponents and the pro-democracy militancy of civil society actors, allowing us to isolate the role of institutionalization for the dramatic events that led both to the fall of Compaoré and the reassertion of democracy and constitutional rule in Burkina Faso.

DEMOCRACY IN BURKINA:
THE ROAD TO INSTITUTIONALIZATION

Upper Volta, as Burkina was then known, first experimented with pluralist democracy during the process of decolonization in the 1950s. The colonial administration was far from neutral, and elections organized in that period were competitive, but neither fair nor transparent. "Irregularities and fraud were many," writes Madiéga, adding that, "the administration and traditional chiefs cared little for lawfulness: refusal to register opposition lists, intimida-tion of voters, vote cast by a single voter (the chief for instance), ballot stuff-ing, manipulation of results. All of these methods were used by the chiefs and administration officials to support candidates from 'conservative' or 'moder-ate' parties" (1995, 438).

The initial elections organized by the Ministry of the Interior after inde-pendence were no better, indeed not even competitive, as they were used by President Maurice Yaméogo to gradually suppress opponents and manipulate voting to impose a single-party regime. After a popular insurrection ended Yaméogo's authoritarian rule in January 1966, Upper Volta was run by the military for the following four years, before power was returned to civilians in another attempt to establish a democracy. Politics in the first two decades were, in Chérigny's words, "dominated by a kind of pendulum movement which successively led the country in a quadrennial tempo, in which a 'laid-back [military] regime' (1966–70) made way for a constitutional govern-ment with the advent of the Second Republic (1970–74), followed by a full takeover by the military in February 1974 and finally a restoration of civilian governance with the establishment, in late 1977 to early 1978 of the institu-tions of the Third Republic" (1979, 163–164).

Under successive constitutional regimes, elections were characterized by "tribal-regionalist" discourses, the role of "great electors" (traditional chiefs) and, above all, the practice of vote-buying. Despite these irregulari-ties, however, there was also increasing room for popular will. As Chérigny noted at the time, "for the first time . . . a military head of the state—General Lamizana—had to stand for a second round of elections after an open first round, eventually winning in the runoff election only by a small margin" (1979, 171). But that experiment in democratization also did not last long, ending when a motley coalition of army officers staged a military coup on November 25, 1980. The revolutionary wing of the coalition prevailed on August 4, 1983, when another coup d'état brought Captain Thomas Sankara to power. Proclaiming a "revolution," Sankara undertook a series of radical social and political reforms. In the process, Upper Volta was renamed Burkina Faso ("the Land of the Upright"). Wildly popular in some quarters, the Burkinabé revolution also had its discontents and inspired resistance in others. When Captain Sankara was assassinated in another coup on October 15, 1987, his successor and the erstwhile "second in command" of the regime, Captain Blaise Compaoré, gradually put an end to the revolutionary experiment.

After a decade of "special regimes" (*régimes d'exception*—meaning, military rule) during which constitutional rule was suspended, Burkina started a new democratic transition in the early 1990s, during the "wave" of democratic reform on the continent. This took the form of a "progressive change within a regime instead of being a progressive change of the regime" in a process that was carefully supervised and controlled "with a top-down impulse in many regards" (IDEA 1998, 5, 26). At first, the new Compaoré regime wavered between two seemingly conflicting orientations: either continuing the revolution, or opening up to democracy. Political life was liberalized and yet, at the same time, official discourse insisted on the "rectification" of a revolution that, it was said, had lost its way under President Sankara.

In June 1991 a new constitution was adopted by referendum, and in December a presidential election was held, but in a context with no consensus on the conduct of a democratic transition. The opposition consequently boycotted the polls (Loada 1996, 291), and as the sole contender Blaise Compaoré was elected. The system of political control that he developed was to allow him to go on to win elections again in 1998, 2005, and 2010, thus breaking records of political longevity in West Africa. That longevity was based on a ruling coalition of elites from parties in the so-called presidential camp (*mouvance présidentielle*), notably from the ruling *Congrès pour la Démocratie et le Progrès*, controlled by people close to Compaoré and to his younger brother, François. The regime also extended its tentacles into the military by placing high-ranking officers in strategic positions in the state apparatus and in the economy. In addition to these spheres, the regime developed close ties with the traditional chieftaincies, in particular the Mossi hierarchy. Leading senior officials of the civil service and of businesses and public enterprises with strategic significance were recruited essentially from among the militants of the ruling party. And religious communities—in particular Muslims and Protestants—were successfully courted by the regime. A consummate politician, Compaoré also managed to coopt some leaders of the opposition and of civil society into the ruling coalition.

However, the presidential camp was not free from internal tensions. Rivalries between Compaoré's younger brother and then-minister of state Salif Diallo (who was to fall from grace in 2008 after years at the center of authority) were evidence that the ruling coalition was subject to fissures. These were downplayed by Compaoré, who characterized them as healthy expressions of a system of internal democracy that he had developed. In reality, this discord grew out of the increasing disenchantment of some factions of the coalition, no longer satisfied with the status quo and aspiring to more access to important posts, and a wider redistribution of rents beyond Compaoré's family and inner circle. Momentously, this culminated in January 2014 when several important members of the party broke with the regime and joined the ranks of the opposition.

Until that point, Compaoré had been quite successful in stabilizing his ruling coalition by mixing elements of liberal democracy and authoritarian governance (Hilgers and Mazzocchetti 2006, 10–11). On the one hand, the regime allowed—perhaps even encouraged—a proliferation of parties, civil society organizations, and the free press, essentially to ensure support from the West. On the other hand, the political game was closely controlled through manipulation and informal arrangements. As a result, as Hilgers and Mazzocchetti noted "politics play[ed] out on two levels: the official level, a shadow theater offered up to donors, and an unofficial one, where the reality of political relations develop[ed]." This was thus not "a regime that [was] necessarily on its way to improve and consolidate democracy; rather, it [was] a political system which, through maintaining the appearance of democracy, shield[ed] the powers that be from the risks of pluralism and free competition" (2006, 10–11).

It is through this concept of a hybrid regime that the democratic institutions put in place in Burkina in the early 1990s must be examined. Even before the end of the first presidential term of the new republic (1991–1998), the regime undertook a series of reforms of the institutions that had been created at the beginning of the process. The central question for our purposes thus concerns the impact of these processes on the institutional framework of democracy. More specifically, to what extent did the tinkering with reform and the creation of new institutions—which lasted for over two decades—strengthen or weaken specific democratic institutions?

I use two criteria for the definition of a democratic institution: origins and function. In that regard, an institution is democratic when it results from universal suffrage, and is thus legitimated by voting and popular consent (Rousseau 2010, 57). However, for voting to lead to a democratic institution, it must occur in a context of freedom, authenticity, fairness, legality, and respect for constitutionally guaranteed rights. Therefore, an institution acquires a democratic nature only when it transforms an individual into a citizen. As was stressed by Rousseau, "any institution that has as its function, implicitly or explicitly, to 'extract' the citizen out of the man, to change an individual, a person, a human being into a citizen, deserves to be called democratic" (2010, 61).

In that light, the chapter will focus on key democratic institutions: the constitution of June 2, 1991; electoral institutions; and the institutions that provide checks and balance such as opposition parties and the courts. I will analyze whether a particular institution was strengthened, remained weak, or was further weakened during the democratization process, through the criterion of institutionalization. Thus, I consider than an institution has been strengthened when it can be shown to have reached a higher degree of institutionalization as a result of reform; and it will be said to have weakened if the opposite is true. By institutionalization, I mean the "process through which social models get organized in a stable manner" (Badie and Birnbaum 1991, 70–71). Such a process implies the flexibility of institutions, manifested in their independence from the individuals who staff them, in their autonomy relative to the forces that surround them, in their permanence or stability, and in their democratic orientation—all elements that allow institutions to adjust to changes within the political system.

Of all criteria developed in the literature, autonomy appears the most significant. As Rousseau writes, "in order for institutions to derive their democratic quality from their function, each function must be separate and, as a consequence, each institution must be autonomous" (2010, 63). The autonomy of institutions in relation to each other is a guarantee of their ability to fulfill their democratic function. Consequently, in this paper, an institution will be considered to have been strengthened when it has successfully become autonomous in relation to the ruling elites who have established it, and, conversely, it will be considered weak—or weakened—when it has been kept under the control of those elites. The analysis of democratic institutions under the hybrid regime of President Compaoré shows in effect that their autonomy was hampered by political strategies, in particular those of the ruling elites. In the two following sections, I will show first how ruling elites tried to control and manipulate institutions to suit their interests, and second, how under pressure from other political forces with different interests, those institutions successfully demonstrated resilience and partially escaped the control of the ruling coalition, which then opened the door for more autonomy.

MANIPULATION: UNDERMINING INSTITUTIONALIZATION

As democratization progressed in Burkina Faso, ruling elites developed strategies of adjustment to democratic institutions, seeking to undermine them while claiming to do the opposite. Interestingly, however, the rulers also needed to substantiate those claims, since democratization was also a political gambit in the effort to preserve power. Therefore, manipulation paradoxically meant that some strengthening of democratic institutions had to be allowed, while still limiting and constraining them.

The controlled democratic transition—started in 1991—defined new rules of the game, enshrined in a new constitution and electoral institutions. Nevertheless, by keeping the process of writing a constitution under his watch, Compaoré ensured that the outcome would be tailored to his interests and could be revised if necessary. To guard against the uncertainties inherent in the political process of democracy, he also made sure to maintain control of the body in charge of running elections. Democratization had led to the creation (or reestablishment) of a number of checks-and-balances institutions, which had been dismantled, forbidden, or instrumentalized under the *régimes d'exception*. As a result, an informal strategy was developed to neutralize those institutional counterweights. In this new context, the objective was not to formally or officially abolish such institutions, but rather to prevent them from operating efficiently through informal practices, hidden from the casual observer.

A Constitution for the Ruler

Writing in the early years of the new regime, Arsène Bongnessan Yé, former second-in-command of the revolutionary regime of the Popular Front, declared that the democratic opening of the late 1980s came about through the political will of Blaise Compaoré himself. It was Compaoré who—independent of any internal or external pressures—decided in early November 1989 to grant a constitution to his people (Yé 1995, 15). In response, the executive committee of the Popular Front met in April 1990 to compile a number of criteria that a constitution drafting committee would need to take into account. Among other things, there was the question of putting in place a multiparty system that would recognize the Popular Front as the state's leading organization and that would adopt the principle of the "preeminence of the head of the state over the Assembly" (Yé 1995, 19).

During his opening speech to the first congress of the Popular Front, Compaoré declared that the new constitution would "codify, in Burkina, a democratic and revolutionary rule of law whose bases existed ever since the advent of the revolution." He added that, "rule of law [would] contrast sharply with the hypocrisies of bourgeois democracy, which, in Burkina as anywhere else in Africa, has demonstrably shown that it could not take root" (Yé 1995, 20). These words portended the contradictions and ambiguities that would mark the democratization process under his leadership. For Compaoré, the main preoccupation was to avoid "selling off" the gains of the Burkina revolution under the pretense of democratization, and above all, to avert any risk of jeopardizing the power that he had won at a high cost in October 1987. The constitutional commission installed in 1990 was therefore staffed so as to ensure that the outcome could be controlled. Under the chairmanship of Bongnessan Yé, most of the commission's members were Compaoré's men.

Despite the efforts, the attempt at constitutional legitimation of the regime did not go smoothly. Some opposition parties and critical civil society actors managed to insert a number of more liberal elements into the final work. Moreover, external influences in the international *zeitgeist* of the early 1990s eventually convinced or pressured the regime to revise the draft of the constitution, removing some vestiges of a revolutionary regime and moving it closer to a liberal democratic constitution. Under the prevailing conditions, the draft constitution adopted by the commission was deemed generally "acceptable," despite some shortcomings. Among such shortcomings, as René Otayek noted, was some ambiguity about the election or appointment of deputies to the single chamber legislature (1996, 317).

Unresolved issues were discussed at a national meeting of the Popular Front in mid-December 1990. The bicameralism that had been rejected by the commission was surreptitiously reintroduced with the institution of a second chamber, which became a point of contention. Opposition parties feared that this would be instrumentalized through popular organizations and could be used to counterbalance the National Assembly in case they won the legislative elections. The supporters of the regime responded with several arguments: first, the chamber would include not only representatives from popular organizations but also from civil society and other social forces (unions, human rights associations, and religious and customary communities). Tensions would thus be easily defused because the voice of the country as a whole would be heard. Finally, it would only be a consultative chamber that would not compete with the National Assembly, which was elected by universal suffrage. The chamber of representatives was eventually instituted in December 1995, but given the legislative dominance of the presidential party this was quickly to become a rather burdensome innovation for the regime. Thus, seven years after its establishment, it was abolished by the constitutional revision of January 2002.

Despite the democratic advances brought forth by the constitution, it remained stained by an original sin: it was designed as an instrument for the legitimation of the military-civilian coalition that came to power in October 1987. The regime that came out of it thus unsurprisingly assigned a predominant role to the president. The exorbitant prerogatives it granted him made the president more than just the head of the executive; he was effectively a sort of elected monarch. Even in the case of an upset in legislative elections and the emergence of an opposition parliamentary majority, the president was under no obligation to resign or to give up his executive power in favor of the prime minister chosen by the new majority. The constitution assured the continued preeminence of the president in case of "cohabitation"; it is he who, in all circumstances, "decides upon the great orientations of state policy" (Article 36), leaving it to the cabinet to "conduct national policy" (Article 61). He also appoints and dismisses the prime minister, even if the latter has to be formally accepted by the absolute majority of deputies.

The lack of flexibility of the Burkinabé constitution in the distribution of powers between the two branches of the executive in case of "cohabitation," unlike that of neighboring Niger[1] for instance, meant that the primacy of the president in Burkina Faso could be contested only at the risk of provoking a crisis at the top of the state. This was in fact what had happened in Niger in 1995–1996, under an older constitution.[2] While it was theoretically possible that the Constitutional Council could regulate conflicts within the executive branch, it is doubtful that the council could have managed to impose an arbitration, given its dependence on the president, who had the prerogative of appointing seven out of ten members to the Council and could dismiss its chairman at any time. Thus, in September 2007, the first president of the Council was sacked because he was perceived to have become a danger to the regime. As a matter of fact, Burkina's history—and the experience of other countries in Africa—shows that in the absence of a political culture of compromise and respect for the institutional and legal framework of politics, there is strong chance that political and institutional crises may be settled by violent means. In Burkina, until its collapse in 2014, the Compaoré regime managed to maintain a monopoly on violence by using its praetorian guard to eliminate (including by physical means) opponents and other troublesome individuals. Despite all appearances, the regime remained essentially military in nature and military personnel played an active and structuring role in the ruling coalition. And in the end, the constitution established a presidency which was not accountable in office, which wielded not only constitutional weapons but also military force, and which could therefore impose its choices in case of a showdown with other centers of state power. There was only one prescribed means to call the president to account: through a constitutional mechanism that stipulated that he could be brought before the High Court of Justice in case of "an attack on the constitution," "high treason," or "embezzlement of public funds." But this court was never much of a threat to Compaoré and his ministers; indeed before 2014, it was never convened.

The preponderance of presidential power was such that there was no real counterweight in other state institutions to temper the regime's authoritarianism. The situation was made worse by the dominance of a hegemonic party which dominated the legislature, and which had control over every aspect of the state. In practice, the relationship between the executive and the legislative branches was deeply out of balance, at the expense of the National Assembly which was prevented from playing its role in any meaningful way. This was partly the result of institutional restrictions stipulated in the constitution, which, by specifying procedures related to voting and the control of government action, restricted the power of the National Assembly. As a result, almost all legislation originated in the executive branch, and amendments of bills by the legislature were scarce. Similarly, mechanisms for control of government action by the legislature were restricted to information requests in the form of oral or written questions. Information was released only to the extent that the executive branch was willing to do so, but it seldom helped in fixing problems in ministerial departments and other state organizations.

As for the provisions for parliamentary investigations—which formally bestow more power on deputies—they were sparingly used and rarely allowed by the parliamentary majority, which took care not to challenge the government. The parliamentary opposition could hardly play the role of watchman in that regard, given its minority position and the strict discipline in the ranks of the parliamentary majority. Only after the legislative elections of December 2012 did a stronger parliamentary opposition emerge on the political stage, opening up better perspectives for the future. Finally, with regard to the mechanisms that helped the deputies to call the government to account before the assembly, in a vote of confidence or a motion of censure, the constitutional provisions for invoking them were so restrictive that they were in fact never activated. In sum, the strict discipline of a docile parliamentary majority and the weakness of the parliamentary opposition until 2012 ended up making government accountability to parliament a rather theoretical notion. Burkina Faso's National Assembly under Compaoré was thus clearly a weak institution, given the undue ascendancy of the executive branch and of the majority party in its operation.

From the beginning, democratization in Burkina Faso was a controlled process, viewed under a constitution serving Compaoré's purposes as mechanism for legitimating the dominance he had claimed in coming to power in 1987. As such, from the beginning the constitution was open to opportunistic revisions and vulnerable to presidential whims, a fact that was only reinforced with the adoption of new procedures with a 1997 law that did away with some initial restrictions on the president's prerogatives in matters of constitutional revision (Garané 1998, 33–59).

Electoral Mischief

After over ten years of non-constitutional *régimes d'exception*, Burkina in the early 1990s was faced with the need to rebuild technical competence in electoral matters, in a rather unfavorable political and institutional context.

From the mid-1980s, the Burkinabé state administration had been deliberately politicized by the young revolutionary elite that had taken power in August 1983. The state bureaucracy was thus purged of elements deemed to be "counter-revolutionary," and its staff were promoted primarily on the basis of their political commitment. The formal separation of the Popular Front from the state, orchestrated by Compaoré in the early 1990s, did not put an end to this phenomenon. Rather, to get access and to maintain strategic positions in the apparatus of the state required adherence to the president's party, and exhibiting zealous commitment to it. It was in this political atmosphere that the first elections of the Fourth Republic were held.

The process of the elections was governed by a code promulgated by Compaoré in an ordinance that managed both the constitutional referendum of June 2, 1991, and the presidential election of September 1, 1991. The initial code was revised several times, for both technical and political reasons, at times as concessions to opposition parties, at others from the desire of the ruling party to maximize its electoral gains.

Under the Compaoré regime, as was also the case in Niger (Tidjani Alou 2002, 34–5), electoral laws were often instrumentalized to bolster the dominance of the ruling coalition. Electoral rules were repeatedly subjected to the vagaries of political conditions, and decreed or modified unilaterally by the governmental majority, according to priorities at specific moments and the prevailing power dynamics. Yet, an electoral system that deprives opponents of any chance to win elections will—in the medium or long term—incite permanent losers to reject the system and resort to antidemocratic tactics that lead to confrontation or violence (IDEA 2002, 8). In an admission of this fact, concessions were at times made to the opposition during sociopolitical crises, such as the one that followed the murder of journalist Norbert Zongo in December 1998, widely believed to have been carried out by Compaoré's praetorian guard. For the first time since the transition of the early 1990s, the regime tottered in the face of a mass protest movement led by the opposition and civil society (Loada 1999).

In 2000, the parliament responded by adopting an electoral code that included many innovations, but which was rejected by the opposition and civil society as inadequate. Faced with threats of a boycott of the 2002 legislative elections, the government, keen to resolve the crisis, formed an all-inclusive cabinet on the basis of an agreement with parties from the moderate wing of the opposition. Thereafter, it began a series of consultations about institutional and political reforms with the political class and civil society, and indeed important concessions were made to assuage the so-called radical opposition. In July 2001, a law modifying the electoral code was adopted in a consensual manner. When the opposition made an electoral breakthrough in the legislative elections of May 2002—the ruling party won only 57 seats out of 111, compared to 101 in the previous legislature—political tensions subsided.

But political consensus on the rules of the electoral game proved to be short-lived; in April 2004, the consensus was again broken following the adoption of another law revising the electoral code. The ruling party, under the pretense of a technical modification of the electoral code as recommended by the electoral commission, changed—to their advantage—both the ballot system for municipal elections and the electoral districts for legislative elections. It reinstated a highest-average proportional representation system for local elections and made the forty-four provinces of the country the electoral districts for legislative elections, replacing the thirteen electoral regions prescribed by the previous code. This revision of electoral law was accompanied by a collapse of the opposition in the legislative elections of 2007 and was seen by many as signaling a step backward in terms of democratic gains in electoral matters (MAEP 2008, 104). In fact, the capacity of Burkina's entire electoral system to guarantee free and transparent elections was called into question (MAEP 2008, 104). Moreover, the regime used informal rules and practices to further reduce uncertainty in the electoral game. Thus, regime supporters infiltrated electoral administration bodies, from the electoral commission down to polling stations, and into the commission's district branches.

On the Independent National Electoral Commission (CENI), where the majority and the opposition were given equal representation, what was at stake was the positions that were to be reserved for civil society. It was easy to maneuver—often with the help of state agents—so that these positions would in fact go to individuals close to the ruling party. This was all conducted in a participatory manner, so as to give an air of transparency, but was in reality quite an exclusionary process that carefully edged out associations deemed too critical of the regime. Similar tactics were used to staff voting stations. Though supposedly these were to be chosen by the branches of the CENI on the basis of personal ability and political neutrality, the reality was very different. Given the politicization of the administration, public officials, and local government servants—who formed the pools from which voting stations staffers were chosen—were most often closer to the ruling party than to the opposition.

The informal practices used most systematically to control the electoral process and to reduce the uncertainty of electoral outcomes were fraud and electoral bribery. Such practices harkened back to the colonial period (Madiéga 1995, 438) and survived into independence, as was seen during the elections that were organized in the 1960s and 1970s (Chérigny 1979, 168). But they became systematic after 1991 under the Fourth Republic. In the culture of the ruling coalition, elections were perfectly compatible with such practices as long as they left no material evidence. Fraud or bribery committed under the nose of elections observers—and not caught—was not deemed a transgression, but rather a display of legitimate know-how. The repertoire seemed inexhaustible: buying the voting cards of those believed to be close to the opposition; providing gifts to voters—in particular to the "great electors" (i.e., traditional and religious leaders); using state resources and personnel for canvassing and campaigning; and manipulating electoral institutions. All of these strategies were considered to be perfectly legitimate efforts to mobilize voters and win elections.

In that same vein, regime elites took pains to control the selection of civil society representatives, both at the national CENI and in the districts. At times, they would manage to "place" their men in these positions; at others, people officially from civil society would offer their support in an attempt to build clientelistic ties with the regime. The lack of professionalism that came from this was especially glaring in district branches of the CENI. Local CENI officials were constantly criticized for forfeiting obligations to impartiality and neutrality. The tripartite principle of representation (majority, opposition, and civil society) was even further undermined in regions were opposition parties had a very weak presence.

The commission recognized these shortcomings in a 2007 report on the legislative elections, stressing that the parties and civil society organizations were not always "judicious" in their choice of representatives, especially in appointing illiterate people. In such contexts, the ruling party's control of greater political resources facilitated its capacity for political manipulation and influence. It could mobilize people locally across the country, as well as its supporters within the state administration. It could ensure that its supporters in the civil service were appointed by the branches of the CENI to head polling stations. While all parties and candidates attempted to manipulate the electoral process, the ruling party evidently had the advantage in this game.

These issues were compounded by the recurring problem of the limited capacity and skills of CENI staff in district branches. The commission had to develop strategies to cope with repeated absences or even desertion of posts. It also had to supervise officials of dubious morality, themselves without experience or sufficient skills, who often gave the impression that their only motivations were either money or party interest. All of these eroded public opinion about the quality of the electoral process, contributing to low voter turnout in elections. Moreover, the adoption and implementation of the CENI budget quite often led to bargaining and deals with the relevant government ministries (Finance, and Territorial Administration), and sometimes with donors. Such practices affected the independence of the CENI, and the high costs of its operations and of the entire electoral process became an object of frequent criticism.

Under pressure from opposition parties and civil society, there were frequent debates about the fight against electoral fraud and bribery. Paying lip service to democratic fairness, and in an effort to show that its power was legitimate and not based on fraud, the ruling party would at times respond to its critics by undertaking some practical improvements, such as the use of transparent ballot boxes, reform to the form of the ballot, or a biometric registration system. Such technical refinements likely ended up reducing opportunities for fraud, but they had little impact on the manipulation of voters through methods which, though certainly dishonest, were not explicitly illegal. Such was the case of electoral bribery. Neither the Burkinabé electoral code nor the penal code address this practice, which can alter the outcome of elections in ethically questionable ways, but ones which many voters found perfectly acceptable. Before, during, and after the vote, for example, goods, services, and gifts might be promised and clientelistically distributed. While all parties engaged in such practices using the means at their disposal, the ruling party clearly had the greatest redistributive capacities through its control of state coffers and its domestic and foreign economic networks.

Given the efficacy of this strategy, and its capacity to undercut the real possibilities of democratic alternation in power, the regime was able to gradually relax its hold on the electoral commission, while also undermining institutional checks and balances.

Unbalancing Checks and Balances

The democratic process of the early 1990s in fact established or restored a number of important institutions that had been dismantled or neutralized. But this apparent progress was accompanied by informal strategies for undercutting the power of these institutions to provide checks and balances on the regime. This was done in subtle ways that were not always obvious to outside observers. Two examples illustrate this strategy well: the situation of the judiciary and the status of opposition parties.

The judiciary was a weak and ineffective institution until the democratic transition in 1991. Yet despite appearances of it being restored to its formal powers at that point, it was to remain limited in its capacity. The leadership under the revolutionary regimes of Sankara and the Popular Front had considered that the judiciary was an instrument of oppression. As a result, they had had no qualms about purging judicial personnel and breaking "the apparatus of bourgeois law" in order to replace it with "popular courts" that were to thenceforth apply "revolutionary law." The head of the Ministry of Justice, the regime's second-in-command, was no less than the future President Compaoré.

The democratic opening that Compaoré put in motion after seizing power led to an ostensible "normalization" of the judicial system, and in the constitution of 1991, it was established as an independent power with guarantees offered by the head of the state. During a meeting of the highest judicial body, known as the *Conseil Supérieur de la Magistrature* (CSM), on October 31, 1997, Compaoré decided to convene a "national forum on the justice system" in order to contribute to the "existence of a well-organized, efficient, independent and credible judicial power" (Burkina Faso May 2001). The forum was held on October 5–7, 1998, at the end of Compaoré's first seven-year term, and a few weeks before the presidential election of November 1998. It ended with the adoption of four recommendations, which aimed at ensuring decent living and working conditions for members of the judiciary; strengthening recruitment and training of judges and support staff; ending the politicization of the judiciary; and establishing a communication service in the Justice Ministry in order to provide information to the public.

Following the forum, in April 2000, the government adopted a strategy and an action plan for justice system reform. Yet despite the reforms, which were implemented with the support of many foreign donors, the justice sector in Burkina Faso remained in poor shape. According to a 2012 Afrobarometer survey carried out by the *Centre pour la Gouvernance Démocratique*, though two-thirds of Burkinabé trusted the courts, well over half of them (56 percent) thought that judges were involved in corruption. The same proportion of Burkinabé thought that crimes by well-placed people generally—or always—went unpunished, while 73 percent were of the opinion that ordinary people's crimes were generally punished.[3]

Among the most notorious cases of injustice and impunity that tarnished the Compaoré regime was the 1998 murder of journalist Norbert Zongo and three of his companions. Despite domestic and international protest, the regime successfully swept the affair under the rug. Political pressures and the complicity of judges close to the dominant coalition led to a denial of justice, as the courts dismissed all charges against arrested suspects in July 2006. In a later ruling in March 2014, a court stressed the many deficiencies of the Burkinabé justice system in processing the Zongo case: the excessive length (close to eight years) of the procedure, late hearings for those who filed civil suits, and the ending of the investigation after the 2006 decision, even though no perpetrator had been identified. Public opinion grew convinced that as long as the Compaoré regime was in place, there was little chance justice would be served in the Zongo case.

Impunity under Compaoré resulted from both formal and informal institutional dealings that linked the justice system to the president. The CSM was more of a rubber-stamping organ of the executive branch than an impartial, independent organ that would oversee the neutrality of the judicial power, as was its constitutional mission. The CSM was so beholden to the executive that it was not really capable of an impartial management of the careers of magistrates. Judges who were not docile had little chance of gaining access to strategic positions in the justice system, and those whom the Minister of Justice Boureima Badini deemed committed to supporting the executive (*juges acquis*)[4]—were assured of a meteoric career. When faced with an independent judge, members of the ruling coalition could appeal to the justice minister, who did not hesitate to directly contact the recalcitrant magistrate.[5]

But the Ministry of Justice did not only settle for hampering the work of independent judges—an insubordinate judge could also be marginalized or harshly punished for the smallest shortcoming. Illustrative of this was the case of the investigative judge Alexis Kambiré, who was bold enough to launch a preliminary investigation in 1997 into the "David Ouédraogo case," and in 1998 into the "Thomas Sankara case," against the will of the public prosecutor's office. The "impertinent" judge was eventually brought to the disciplinary board, demoted, and transferred. On the other hand, the regime knew how to show its gratitude to the judges who defended the interests of the ruling coalition.[6] It is therefore unsurprising that the term that was most often in use to describe the justice system was that of a "obedient judiciary" (*justice aux ordres*), following the phrase of Judge Kambou, the magistrate who presided over the independent commission that investigated the assassination of journalist Norbert Zongo.[7]

Opposition parties are another central institution for checks-and-balances in a pluralist democratic regime. In theory, Burkina's opposition enjoyed the rights and liberties that would have enabled it to compete in fairness. In April 2000, Burkina Faso was even one of the first states in West Africa to legally grant the opposition a formal status, following the recommendations of a "committee of wise men" (*collège des sages*) appointed by Compaoré. But as it was wont to do, the regime took away with one hand what it gave with the other. Most of the rights bestowed on the opposition were in fact redundant, since they already existed in the constitution and in many other provisions of substantive law.[8] Some other supposed new rights were, moreover, insecure since they were presented in the law as mere options, which posed no obligations on the government. The law also created the official position of "head of the opposition," (*chef de file de l'opposition*) which was to be filled by the leader of the opposition party that had the greatest number of deputies. In a context where political parties were fragmented, and ideologies heterogeneous, this measure was interpreted by some analysts as another way to further divide the opposition. Indeed, some opposition leaders vowed they would not compromise their independence by lining up behind a "head of the opposition" which they interpreted as imposed on them.

In addition, the law was applied opportunistically. When a "radical" opponent was in line to be "head of the opposition," the government would delay the appointment or refrain from initiating the adoption of the necessary regulatory texts to implement it. On the contrary, when the leading opposition party happened to be in the good graces of the ruling party, it was immediately recognized in the position by the chairman of the National Assembly. As the presidential election of 2005 was approaching, the official "spokesperson" of the opposition—in this instance Gilbert Ouédraogo, chairman of the ADF-RDA party—lifted his "mask," gave up his status, and announced that he was supporting Blaise Compaoré's candidacy.

That action was symptomatic of the degree of control that the regime in fact exerted over the Burkinabé opposition. In practical terms, the opposition was confronted with numerous traps and roadblocks, often deliberately put in place by the regime to delay or even thwart democratic alternation. The presidential party was the backbone of this strategy. To buttress its hegemony in the political arena, the regime had no qualms about resorting to informal tricks, including the fragmentation of the opposition, or co-optation. In 1996, the ruling party was strengthened by the merger-absorption of a dozen opposition groups, including the main opposition vehicle, thereby ensuring an all-powerful party. When a new leading party came into being afterward, the regime was quick to "poach" it and to integrate it into the presidential majority. This poaching practice—used effectively with the CNPP/PS in 1996, and the ADF/RDA in 2005—was partly at the root of the decline of the Burkinabé opposition, at least until 2012, when new dynamics started to take shape.

Not only did the dominant party encourage the creation of parties that claimed to be part of the "presidential camp" or of the "moderate opposition," it also promoted rifts within opposition parties that were thought to be a threat to its political dominance.[9] Former State Minister Salif Diallo in fact admitted to his role in impairing the opposition in an interview shortly before his fall from grace in 2008:

> We've had to deal with political antagonists whose stated goal was the conquest of state power, and we, in our capacity as the majority party, our principle is also that we need to keep hold of state power. These are two attitudes that cannot be reconciled. They develop strategies to effectively seize state power. And as for us, we put in place measures that will help us to keep it. So from time to time, if we can hasten their internal decomposition, we do it, that is completely logical . . . I've often given some blows at that level . . . otherwise, they would be in power now. I admit that it is not easy being in the opposition. We do have an advantage, let's be honest and recognize that. We control the state apparatus, and in Africa, when you have the state apparatus, you are a step ahead of the opposition.[10]

Despite its regular undercutting of the opposition behind the curtains, the Compaoré regime took its official standing as a "formal democracy" seriously in order to sustain its domestic and international legitimacy. Under Compaoré,

Burkina often took pains to be among the first states to ratify international legal instruments and agreements protective of human rights, democracy, and good governance, even though the implementation of these instruments was undertaken with much less haste. The point was to attempt to show the world that Burkina Faso was a model country. Thus, for example, President Compaoré did not hesitate to call for the assistance of the African Peer Review Mechanism (MAEP in its French acronym) in 2003. Such acts however, could backfire. In this instance, the MAEP evaluation report uncompromisingly enumerated the many blemishes of the Burkinabé party system and traced them mainly to the existence of a hegemonic ruling party. The report detailed the shortcomings:

> monopoly over the structures and infrastructures that came out of the Revolution; advantage taken of the resources of the state and the administration; abusive use of a dominant position; influence peddling and intimidation of the population; subtly maintained confusion between the state and the party; active cells of the party within the administration. . . . Combined with a favorable ballot system, the excessive weight of the majority party compromises in practice the chances of any real political alternation. The recurrence of such recriminations means that greater attention must be paid to that fundamental issue for fair balance between institutions, and for building democracy. (MAEP 2009, 102)

RESILIENCE: SUPPORTING INSTITUTIONALIZATION

Despite the seeming success of the Compaoré regime's strategy of manipulating the institutions of democracy and neutering institutional checks and balances, there was a clear resilience of democratic institutions in the country. Thanks in part to pressures from the external political environment, democratic institutions had some success in resisting the ruling party's systemic strategy of manipulation. Moreover, the political forces generated by the establishment of these institutions were able to put some pressure on the regime to make it relax its grip. This created a gradual and cumulative counter-hegemonic process, which relied on steps toward the strengthening of democratic institutions to incrementally stack the cards against the regime.

The Relative Emancipation of the CENI

As discussed earlier, electoral legitimation became key to Compaoré's political survival in the early 1990s. Ad hoc electoral commissions—themselves controlled by the executive—organized the first two presidential elections of 1991 and 1998, the legislative elections of 1992 and 1997, and the municipal elections of 1995 and 2000. But, under pressure from the opposition and civil society, a process was begun to push for the independence, and even institutionalization, of the body in charge of organizing elections. The process took place in three stages, with laws adopted in 1998 and 2001: the establishment of a national commission for the constitutional referendum, the creation of a national commission for the organization of elections, and the setting up of an Independent National Electoral Commission (CENI).

The first CENI had twenty-seven members appointed according to a specified formula: twelve members represented political parties, six each from the majority and the opposition; six represented the religious communities (Muslim, Catholic, and Protestant) and the traditional chieftaincy; six represented the unions; and three represented human rights associations. Its chair was officially appointed after being elected by the members. Neither the chairman nor his assistant could come from the political parties. CENI members were all protected by rights of immunity, and their terms ended ninety days after the final electoral results were announced. The Ministry of Territorial Administration and Security continued to play a strategic role, since it was in charge of establishing and revising the electoral registry, though this was done under the supervision of the CENI.

This institutional configuration of the 1998 CENI was rejected by the opposition and a segment of civil society because, in their view, it featured many of the same problems that had marred previous electoral bodies. To show their discontent, the opposition parties set up the so-called *Groupe du 14 Février* ("February 14th Group"), which decided to boycott the presidential election of November 1998. The February 14 Group criticized the lack of independence and financial autonomy of the CENI, as well as the fact that it did not have the power to establish electoral lists, process voter ID cards, or create polling stations. But they were also unhappy with what they saw as a lack of dialogue on electoral matters. Given their boycott of the 1998 presidential election, the regime was compelled to recruit for "companion candidates" to avoid the embarrassing spectacle of having Compaoré as sole candidate, something which had happened in 1991.

Compaoré was reelected with over 86 percent of the vote in the first round but found his legitimacy limited by the dubious conditions of this election; this was further aggravated by the severe legitimacy crisis that followed the assassination of the journalist Norbert Zongo in December. The "Committee of Wise Men" (*Collège des Sages*) that Compaoré convened made a number of recommendations for reform, including that he ensure the effective independence of the internal workings of the CENI, and suggested the eventual creation of a permanent electoral administration. In fact, following two revisions of the electoral law in 2000 and 2001, a consensual CENI, which was to continue into the post-Compaoré era, emerged from this episode. Among other characteristics, it was now a permanent body that had authority over most of the electoral process (with the exception of the electoral campaign). Its composition did not change much from the previous CENI, but the new law stipulated that members who belonged to a political party must come from the rank and file and must give up any elected office during their tenure in the CENI. Members were chosen for five years, except in the case of the local branches of the CENI—whose mandate ended with the proclamation of their district's final results. While this provision was intended to limit costs, it also implied a loss of experience and institutional memory at local levels. This explains much of the efficiency deficit and logistical failures in key domains of electoral management, including in respecting the timetable for elections. Yet, despite these flaws, it is also the case that these reforms produced a marked improvement in the transparency of electoral institutions over time, to the point that Burkina's electoral management system became a model across West Africa—even if remained subject to the possibility of partisan manipulation. As such, the institutionalization of electoral administration made real progress under the Compaoré regime. The same was not quite true with regard to institutional counterweights. Yet, even at this level, a certain level of resilience existed.

Rebirth of the Opposition

An institutional counterweight is any institution which, by its very existence or through its action (and whatever its objectives), may limit the power of the central apparatus of the state. Both the opposition and the judiciary are notable counterweights. From 1991, President Compaoré strove, more or less successfully, to control these two elements, seeking to prevent the former from offering an alternative to his rule, and the latter from becoming a problem for his allies. Yet, despite the difficult political environment that these efforts created, these institutions resisted with the support of key opposition leaders and also—as we will see below—thanks to the activities of social movements capable of countering the hegemony of the regime.

After Gilbert Ouédraogo renounced his status as head of the opposition in 2005, he was succeeded by Bénéwendé Sankara. At the presidential election of 2005, Sankara garnered less than five percent of the vote. Like other leaders of the so-called Sankarist parties, he tried to mobilize the Burkinabé around the memory of the murdered young revolutionary hero (Joly 2009), but he did not pose a real threat to the Compaoré regime. The opposition, however, found renewed momentum with Zéphirin Diabré. One of Compaoré's former cabinet ministers (from 1992 to 1996), Diabré had worked for the U.N. Development Program and also for the French company AREVA until 2011. Given his career base outside the country, he was able to convene a forum for political change in Burkina Faso that was held in Ouagadougou in May 2009. Much to the annoyance of the regime, it was a resounding success. Building on this, Diabré then founded a party in 2010, the *Union pour le Progrès et le Changement*. This party experienced a remarkable breakthrough during the legislative and municipal elections of December 2012, emerging as the country's second political force after the ruling party.

Zéphirin Diabré thus emerged as the official head of the opposition. During a meeting with the opposition parties on April 17, 2013, he defined this role not as that of a "chief" or a "messiah," but rather that of a facilitator who would carry the voice of the opposition. "It therefore behooves the opposition to know what they want," he declared. In his view, the objective conditions for an alternation in power already existed in Burkina Faso, but the subjective ones were still not achieved given the lack of credibility of the opposition. To change this, he proposed working on five fronts: strengthening the institutional rootedness of the opposition by getting it to pronounce itself on all major issues; establishing rules that could regulate the fifty or so political parties that collectively made up the opposition; consolidating the national presence of the parties; proposing a "minimal alternative program" different from that of the majority; and mobilizing the resources needed for the effective functioning of the opposition, independently of the government.

As Compaoré's schemes for a referendum for revising "Article 37" of the constitution—which limited presidential term limits—became clear, Diabré was provided with the opportunity to respond to the challenge of credibility. To ensure the success of protest mobilization, the opposition parties encouraged the creation, across the country, of anti-referendum committees, launched a subscription to fund its activities, and struck a strategic alliance with several civil society organizations. In this way, they successfully mobilized thousands of Burkinabé in repeated demonstrations in May, June, and July 2013 to protest Compaoré's plan to hang on to power. Simultaneously as the opposition was gathering strength, the dominant party was slowly eroding, as if in a zero-sum game.

Although it retained its parliamentary majority, in the legislative elections of 2012 the ruling party had earned less than half of the popular vote, the poorest it had done in twenty years (in 1992, it had garnered just 48 percent of the vote in the legislative elections). In this context, the internal cohesion of the party began to fray. When the 2012 party convention tightened things around the Compaoré family and the effort to revise Article 37, some of the party's top brass was sidelined, including former mayor of Ouagadougou Simon Compaoré and, most importantly, former chairman of the National Assembly Roch Marc Christian Kaboré, who had been seen until then as a potential successor to Compaoré.

Following their fall from grace, these two men joined forces with former State Minister Salif Diallo who had suffered a similar fate before them. The trio, which had been the backbone of the presidential party, eventually chose to defect and—together with other former party executives—founded, in January 2014, the *Mouvement du Peuple pour le Progrès*. The newly energized opposition that emerged from this intensified social mobilization in collaboration with civil society organizations. The protest demonstrations of October 28, 2014, organized two days before a scheduled vote in the National Assembly on a bill revising Article 37, was an unprecedented success. The regime, however, held out stubbornly, with dramatic consequences.

The Citizen Factor

As we will see later, the institutional strength of the constitution served as the focus point, transforming resilience—normally a defensive force—into a force of attack. But we cannot understand this transformation without taking into account the "citizen factor."

Compaoré's strategy for the neutralization of institutional counterweights did not stop the gradual emergence of citizen movements which escaped his control. In the 2000s, these processes of social mobilizations gathered enough strength to take back the public space and compel the regime to stand back. The earliest of such movements was unquestionably the one that clamored for truth, justice, and the fight against impunity following the 1998 assassination of journalist Norbert Zongo. The continuing impunity in relation to that affair during Compaoré's tenure stimulated the development of a collective memory and consciousness regarding the murdered journalist, whom many viewed as the "first martyr of Burkinabé democracy."

The regime was also shaken by other social movements, such as those which developed around the issue of the high cost of living. In 2008, urban riots led to the creation of a national coalition against the high cost of living (*Coalition Nationale contre la Vie Chère*, CCVC) (Loada 2009). The movement brought together unions and civil society organizations with a mission to fight not only the high cost of living but also corruption, fraud, and impunity. It organized a number of demonstrations and meetings aimed at educating and training the public to critically engage with the entire "political class." The opposition, the movement leaders insisted, "attempt to present themselves as an alternative to those in power, [but they] in fact share their beliefs in neoliberal policy." The opposition and other segments of civil society did not welcome this anti-neoliberal stance, as they judged it inopportune at a time when the priority, in their view, was to mobilize against the revision of the constitution. Despite the CCVC's defiant discourse toward the opposition, many of its members later joined Zéphirin Diabré's political protest movement. But, in their insistence to distance themselves from the opposition, the leaders of the CCVC, in particular those from the unions, missed out on the opportunity to spearhead the protest movement. They were instead supplanted by people from newer social movements that cropped up in response to the efforts to revise Article 37. Prominent among them were two organizations born in 2013 and that developed different styles of engagement to contribute to the protest movement: the *Front de Résistance Citoyenne* (FRC) and the *Balai citoyen* (Citizen's Broom). The FRC was the brainchild of university scholar Luc Marius Ibriga, the chairman of the *Forum des Citoyens de l'Alternance* (FOCAL), which had been launched in 2009 by Zéphirin Diabré himself, before the creation of his own party.

The 2011 and 2013 editions of the forum were instrumental in stirring up resistance to Compaoré's project of holding onto power, and the last FOCAL framed the intended revision of Article 37 as a "constitutional coup d'état" that called for "civil disobedience." The argument relied on Article 167 of Burkina Faso's constitution and denounced an attempt at an "anti-constitutional change of government," which is explicitly condemned by the African Charter on Democracy, Elections, and Governance. President Compaoré and his parliamentary majority—who had speedily ratified that charter in 2010— did not imagine at the time that it would give the opponents of the revision project legal arguments against them. In a key provision, the African Charter stipulated that "any amendment or revision of the constitution or the legal instruments that impairs the principle of democratic alternation" was to be avoided as a form of anti-constitutional change of government.

In contrast to the FRC, which was a coalition of organizations led by university scholars, and which imparted a high degree of intellectual credit to the protest movement, Balai citoyen was more of a mass movement. It had been formally launched on August 25, 2013, by musicians Smockey and Sams'K Le Jah, themselves very popular with Burkinabé youth. While the FRC's idea of action was to organize colloquia where they would challenge the legal arguments of the regime, Balai citoyen chose to work in the trenches. This often meant that they would walk the capital's outlying neighborhoods with loudspeakers, calling on citizens to raise their consciousness. The stated aim of Balai citoyen was to "contribute to the effectiveness of change in 2015." Defining itself as a political movement, not a political party, it vowed to keep agitating beyond the elections scheduled for 2015, since it was "not created only for alternation, but also for deep change," and must remain a "watchful sentinel" against corruption from on high, whatever the ruling party. The movement endeavored to establish so-called *Club Cibals*[11] across the national territory and abroad, and collected donations from members, and funding from other sponsors who remained anonymous to shelter themselves from political reprisals.

The formulation of a strategy to combat the regime's project of remaining in power proved to be a divisive issue among all the parties and organizations involved. The divisions harkened back to the differences of the early 2000s between the two branches of the *Collectif des Organisations Démocratiques de Masse et de Partis Politiques* (Collective of Democratic Mass Organizations and Political Parties, CODMPP) that had arisen after the murder of Norbert Zongo. Against the will of civil society organizations in that collective, which did not want to ease the pressure on the regime, the political parties ended up compromising with it. Some of them agreed to enter into a government of national union and to take part in the legislative elections of May 2002. Civil society organizations felt betrayed and accused the parties of pushing aside the Burkinabé people's interests to pursue their own personal good, and the event stoked civil society's distrust of the political opposition.

Building on this experience—and also on lessons drawn from the success of the Senegalese protest movement M23, which had defeated a project at constitutional revision promoted by President Wade—several civil society organizations agreed to strike a strategic alliance with the opposition, but only for the duration of the struggle against the revision of Article 37. It is also worth stressing that Burkina's civil society profited from the support of a number of African social movements. Fadel Barro and Landing Mbessane Seck, the founders of the Senegalese movement *Y'en a Marre*, took part in the third FOCAL in November and December 2013, and were later involved in the activities of Balai citoyen. Like their Senegalese counterparts, the new leaders of Burkina's civil society learned how to make common cause with the opposition while still preserving their autonomy. But for more conventional organizations, such as the unions, it was out of the question to join in a protest movement led by political parties. As a result, the unions were not to be part of the popular insurgency of October 2014, and had to leave to the new citizen movements the glory and benefits of being at the vanguard.

A Constitutional Uprising

Despite the custom-made constitution he engineered, President Compaoré initiated or endorsed several constitutional revisions, with the strategic goal of strengthening the dominance of the ruling coalition. But this tinkering with the constitution was to lead to social and political resistance.

Between its adoption in June 1991 and 2014 the constitution of the Fourth Republic was revised seven times.[12] This was possible during the first two parliamentary terms because Compaoré had the support of the necessary majority in the National Assembly. These revisions were presented as a way of deepening democracy, but the real motivations behind this claim were less admirable. While there were some effective innovations, most of the constitutional changes aimed at increasing—not decreasing—the imbalance in power between the executive and the other institutions established by the constitution.

The first revision, in January 1997, did away with the initial presidential term-limit provision, despite protests from a segment of civil society and from the political opposition, who boycotted the vote. This broke the compromise which had been established within the constitutional commission of 1991, when the representatives of the opposition were conceded the term-limit provision in exchange for accepting a seven-year presidential term, instead of the five-year term they were demanding (Loada 2003, 5). But the crisis following the Zongo assassination opened a window of opportunity for the reestablishment of the term-limit provision. Upon the recommendation of the "college of wise men" which he himself had installed in 1999 to help him weather the post-Zongo storm, President Compaoré accepted a new constitutional revision in April 2000. Not only was the term-limit provision reinstated, but the term length was also reduced, from seven to five years. However, the question then arose whether the provision was applicable to the current term of the incumbent, which was still underway—a question to which constitutional law gave no answer.

After two consecutive seven-year terms, President Compaoré decided to stand for reelection in 2005. In spite of protests from a large section of society, the Constitutional Council ruled, in October 2005, that he could in fact stand for two more terms, on the basis of the principle of non-retroactivity of the 2000 law. Reelected, President Compaoré could therefore be a candidate for a final term in November 2010. In anticipation of this closure, the presidential party decided, in July 2009, to initiate discussion about a revision of the constitution, without specifying the real intent. The opposition and a segment of civil society interpreted this to mean that the majority intended to again remove presidential term limits, which the chairman of the presidential party at the time, Roch Marc Christian Kaboré, himself characterized as "anti-democratic."[13] Meanwhile, Ouagadougou mayor and ruling party baron, Simon Compaoré, cynically replied to those who invoked the advice of the "college of wise men" that had led to the reestablishment of the term limit provision that "the truths of yesterday are not those of today." In that context, civil society, the Catholic Church, and the opposition parties started a campaign to enlighten Burkinabé citizens about the real stakes in the reform: blocking any chance of democratic alternation by helping the incumbent remain in power beyond the term limits specified in the constitution. The African Peer Review Mechanism, to which President Compaoré had adhered in March 2003, further embarrassed the regime by recommending, in 2009, that "the solution to be adopted should rest on a wide political consensus and take good account of the need to consolidate democracy, peace and stability in Burkina Faso" (MAEP 2009, 115). Quickly, the issue divided Burkinabé society.

One of the first political forces to sound the charge was the Catholic Church. After a meeting held in February, the Church's Episcopal Conference of bishops, while recognizing that it was "normal that regular reforms, made with wisdom, help the institutions to work for the superior good of the populace," went on to state that "in the case of this Article 37, we ought not shut our eyes to the recent history of our country, or our regional and global environment." The bishops pointed out that the issue at hand had already been the cause of a serious crisis in the past, forcing the government to convene a "college of wise men," and they stressed that constitutional change must aim for the common good, not for the advantage of a particular group. The key question, they insisted, was whether removing the presidential term limit would further social peace, or lay the ground for new turbulence, "especially when one knows that there are many open [judicial] cases, notably about unsolved economic crimes." The Church concluded by calling all to "vigilance and responsibility in the task of preserving the gains of our people." This extremely firm standing of the Church was not taken very well by the regime, which counterattacked by accusing the clergy of subversive political activities. When military mutinies and social revolts broke out in the first quarter of 2011, the Episcopal Conference rubbed this in the face of the regime by declaring that those were the very things it had warned about.[14]

Despite these warnings—and similar ones from civil society and the opposition—the regime did not abandon its reform project; indeed, a Minister of State in charge of political reforms was even appointed in January 2011 to oversee it. Yet, at the same time, the regime offered some pretense at a political opening. In June and July 2011, it summoned a "Consultative Council for Political Reform," hoping to secure some legitimacy for its project. The opposition and civil society boycotted the gathering, and although the regime did manage to lure in some interlocutors, it failed to secure a consensus on the revision of Article 37. Worse, most of those who spoke at the meetings—remembering the recent mutinies and riots—wanted the article to remain unchanged, or even reinforced by a stipulation that a revision of the controversial article would be constitutionally prohibited.

On the other hand, the government was successful in pushing through a return to a bicameral legislature, with the reestablishment of a Senate. While the Catholic Church initially was the sole opponent of this measure, it eventually issued a pastoral letter in which it reluctantly bowed to the decision. The reform, however, was difficult to justify given its history. In the 2002 constitutional law that had abolished the Senate, the preamble explained that Burkina's democratic process had matured, and that the National Assembly institutionalized all the mechanisms that were needed to develop and adopt legislation. This being the case, it was better advised not to burden the country's "fragile economy" with a bicameral legislature, which would slow down administrative work and incur high costs of maintenance. That reasoning behind the abrogation of the Senate had been widely accepted.

In 2011, the opposition and a segment of civil society, convinced that the envisioned reestablishment of the Senate was in fact intended as an additional weapon for the undoing of Article 37, took up the old arguments against bicameralism. But the regime also considered resorting to a referendum and, in order to prepare public opinion, launched an intensive communication campaign to put forth the argument that in a democracy, the people, as the sovereign, are the final arbiter when no consensus can be found. Rejecting the people's will would "really go against the principles of democracy. If one were truly a democrat, one should accept that in a situation where debating does not show who is in the right, the final say should belong to the majority."[15]

Given the polarization of the debate and the extreme sensitivity of the issue, religious leaders—with the exception of Roman Catholics and traditional chiefs, notably the powerful Moaga chiefship—opted for caution. Many tried to stay on the fence and refused to come out in favor of either party, calling for social peace instead. However, fault lines began to emerge within religious communities. Thus, in the Muslim community, the old guard was apparently supportive of the regime, while the young intellectuals represented in the *Centre des Etudes, Recherches et Formations Islamiques* and the *Association Musulmane des Etudiants et Elèves Burkinabès* appeared more critical of the regime, and perhaps closer to the views of the opposition (Madore 2016). Similarly, among the traditional chiefs, there were as many supporters of the regime as of the opposition.

After much hesitation, on October 21, 2014, the government eventually adopted a bill for the revision of the constitution that was duly presented before the National Assembly. In a plenary meeting, the Assembly accepted the agenda that had been devised the day before. As a result, the adoption of the revision bill was slated for October 30, 2014. In a context where the key question was whether the regime would secure the qualified majority it needed to dispense with a referendum, Gilbert Noël Ouédraogo, the chairman of the *Alliance pour la Démocratie et la Fédération/Rassemblement Démocratique Africain* (ADF/RDA), announced that his party was backing "the compromise found within the majority."[16] Instead of removing the term-limit provision contained in Article 37 of the constitution, the bill proposed that the president could be reelected twice, and included language to the effect that this particular provision would be applicable beginning with the current term. This meant that Blaise Compaoré would be able to stand for two more terms. The announcement of ADF/RDA support for the regime's project—which it had strongly opposed up to that point—considerably soured the political climate. The opposition and civil society deemed this a betrayal, and the risks of confrontation heightened as the government hastened to close the deal as quickly as possible.

On October 28, the opposition mobilized thousands of demonstrators to voice their opposition to the law. That same day, under pretense of protecting the deputies from the ruling party from threats and intimidation by the supporters of the opposition, the regime put them up in a luxury hotel not far from the National Assembly building, where they were to wait for the vote to take place on October 30. The opposition and civil society kept up the pressure and called upon their partisans to prevent the vote. Thousands of people responded to the call, in spite of the impressive positioning of defense and security personnel around the perimeter of the Assembly. The demonstrations turned into an insurgency as the National Assembly building was attacked and the rioting demonstrators set it on fire. Elsewhere in the capital, as well as in the main towns of the provinces, the regime's dignitaries were hunted down, and their property was ransacked, plundered, or burned down. The government's spokesperson announced the cancellation of the bill, but it was already too late, as the demonstrators were now clamoring on the public television and radio—which they had managed to seize—for no less than the resignation of President Compaoré.

The opposition itself was overwhelmed and completely lost control of the insurgents. When the formal head of the opposition requested that the demonstrators return to their homes since the goal—the withdrawal of the controversial bill—had been accomplished, the demonstrators who were massed in front of his headquarters shouted him down. He then delivered a second speech, more in sync with the wishes of the insurgents, calling for the immediate resignation of Compaoré. The mood became festive. In the evening, Compaoré delivered an address to the nation, saying that he had heard the message and was dissolving parliament and the government in response. But the insurrectionary movement, now led by civil society activists, was not about to put the brakes on their momentum at that point.

The following day, thousands of demonstrators flocked to the headquarters of the army high command to demand the unconditional resignation of President Compaoré. By then, thirty people had died and hundreds had been injured in the demonstrations. With no choice really left, Compaoré abdicated and fled into exile in Côte d'Ivoire. The military stepped in, and, under political pressure from both internal and external forces, agreed to set up a civilian transition process to restore constitutional order. To that end, a constitutional charter was quickly drafted and adopted, after several days of negotiation, and was signed on November 16, 2014, by representatives of the military, the political parties, and civil society. The charter supplemented the constitution and put in place a transitional government, with the mandate to organize new presidential and legislative elections. A career diplomat, Michel Kafando, was selected to preside over the transition.

CONCLUSION

The analysis of the functioning of the institutions of democracy under the Compaoré regime shows that the regime tried to control them and limit their autonomy, using both formal and informal weapons, with some success. Given the overriding central goal of staying in power, granting the autonomy of institutions was a risk the regime was not willing to take. Given this attitude, the regime's reforms had the paradoxical effect of developing democratic institutions without institutionalizing democracy.

The condition of the Burkinabé parliament is evidence of this contradiction. While it sat without interruption from 1992 to 2014—a record in Burkina's history, the parliament, which oscillated between mono-cameralism and bicameralism according to the whims and interests of the ruling coalition, was ultimately a weak institution, given the excessive power that the executive and the majority party exerted over it. It should not come as a surprise that its physical seat was burned down by insurgents on October 30, 2014, since it was seen as the puppet of President Compaoré.

In the early 1990s, Compaoré had successfully pushed for the adoption of a constitution specifically tailored to suit his political ambitions. This served him well for a long time, yet it was the repeated manipulation of the constitution that ultimately led to the emergence of a multifarious movement of resistance that changed the script. Political consciousness was whipped into action by the efforts of the opposition parties and civil society organizations, and, quite ironically, the same constitution that Compaoré had manipulated eventually came to be used against him as the crowds of 2014 demanded the respect of its provisions, including Article 37. This also points to the fact that Burkinabé constitutionalism came into being through struggle. Indeed, the constitution has now become a totem, which cannot be desecrated with impunity, and which carries red lines that cannot be crossed without retribution. The political elites have been made aware that they must take into account the watchfulness of the citizens, who stand ready to defend what they perceive as the key gains of democracy, such as presidential term limits.

For its part, the electoral administration, through the CENI, experienced an appreciable level of institutionalization. Its independence and professionalism were strengthened, and even though the outcomes of electoral competition remained tainted by electoral corruption, they are less marred by electoral fraud, a phenomenon that is increasingly held in check by the sophistication of new technologies of voting transparency. If, for many years, President Compaoré had managed to neuter the opposition and prevent it from becoming a viable alternative to his regime, his persistent efforts to overstay his term—and the way in which he obstructed the circulation of elites within his coalition—ultimately weakened his grip on power. The defection of several prominent members of that coalition brought strength to the opposition, which also profited from its formal status conceded by the regime.

While the initial objective of that concession was to further buttress the internal and international legitimacy of the regime, the tables were turned in 2012, thanks to changes in the leadership of the opposition. The episode gave the opposition greater credibility and made alternation a real possibility in the eyes of the citizenry. In the end, the institution that did not fare as well was the judiciary. Even so, it seems that there is hope to be found in the very strong aspirations of Burkina's citizens for an independent justice system. After the fall of the Compaoré regime, in this respect, as in others, it might just be the case that "nothing will be as before," to use the words of the president of the political transition, Michel Kafando.

To return to the question raised in the introduction to this chapter, the case of Burkina Faso presents us with the interesting problem of understanding what eventually led to the entrenchment of democracy: the logic of gradual institutionalization, or, rather, the contingent actions of political and civil society actors, including the mistakes of the ruling elite or the often undemocratic behavior of the opposition. The analysis of the case presented here leads me to argue that institutionalization was the driving force—or the independent variable, as social scientists would have it—behind the Burkinabé outcome.

For one thing, as we have seen, neither the majority nor the opposition consistently cared about or worked to build strong democratic institutions during much of this history. Rather, they were more interested in exploiting institutions to serve their own goals, of either winning or preserving power. Certainly, given their weaker position, opponents were in general more invested in strengthening democratic institutions than was the ruling coalition, but that investment derived precisely from the fact that there was a genuine process of institutionalization underway. Institutionalization took shape not from the calculations of specific actors, but because no single actor could control it—not even the powerful presidential camp with its robust strategy of political and social entrenchment. The institutionalization of democratic procedures could be successfully defended, as was shown by the engagement of citizen movements and some principled political actors, but it could not be curbed, as was demonstrated by the collapse of Compaoré's regime. Even more importantly, the collapse of the regime and the appearance of a power vacuum at the top of the state did not lead Burkina to fall into the hands of a dictator, nor was the military able to step in. The Burkinabé state and its democracy were protected by institutions that had grown incrementally stronger in their resilient struggle against twenty-seven years of autocratic manipulations.

NOTES

1. In the Francophone semi-presidential systems, "cohabitation" refers to a situation in which the president and the prime minister, chosen by the parliamentary majority, are not from the same party. In such circumstances, the relative power of each executive office is central to how the situation is managed politically. In Burkina, the constitution strongly tilted the power toward the president. The Constitution of Niger's Seventh Republic stipulates a sharing of responsibilities between the president and the prime minister when the presidential and parliamentary majorities diverge.

2. Under the Constitution of Niger's Third Republic, a divergence between the presidential and parliamentary majorities led to a "cohabitation" stalemate that ended in a coup in January 1996.

3. See: http://afrobarometer.org/fr/publications/sommaire-des-resultats-du-round-5-enquete-au-burkina-faso-2012.

4. Badini admitted that "only those judges who committed to support him were appointed to important positions." See articles in the press: *L'Événement*, No. 58, December 25, 2004 and No. 59, January 10, 2005; and *L'Indépendant*, No. 593, January 18, 2005.

5. A well-known case was that of the general director of the customs office, Ousmane Guiro—who was saved (at the last minute, from a committal order) by Minister of Justice Zakaria Koté with the extraordinary explanation that Guiro "was not a nobody." Questioned on the blatant interference with due process, Prime Minister Tertius Zongo, far from disowning the minister, approved his behavior and denounced the justice system's exposure to the media (*la justice spectacle*), saying, "if manifestly the Ministry of Justice, which is there to supervise, believes that things must go on following the norms, I think it must intervene." See the newspaper *Le Pays* No. 4033 of January 15, 2008.

6. Some prime examples: Public prosecutor Dramane Yaméogo was rewarded with an ambassadorship to Nigeria in 2003 and became justice minister in 2012, a position he kept until the fall of the regime. Attorney General Abdoulaye Barry, a zealous defender of the regime throughout the Norbert Zongo affair, became special advisor to the president. Judge Emile Somda, who, together with other representatives of the state, refused to sign the independent commission's investigative report on the Norbert Zongo affair, enjoyed a stellar career that led him from one important post to another: president of Bobo Dioulasso's court of appeal, minister in charge of the public service and the institutional development of Burkina, member of the constitutional council, judge at the African Court on Human and People's Rights in Addis Ababa, advisor for judicial affairs at the office of the special representative of the facilitator

for the inter-Ivorian dialogue in Abidjan, councilor at the court of cassation, and, after 2013, president of the court of appeal of Ouagadougou.

7. See: *Le Pays* No. 4882 of Thursday June 9, 2011.

8. For instance, the Charter on Political Parties; laws on the funding of political parties and on the High Council for Communications; the internal regulations of the National Assembly; or the general code for territorial collectivities.

9. The example that drew most interest for analysts of Burkina Faso's judicial affairs in the past few years is undoubtedly that of the *Parti Africain pour l'Indépendance* (PAI). The faction of that party that was supportive of the regime—led by Soumane Touré—received a convenient decree (*arrêté*) of official recognition by the authorities. The decree was cancelled by an administrative court in June 2005 and later reinstated by the Conseil d'Etat in January 2011. One might also mention the collapse of the "United Burkinabé Opposition" set up by Laurent Bado and Emile Paré. According to the press, the two leaders were divided not only over the candidacy to be put forward for the presidential election of 2005 but also over the management of thirty million francs that President Compaoré would have given their coalition to organize and strengthen the opposition. The publicity given the affair in the press damaged Laurent Bado's reputation of integrity.

10. Quoted in the newspaper *L'Evènement* No. 133 of February 10, 2008, p. 12.

11. *Cibal* is a contraction of *citoyen balayeur*, that is, "citizen sweeper."

12. These revisions occurred on January 27, 1997, April 11, 2000, January 22, 2002, April 30, 2009, May 18, 2012, June 11, 2012, and November 12, 2013.

13. Kaboré later admitted his error, in 2014, after his defection from President Compaoré. He was subsequently elected president of Burkina Faso in the presidential election of November 29, 2015.

14. Message issued after a meeting on the crisis held on June 14–17, 2011, as reported in the Burkinabé press.

15. This statement was put forth in an interview with the Minister of State in charge of reforms, Arsène Bongnessan Yé, published in *Le Progrès,* the CDP's periodical, December 2011.

16. See: http://lefaso.net/spip.php?article61414.

REFERENCES

Badie, Bertrand and Pierre Birnbaum. 1991. *Sociologie de l'Etat*. Paris: Grasset.

Burkina Faso. 2001. "Stratégie et plan d'action national pour la réforme de la justice au Burkina Faso, 2002–2006." Government document.

Chérigny, Bernard. 1979. "La Haute-Volta ou le 'luxe' de la démocratie: les élections législatives et présidentielles d'avril-mai 1978." *Pouvoirs* 9: 163–181.

Hilgers, Mathieu and Augustin Loada. 2013. "Tensions et protestations dans un régime semi-autoritaire: croissance des révoltes populaires et maintien au pouvoir au Burkina Faso." *Politique Africaine* 131: 187–208.

Hilgers, Mathieu and Jacinthe Mazzocchetti, eds. 2010. *Révolte et Opposition dans un Régime Semi-Autoritaire*. Paris: Karthala.

Hilgers, Mathieu and Jacinthe Mazocchetti, eds. 2006. "Le Burkina Faso: l'Alternance Impossible." *Politique Africaine* 101: 1–218.

Garané, Hamidou. 1998. "L'Acte II du processus démocratique au Burkina Faso: portée juridique et politique de la loi du 14 février 1997 portant révision de la Constitution." *Revue Burkinabé de Droit* 33.

IDEA (International Institute for Democracy and Assistance). 2002. *La Conception des Systèmes Electoraux: un Manuel de International IDEA.* Stockholm: IDEA.

IDEA (International Institute for Democracy and Assistance). 1998. *Rapport sur la Démocratie au Burkina.* Stockholm: IDEA.

Joly, Christophe. 2009. "Mémoire et Compétition Politique: 'la galaxie sankariste' et la production mémorielle au Burkina Faso." Master's thesis, Université de la Sorbonne Paris I.

Loada, Augustin. 2009. *Burkina Faso: petites manoeuvres et grandes résolutions face aux mobilisations, in Etat des résistances dans le Sud. Face à la crise alimentaire.* Louvain-La-Neuve: CETRI.

Loada, Augustin. 2003. "La limitation du nombre de mandats présidentiels en Afrique francophone." *Afrilex* 3: 139–174. Available at: http://afrilex.u-bordeaux4.fr/sites/afrilex/IMG/pdf/3doc8loada.pdf.

Loada, Augustin. 1999. "Réflexions sur la société civile en Afrique: le Burkina de l'après Zongo." *Politique Africaine* 76: 136–151.

Loada, Augustin. 1996. "Blaise Compaoré ou l'architecte d'un nouvel ordre." In *Le Burkina entre Révolution et Démocratie*, edited by René Otayek, Filiga Michel Sawadogo and Jean-Pierre Guingane, 277–297. Paris: Karthala.

Madiéga, Georges. 1995. "Partis Politiques et Élections en Haute-Volta." In *La Haute-Volta Coloniale: Témoignages recherches, regards*, edited by Gabriel Massa and Georges Madiega. Paris: Karthala.

Madore, Frédérick. 2016. "Islam, médias, mise en place du Sénat et article 37 de la Constitution: changement de paradigme au Burkina Faso (1991–2014)?" *Canadian Journal of African Studies / Revue canadienne des études africaines* 50(1): 7–27.

MAEP (Mécanisme africain d'évaluation par les pairs). 2009. *Rapport sur le Burkina Faso.* MAEP.

Otayek, René, Filiga Michel Sawadogo and Jean-Pierre Guingane, editors. 1996. *Le Burkina entre Révolution et Démocratie.* Paris: Karthala.

Rousseau, Dominique. 2010. "Qu'appelle-t-on institutions démocratiques?" In *La démocratie. Histoire, théories, pratiques*, edited by Jean-Vincent Holeindre and Benoît Richard. Paris: Sciences Humaines.

Tidjani Alou, Mahaman. 2002. "L'avenir des processus de démocratisation en Afrique: les avatars de la consolidation démocratique." *Bulletin du CODESRIA* 3&4: 31–38.

Yé, Bongnessan Arsène. 1995. *Burkina Faso: les fondements politiques de la IV République.* Ouagadougou: Presses Universitaires de Ouagadougou.

Chapter 6

The Nigerien Paradox

Institutional Consolidation through Political Instability

Mahaman Tidjani Alou

Democracy in Africa provokes heated debates around central questions of power and governance. Indeed, democracy itself remains a controversial concept in terms of its relevance and efficacy for African societies in search of solutions to persistent social and economic ills. While the democratic question in Africa thus remains central to scholarly concerns, studies of democratization have tended to focus their attention on the development of new political structures and institutions, and on the capacity of new political actors to anchor new systems of representation in behaviors and practices.

Scholarly attention and research on Niger has reflected this approach, and hence has privileged a number of themes. Toward the end of the 1980s, in the aftermath of the fall of the Berlin Wall and as Niger embarked on its National Conference of 1991 in the context of the democratic wave in Africa, there was a renewed interest in understanding the transformations of political power in Niger. Thus, Niandou Souley (1990) examined the relationship between army and political power as the winds of democracy were blowing across the country. In a concise and insightful book, Charlick (1991) examined the personalization of power in Niger and the ways in which this structured and shaped processes of institutionalization. In the new political context, debates on these previously taboo topics were also reflected in the burgeoning media sector; the independent weekly publication *Haské* was in this respect a symbol of this new media boom.

The 1990s was a decade of significant political turmoil in Niger: beyond elections and the transitions from the Third to the Fifth Republics, the decade was marked by military mutinies in 1992, coups in 1996 and 1999, and persistent Tuareg and Toubou rebellions. Analysts thus directed their attention to a variety of topics, including recurring military involvement in politics (Issa

Abdourhamane 1996); electoral processes (Illiassou and Tidjani Alou 1994), the legal bases of transitional regimes (Laouel Kader and Mindaoudou 1993); power sharing (Grégoire 1995; Tankoano 1996); and democratization and the restoration of authoritarian elements in Niger's political life with the return of the military to political affairs (Idrissa 2001). Insightful studies by Gazibo (2005, 2010) also focused on the paradoxes of regimes born of democratic elections in Niger.

In retrospect, however, there are a number of important issues that seem to have escaped the attention of researchers, despite their importance. Democratization efforts and the repetitive political crises that followed seem to have produced a smoke screen that distracted scholars from the complex dynamics of political and administrative institutionalization that were simultaneously underway, and which were linked to political dynamics. Considered from an operational angle, institutionalization refers to the permanent construction of institutions through the intersection of the actions of relevant actors (Lagroye and Offerle 2011). This process thus shapes institutions by the ongoing behavior of varied actors, and consequently the building of an institution is the outcome of heterogeneous activities and commitments. In this sense, we can imagine processes by which democratization redesigns the state both in terms of infusing it with new philosophies and by restructuring its institutions. Concomitantly, democratization triggers highly varied processes involving a plurality of actors in specific, normative and organizational frameworks aimed at producing political meaning. It is also the case, of course, that especially in its early stages, democratization also entails the transfer of existing institutional models. These processes occur as varied actors selectively claim ownership of imported models in their struggles to claim power.

This chapter examines the case of Niger via the central question posed in this book; I seek to examine the effects of the politics of democratization—that is the elaboration of institutions via the interaction of actors seeking to shape and to utilize them to their own ends—on the structuring of the state in the Sahel, and in Africa more broadly. This approach departs from the more common one focused on democratization as a sequence: the breakdown of authoritarian regimes, the study of transitions, and the examination of processes of attempting to consolidate democratic gains. This latter preoccupation has produced a significant literature focused on the content and nature of democratization processes in posttransition settings.

Reviews of this literature (see: Buijtenhuijs and Rijnierse 1993; Buijtenhuijs and Thiriot 1995; Thiriot and Van Walraven 2002) highlight the wide diversity in approaches and fields of interest. Among the preferred topics, we find, in no particular order: conceptions of democratization; relations between state and civil society; multiparty systems and democracy; good governance; rule of law and democracy; democracy and development; the legacy of national conferences; electoral models and electoral procedures;

constitutional commissions and revisions; the role of the press; religion and democratization; women and democratization; and externally controlled economic and political conditions. As this list suggests, the range of topics addressed by scholars of African democracy in the 1990s covered much ground, with many interesting insights.

More recent research has sought to critically evaluate African democratic experiences. Regarding the latter, for example, Patrick Quantin has written about the rise of "hybrid regimes," which he describes as "regimes in which elements of democracy (i.e., elections) survive but are mixed with authoritarian practices" (2010, 23). Similarly, Levitsky and Way (2010) have described the rise of what they label "competitive authoritarianism." Alexandra Goujon echoes their argument in tracing the wave of democratization. Building on the work of Loada and Wheatley (2014), she argues that "In many countries, competitive elections as avenues for legitimate access to power has grown, and citizens have developed ownership of the institution of competitive elections. We note that multiparty systems have become commonplace, as well as the liberalization of the media and the acceptance of freedom of assembly and association, which leads to the development of a civic culture." She builds on this observation, noting the expansion of "the idea of political responsibility, . . . which heralds the transformation of the relationships between those who govern and those who are governed." By contrast, and citing the work of Diamond and Plattner (2010), she notes that "military coups persist, and the generalization of elections often leads to the establishment of electoral autocracies based on clientelism and the personalization of power." Finally, she argues that "elections are not always synonymous with the renewal of governing elites, and even if we can observe that there has been a slow but steady decrease in the longevity in power of political leaders, this does not end the continuity of authoritarian practices" (Goujon 2015, 164–165).

While this body of work has produced a number of interesting insights, it has had relatively little to say about the central interests of this book. Thus, my approach here, anchored in a reflection on the dynamics of state institutionalization, attempts to offer a novel perspective on democratization processes in Africa. In doing so, we bring the state squarely into our analysis. The focus, however, is not on public services (for that, see, for example, Bierschenk and Olivier de Sardan 2014) but rather it is on democratization processes in Africa, fully recognizing that these processes took place in countries where the state had been seriously weakened by the structural adjustment programs of the 1980s (Médard 1991) and where these processes remain, to a large extent, work in progress.

In this regard, and despite the relatively high degree of instability it has experienced, Niger is not an isolated case. Indeed, democratization in Niger occurred in the context of a state that had been significantly weakened by the privatization policies it had embraced under conditions of limited choice

(Liman-Tinguiri 1990; Guillaumont and Guillaumont 2000). These policies had been implemented through various programs that Niger had contracted with its development partners before the era of democratization, and that were resumed in 1996, following a period of denunciation of external financial pressures in the political contexts of the National Conference and the first post-transition regime. In this respect, the political rhetoric of the National Conference was only a short-lived game change; Niger was to remain a largely non-performing state whose legitimacy had been eroded by its incapacity to assert its power and to implement public policies.

In a country like Niger, then, democracy has developed progressively within the framework of a state that has historically enjoyed very little autonomy (Tidjani Alou 2000). It shares much in common with the earlier authoritarian political regimes (the colonial regime, one-party regimes, military regimes) that have shaped it throughout its history. This observation may seem, on the face of it, overly pessimistic, as it postulates that authoritarianism still influences political behavior and more generally, relationships to power. We must recognize that this vision has fed nostalgic political ideologies that have often depicted fledgling democracies in grim terms, portraying them as incapable of surviving in the unfavorable socioeconomic and cultural environments of the region, and suggesting a preference for authoritarian order.

While not focusing on an assessment of the quality or suitability of democracy, the approach I take here distinguishes itself from such perspective. Rather I seek to focus on the *dynamics of institutionalization as shaped by processes of democratization that themselves incorporate new sectors of activity into the domain of the state*. My approach seeks to examine the strengthening of existing sectors while giving them a novel orientation. This reflection leads to a vision of the state that encapsulates areas of administration beyond the traditional boundaries, but which also allows us to perceive how the state conducts reforms of core structures that are the very foundation of its authority. Three substantive areas will be highlighted in the analyses that follow: (1) The rooting of the concept of a republic, as induced and shaped by political instability; (2) The expansion of state activities to new sectors; and (3) The dynamics of territorial oversight, born of the need to deepen democratic processes and ownership of the state at the local level.

POLITICAL INSTABILITY AND ROOTING
THE CONCEPT OF REPUBLIC

Niger became independent on August 3, 1960. As in most countries of the subregion, the pluralistic political system instituted in the late colonial period and inherited from the short-lived "*Communauté Franco-Africaine*" of 1958–1960 did not last long (Raynal 1993). The constitution of the First Republic (November 10, 1960) established a multiparty democracy and a presidential regime. Very quickly, however, the ruling PPN-RDA party moved to institute a de facto one-party system and an authoritarian regime in the context of a turbulent political struggle for control of the state (Van Walraven 2013). This single-party regime was to remain in power until the military coup of April 15, 1974 formally put an end to constitutional order and instituted the first period of military rule in Niger.

The leader of the 1974 coup, Lieutenant Colonel Seyni Kountché, assumed the chairmanship of the Supreme Military Council (*Conseil Militaire Suprême*, CMS). Kountché was to oversee a gradual and partial return to constitutional government in the early 1980s, but remained in power until his death in office in November 1987. Upon Kountché's death, the Supreme Military Council chose Ali Saibou, a longtime supporter, to replace him. Saibou initiated a limited political opening, freeing all political prisoners and liberalizing a regime that had continued to operate outside the norms of a constitutional order. A new constitution to inaugurate the "Second Republic" was adopted in 1989, with the *Mouvement National pour la Société de Dével-oppement* (MNSD) which Saibou had founded, as the sole political party. In December 1989, Saibou was "elected" president in an election in which he ran unopposed (Robinson 1991).

The Second Republic was thus organized from the beginning as a party-state and was largely managed by the former leaders of the Supreme Military Council, now replaced by a new *Conseil Supérieur d'Orientation Natio-nale*. Given both the domestic and the international context of pressures for democratization, the Second Republic was challenged from the start. Following the violent crackdown of a demonstration organized by students at the University of Niamey, in which a number of students were killed, the regime found itself seriously challenged by popular mobilization on various fronts. This coincided with the regime's efforts to negotiate a second round of structural adjustment programs, as well as reforms to the educational system included in the "Education 2 Program" agreement with the World Bank. These reforms envisaged budget cuts to the higher education system that considerably restricted access to scholarships and social aid, as well as called for a double-shift schedule in the elementary education system, and quickly sparked major protests among teachers and students. Trade unions took up the cause, and mobilized to vigorously oppose these programs, even though Saibou's government insisted they were crucially important. As the political climate degraded and was marked by ongoing protests and mobilization in the form of strikes, demonstrations, and rallies, President Saibou found himself obliged to address the National Assembly and to declare that Niger would henceforth adopt a multiparty system.

Table 6.1   A Chronology of Transitions and Political Regimes in Niger

July 1991 to November 1991	National Conference
November 1991 to March 1993	First Transition
November 1992 to January 1996	Third Republic
January 1996 to July 1996	Second Transition
July 1996 to April 1999	Fourth Republic
April 1999 to December 1999	Third Transition
December 1999 to September 2009	Fifth Republic
September 2009 to February 2010	Sixth Republic
February 2010 to April 2011	Fourth Transition
April 2011–	Seventh Republic

This tumultuous period heralded Niger's descent into a long period of cyclical political instability. As we will see later, the following decades would witness the alternation of "republican" (constitutional) regimes with transitional ones, punctuated by military interventions. The first of these transitions grew out of Niger's National Conference, which was convened in 1991 when Saibou was forced to accept the inevitability of reform. It was patterned on a model of political transition which was first set by Benin, and which was to become widespread in Francophone Africa (Robinson 1994; Apard 2015). All subsequent transitions in Niger were to follow military coups, as summarized in table 6.1.

The core mandate of Niger's first transition to democracy, launched in November 1991 at the conclusion of the National Conference, was to establish the bases for what was to be called the "Third Republic." A transitional government including representation from all political parties, as well as some civil society activists, was charged with a number of tasks by the National Conference, most notably the elaboration of a new constitution and other "fundamental texts" (including an electoral code), to be followed by the organization of legislative and presidential elections. The transition was hampered by an extraordinarily difficult economic situation and fiscal crisis. Unable to meet its obligations, the state accumulated serious salary arrears in the payment of the civil service, with all state employees including teachers and healthcare workers going months without pay. As the military began to grumble and various mutinies threatened in the barracks, the government was obliged to scramble for support. It thus took such unexpected steps as recognizing the government of Taiwan in exchange for financial support (and hence foregoing potential future cooperation with the People's Republic of China). Despite these extreme difficulties and some delays beyond the initially mandated one-year timetable, the transitional government in the end managed to hold elections, and by April 1993 to put in place the new leaders who were to govern the Third Republic.

Nine parties won seats in the first democratic elections for the legislature, held in February 1993. While the old ruling party, the MNSD, had the largest number of seats, it failed to win a majority. In the presidential elections which followed the MNSD's candidate, Mamadou Tandja, again received the largest number of votes in the first round, but failed to win an outright majority. As the second round approached, the remaining parties united to create a coalition, the *Alliance des Forces du Changement* (Alliance of the Forces of Change, AFC), which collectively gained more seats than the MNSD. The main parties composing this alliance were the *Convention Démocratique et Sociale* (CDS) whose leader Mahamane Ousmane was elected president in the second round; the *Parti Nigerien pour la Démocratie et le Socialisme* (PNDS) whose leader was eventually appointed Prime Minister; and the *Alliance Nigérienne pour la Démocratie et le Progrès* (ANDP) whose leader became the Speaker of the National Assembly. Other political parties were also members of the Alliance, and were rewarded with various positions in the administration. In this new political context, the MNSD—as the old ruling party of the Second Republic—found itself leading the opposition.

The new regime was quickly confronted with enormous problems in the payment of the accumulated salary arrears, and consequently challenged by recurrent worker strikes (Gervais 1997). In addition, the distribution of high-level administrative positions among key party members of the AFC Alliance became a source of tensions, leading to the politicization of the civil service. As these dynamics created rivalries within the Alliance, tensions came to a head with the resignation of the Prime Minister and the defection of his PNDS party. A new majority coalition was thus born in the legislature, now uniting the PNDS with the MNSD, as well as some other smaller parties that joined them, to form a new opposition. When President Ousmane appointed a new Prime Minister, he was quickly toppled by the National Assembly through a vote of no confidence.

Gambling unsuccessfully on trying to reconstitute a majority, Ousmane dissolved the National Assembly and called for early legislative elections. But when the opposition alliance of the PNDS and the MNSD again won a majority in parliament, Ousmane was obliged to appoint a Prime Minister from that alliance, and the former Prime Minister, head of the PNDS, became the Speaker of the National Assembly. This sequence of events ushered in an unprecedented experiment in "cohabitation" or shared government, which quickly led to institutional paralysis and a breakdown of constitutional procedures. In a context of crisis and a widespread sense that existing institutions were unworkable, in January 1996 the first military coup of Niger's democratic era brought an end to the Third Republic.

Colonel Ibrahim Baré Mainassara, Joint Chief of Staff of the Armed Forces, led the coup, and assumed the position of president of a *Conseil de Salut National* and head of state. Given the instability and crisis that had provoked it, the main political parties of Niger in the end accepted the coup, and indeed joined the government. However, the consensus around the need for institutional reform to fix the system and return to democratic rule was short-lived. The forum convened by the military junta to draft a new constitution was quickly contested as it became clear that the military had clear expectations regarding the outcome. Most centrally, it pushed for the establishment of a so-called presidential regime, arguing that it could counter both the institutional shortcomings of the Third Republic's semi-presidential regime and its "lack of resonance" given an alleged Nigerien political culture of centralized power.

Following a referendum to adopt the new constitution for the Fourth Republic, new elections had to be organized to complete the transition phase. The process moved quickly and new elections were planned for just six months after the coup. While much of the political class was initially willing to accept the process, election preparations were quickly mired in controversy when Baré Mainassara seemed to indicate that he would himself be a candidate for president, despite his earlier assurances to the contrary. What was initially a rumor became hard reality when a committee in support for Baré Mainassara's candidacy (known as COSIMBA) was created.

In a context of strong contestation and political challenges, the presidential elections were flawed from the start, and the process quickly proved chaotic. Most controversially, the Independent National Electoral Committee (CENI) was dissolved and replaced by a new entity in the midst of the vote counting process, when early results seemed to suggest Baré Mainassara's defeat. The new commission then declared him elected in the first round, with no need for a run-off. All the country's major parties, including the MNSD, PNDS, and CDS, flatly rejected the results and dubbed the elections an "electoral hold-up." Most of the major political parties then also boycotted the legislative elections organized in November, although there were a number of defections from these parties by politicians who opportunistically joined the new regime.

The Fourth Republic was thus born with a deep legitimacy deficit, both at the national and international levels. At the national level, the political structure remained formally democratic even though most of the major parties were not represented in the parliament. Consequently, the regime was confronted with a very strong extra-institutional opposition from its inception. At the international level, it had to attempt to resume its cooperation with foreign partners, most of which had suspended their aid programs following the coup. This resumption of aid was critical given Niger's level of dependency on outside support. Moreover, the regime signed a structural adjustment package with the International Monetary Fund, something which the previous government had wanted to do, but without being able to conquer the resistance of unions and other sectors of public opinion. Throughout its entire precarious existence, the new regime was obliged to focus its energy on these two fronts, using well-rehearsed seemingly democratic ploys, combined with severe repression against political leaders and civil society activists who voiced their disagreement with the political process.

In these ways, the regime found some avenues to begin to mitigate the crisis. The resulting detente in the country's political situation led to a gradual resumption of international cooperation with partners. At the national level, following a negotiated agreement in July 1998, it managed to organize local elections for February 1999 in which opposition parties agreed to take part. These elections, however, did not go well. Electoral equipment was ransacked on the day of the vote, and the Supreme Court refused to proclaim results on the basis of polling station reports, and then in April completely nullified a significant portion of the electoral results. The opposition called for a day of civil disobedience, and the following day, April 9, 1999, President Baré Mainassara was assassinated on the tarmac of the airport while he was about to board a helicopter for a trip to the Tillabery region. The incident, officially described as an "unfortunate accident," marked the beginning of another coup, the second to cut a democratic Gordian knot in the country.

A military "Council of National Reconciliation" quickly took charge and announced a new transition process under the leadership of Colonel Daouda Mallam Wanké. This accelerated transition was to last less than eight months. A new constitution was adopted by referendum in August 1999, setting in motion the process leading to the organization of new legislative and presidential elections, won in a second round by no less than Mamadou Tandja, the candidate of the MNSD. Tandja's inauguration on December 23, 1999, marked the beginning of Niger's Fifth Republic. Within less than a decade after the launching of the democratic process, then, Niger had experienced two coups and two further transitions, only to return to constitutional rule under the continuation of the old single party, the MNSD.

Tandja was to be reelected in 2004, under acceptable conditions. The same year, local governments were sworn in following the election of municipal counselors. This marked the first time since the first democratic transition that a president of the Republic and deputies to the National Assembly in Niger had managed to complete their mandate for their entire term in office. At the end of Tandja's first term, then, the Fifth Republic had managed to have all democratic institutions stabilized and functioning for the first time in the country's history. It was also characterized by an unprecedented appeasement of political life as the opposition, led by the PNDS-Taraya, distinguished itself by making what seemed to be constructive contributions to the functioning of the regime. Furthermore, apparently reflecting the functionality of institutions, an incumbent Prime Minister's government was dismissed by a vote of no confidence after more than seven years in power, and the Prime Minister Hama Amadou was even indicted by the High Court of Justice. The period thus seemed to indicate real progress in the country's democratization process.

This was not to last, however. By the end of 2008, it transpired that the constructive relations between PNDS and the majority party—or rather the faction of that party that was against Prime Minister Amadou—were in fact part of a ploy by President Tandja to use opposition deputies in the Assembly to undermine Amadou's ambitions to be the party's next presidential candidate. While the PNDS leadership might have hoped that the endgame was for Tandja to favor their candidacy out of some unspecified animus against Amadou—an animus that certainly existed within a faction of the MNSD leadership—Tandja's real objective was to remain in power despite the presidential term limits in the constitution that prevented him from seeking a third term. Thus in 2009, Tandja moved to try to amend the constitution so as to extend his mandate by three years. The only reason given to the intended breach was the need to "complete his projects." The move was immediately contested, inaugurating another period of political turmoil. Opposition parties were joined by some parties in Tandja's own ruling coalition in categorically refusing to accept the president's efforts to have a new constitution tailored to his ambitions adopted by referendum. The Constitutional Court, in turn, nullified the decree setting the dates for the referendum. In response, Tandja declared it dissolved, citing exceptional circumstances which he claimed—with no known legal bases—allowed him to suspend all articles of the constitution relative to the high court. For the second time in the constitutional history of Niger the National Assembly was also dissolved.

Together these moves amounted to what opponents called a "constitutional coup d'état." But they cleared the way for the holding of a constitutional referendum in August 2009 and—with a strikingly low turnout rate—the official results of the vote adopted the new constitution. The new "Sixth Republic" was declared, a new National Assembly was elected in October in an election boycotted by the opposition, and local elections were held in December. Unsurprisingly, this new regime immediately faced a radical extra-parliamentary opposition, and a hostile international community, and proved consequently short-lived. In the context of crisis and contestation, Tandja's ambitions were put to an end on February 18, 2010, when he was toppled in a bloodless coup. The High Council for the Restoration of Democracy (CSRD), led by Major Saliou Djibo, insisted from the beginning that it had seized power only in order to restore democratic order, and quickly announced the beginning of a fourth democratic transition for Niger.

This new transition was to last fourteen months, during which the legal texts for new institutions were drafted. This included most importantly a new constitution, drafted by an appointed committee under the chairmanship of a well-respected academic. The draft constitution was vigorously debated on live television by the National Consultative Council. While previous constitutional debates had mainly centered on the nature of the political regime and the issue of the separation of religion and state, the new draft constitution generated significant interest among Nigeriens and led to much public discussion. This included debates about the length of the presidential term, as well as those of members of parliament. The committee also engaged in vigorous debates about such unprecedented issues as the necessary level of education of candidates aspiring to be president, members of parliament, or mayors. Other questions were also debated: the importance of the judiciary, the scope of parliamentary immunity, the electoral code, the use of religious references in oaths of office, economic and social development, and natural resource management, among others.

While there was significant controversy, the draft was extensively presented publicly, discussed, questioned, and rewritten, finally leading to a compromise text between the positions advocated by the constitutional committee and those of the military transitional council, the CSRD. Following adoption of the constitution in November 2011, a new cycle of elections was launched, for the presidency, members of parliament, and municipal and regional local government councilors. The inauguration of Mahamadou Issoufou of the PNDS as president on April 6, 2011, marked the completion of the transition to Niger's Seventh Republic, under a semi-presidential regime, and with an institutional structure not significantly different from previous republics.

As this brief sketch certainly makes clear, Niger's political life has been tumultuous since the inception of the democratization process in the early 1990s, yet it has also been marked by a continuous commitment to the idea of building democratic institutions (Maigan 2000; Villalón and Idrissa 2005). This unstable political process of democratization, as we shall see, was to have significant effects on institutional consolidation and state building in Niger.

Political Instability and Socialization of Democracy

In spite of this persistent political instability—and indeed perhaps as a consequence of it—the succession of regimes and the debates that surrounded each transition served to familiarize Nigeriens with the concept of democracy, its institutions, and its procedures. This process of familiarization was accompanied with the emergence of a new ideological discourse, centered on the people as the raison d'etre for political action. Moving away from narratives based on the goals of unanimity, consensus, or authority, the new discourse was deliberately populist, presenting the common good as the end goal of politics.

Each time the democratic process was interrupted, debates emerged around the provisions of the new constitution to be proposed for popular approval, centered on the search for the best system that could suit people's aspirations. Political parties in turn discussed potential alliances and points of agreement and disagreement, positioning themselves for the future electoral contests. Elections provided the opportunity for party activists to reach out to the public in the search for votes. Niger's villages rediscovered political pluralism through exposure to political leaders who went out to meet people and present their visions for the country. Via these dynamics, electoral campaigns became moments of political buoyancy, rich with billboards, alternative narratives, and promises of all kinds.

While, as elsewhere in the region, the democratization process has led to a wide proliferation of parties (there are officially more than eighty registered in the Seventh Republic) the major parties that have succeed in ensuring regular representation in parliament (the CDS, MNSD, PNDS and ANDP) have existed since the inception of the democratic process, with a second tier set of parties (such as RDP, RSD) that were themselves born from the flanks of the former. The result is that a set of key parties have been long present on the political scene, and their leaders play an active role in the country's democratic political life. Parties hold meetings and assemblies on a regular basis, and the media reports on their activities. They are visible on the political scene through their colors, their emblems, their activists, and their leaders. They even have their own anthems. Importantly, these parties are present in rural areas, where they compete for a share of the electorate. This dynamic spreads partisan political activities to rural areas, which are visited by party leaders during electoral campaigns.

Incubating the Concept of Republic

Through these recurrent political practices, the concept of a republic has thus gradually taken root in Nigerien society. The official birth of what was to be called "The Republic of Niger" took place in the global context of political emancipation initiated after the Second World War and which led, through various ways (violent or peaceful) to the emergence of new states on the international scene. In this process, the referendum on the French

Community of December 18, 1958, was a significant and historic moment for the West African colonies of France. The referendum offered two options: the accession to an independent republic (a path which only Guinea under Sekou Touré was to choose) or to an integration into a French-African Community (CFA), as part of the blueprint for the constitution of France's Fifth Republic.

As elsewhere, the "republic" that was declared from the September 1958 referendum in Niger was a political system subsumed into a larger entity, in effect marking only a reengineering of French colonization. It was a hybrid and incomplete republic, with some attributes of its own, but it was not sovereign. Its powers were narrowly defined in a set of statutes and regulations. December 1958 was thus the beginning of the new entity of a state in Niger, but its content was very much a work in progress.

In rooting the ideal concept of a republic, however, the elaboration of a constitution is central, at various complementary levels. A constitution is first of all a pact that conveys agreement on the way the people wishes to be governed within the framework of the state. A republican constitution puts the people at the heart of its pursuits and thus becomes the source of legitimacy of political power. The republic as pertinently reflected in its Latin origin, *res publica*, should be devoted to the quest for the common good of the national community. It is therefore in opposition to any form of political organization that does not have a popular legitimacy derived from elections. In this sense, a constitution is not just limited to being a framework for the organization of political power in the context of a republic, it is also a cradle for the values that shape the expression of the forms of society that those entrusted with political power are tasked to implement through public policies. A republic must first and foremost be conceived as a political project to be enacted as a whole, by all members of the national community and without exclusion.

To a degree that has perhaps been under-recognized, the ongoing politics of democratization in Niger, shaped by the political instability that led to debating and adopting multiple constitutions in the name of five successive republics in a quarter century, has produced a significant measure of understanding of the conception of a republic. The republic, after all, has been experienced over and over by the debates over key institutions: the presidency, the National Assembly, local government councils, the judiciary, to name the most obvious. Electoral participation has become routine and therefore constitutes a key form of republican practice that is anchored in Nigerien political culture and practice. Beyond these political dimensions, even the social dimensions of a republic, visible in policies such as in education and health, have been brought into the public debate in Niger via the politics of democratization.

EXTENDING STATE ACTIVITIES TO NEW SECTORS

The process of democratization in Niger as it has operated for over a quarter century fed dynamics that introduced the state into new sectors of activities related to the liberalization of political activities initiated in the 1990s. This expanded role of the state, in turn, has led to the development of new institutions and the reform or expansion of others. Debated, embraced, and at times challenged by political and civil society, this process has been central to the restructuring of the Nigerien state in the course of the ups and downs of Nigerien democratic politics.

Familiarization with Elections and the Building of Specialized Agencies

In this regard, two aspects deserve to be taken into account: the regular organization of competitive elections at institutionally mandated dates and the increasingly central role of the National Independent Electoral Commission (CENI). Organizing competitive elections on a regular basis has become an important feature of Niger's political life (Mamoudou 2010). As the account above indicates, since 1990 Niger has organized an extraordinarily large number of elections—no fewer than 29 elections have been held, as summarized in table 6.2.

In this process, Niger has gained great experience in electoral matters, leading to a high level of technical competence in this domain. Despite numerous criticisms voiced against these seemingly frantic election cycles, there has never been any serious argument proposing that Niger forego the organizations of elections at the key moments of its political life since the early 1990s.

Table 6.2   Elections by Year in Niger, 1992–2016

Year	Referendum	Presidential	Legislative	Regional	Municipal	Total
1992	1					1
1993		2 (runoff)	1			3
1994			1			1
1996	1	1	1			3
1999	1	2 (runoff)	1		1	5
2004		2 (runoff)	1		1	4
2009	1		1		1	3
2010	1					1
2011		2 (runoff)	1	1	1	5
2016		2 (runoff)	1			3
Totals	5	11	8	1	4	29

This broad acceptance of elections is closely tied to the political dynamics of discussing changes in the electoral code. In this regard, the originality of the case of Niger is in the specific procedures that have been used to bring political parties to accept electoral revisions. All laws relative to electoral changes are first discussed by *Le Conseil national de dialogue politique* (the National Council for Political Dialogue, CNDP), which consists of representatives of all political parties, including those without parliamentary representation. The consensus reached in the Council facilitates parliamentary debates preceding the passing of the laws that amend the electoral code. This procedure has largely allowed Niger to avoid the endless post-electoral conflicts that have marked many countries, including its neighbors. It has also allowed the country to establish a sound basis for credible elections.

This dynamic has been gradually reinforced by the increasingly important role of the Independent National Electoral Commission in the organization of elections. Although it is not a permanent institution (i.e., it is only appointed as needed during electoral cycles), Niger's CENI has become a central actor in electoral processes. It has managed to gradually impose its authority through the successes it has achieved and the technical competence it has developed during the course of the many elections organized in the country. The CENI's main advantage is that it is not run by the state, but it has been legally established as an independent administrative agency. Furthermore, all its members are elected and a judge elected by his/her peers presides over the institution. The vice chair is a representative of the Nigerien National Bar Association. The other members are representatives of the state, political parties, and civil society.

Niger's first CENI was created in 1994 for the oversight of the early legislative elections called after the dissolution of the first democratic government. This election was an early test for Niger's political class in the democratic era as questions swirled about whether the government would in fact allow for free and fair elections under normal conditions. The general elections of 1993 had been organized by an electoral oversight committee known as the COSUPEL (*Commission Nationale de Contrôle et de Supervision des Opérations Référendaires, Électorales, et Post-électorales*) which was chaired by the vice president of the High Commission of the Republic (HCR), one of the institutions of the first transition. COSUPEL's performances were widely commended (Illiassou and Tidjani Alou 1994). It was a totally new experience and the political class appreciated that the process took place without any clashes or crisis.

The anticipated elections of 1994, however, necessitated the invention of a new structure since the HCR had been dissolved along with the other institutions of the transition. With broad political consensus, the CENI was thus created, to be presided over by a senior judge, the president of the Court of

Appeals. Its operating methods and the performance it has regularly achieved since its creation have led it to maintain a high degree of trust and legitimacy in the eyes of the political class for much of its history.

There have, however, been occasions during which the CENI has failed to ensure the legitimacy of elections, in each case due to the purposes to which it was put by a regime attempting to subvert electoral processes. The first such incident was in 1996 when the CENI was dissolved in the midst of the presidential elections, to be replaced by an ad hoc structure based at the Ministry of Interior as a means of attempting to legitimize Baré Mainassara's electoral "hold up." Similarly, during the elections linked to Tandja's efforts to prolong his terms in office in 2009, including the referendum of August 4, and the legislative (October), and local (December) elections, the legitimacy of the CENI was seriously questioned by a significant segment of political parties and civil society. In these cases, however, it was the leaders who had been placed at the helm of the CENI who were rejected, and not the institution itself.

The Institutions of the Republic and the Emergence of New State Functions

Most directly, the processes of democratization have led Niger to adopt a variety of new formal institutions widely demanded as a key component of democratic state-building in the region. These include a renewed National Assembly; an Economic, Social and Cultural Council (*Conseil Economique, Social et Culturel*, CESOC, which replaced the older Economic and Social Council of earlier regimes); a High Council for Communication; and an Ombudsman's Office. These independent institutions with their dedicated staff and offices have all expanded the Nigerien state's jurisdiction to new areas of activities.

Through the evolution of the role of the National Assembly since the early 1990s, Niger has revived and expanded a core institution of a democratic state. This institution has long historical roots. Indeed, even during the colonial period under France's Fourth Republic all colonies used to send representatives to the French National Assembly to participate in legislative processes (Djibo 2001). In 1958, when the Franco-African Community was established under France's Fifth Republic, legislative jurisdiction was transferred to the respective colonial Territorial Assemblies, which then in turn became national parliaments at independence. During the fourteen years of Niger's First Republic, the National Assembly's legislative activities were institutionalized and performed on a regular basis. With the coup of 1974, however, the army suspended the constitution and eliminated the legislative branch, and the executive branch assumed the role of legislating through executive orders. While the National Assembly was officially restored during the Second Republic, it functioned under the constraints of a one-party system, effectively controlled by the single party, the MNSD. With the advent of the Third Republic in the early 1990s, the National Assembly was again elected under a multiparty system. Over the course of the subsequent period, and despite the turbulence of successive coups and transitions, the institutionalization of the Assembly has become stronger; it has developed an increasingly specialized staff, has adopted rules for the management of its employees, and has acquired its own assets.

Through the parallel institution of the CESOC, the state established a form of consultative assembly. This assembly's jurisdiction included the ability to initiate studies and to advise the government on a variety of issues pertaining to the country's economic, social, and cultural development. In addition, through its composition, the CESOC allows the state to tap the expertise of leading figures whose intellectual abilities and experience can be beneficial to the state under the auspices of a formal public institution.

The Ombudsman's Office (*le Médiateur de la République*), as indicated by the name, is an institution mandated to mediate between the representatives of other government institutions and individual citizens in cases of conflict or complaints about bureaucratic processes. Although a form of this institution predates the democratization process, it is only during the post-1990s period that it was in fact able to assume its role and fully establish itself within the institutions of the republic. This office allows the state to place the citizen/customer at the core of its activities, and as the end goal of public service. Consequently, the establishment of this new institution has been accompanied by the emergence of the notion of state in service to citizens rather than only the state as ruling public power.

Finally, the High Council of Communication (CSC), the entity that regulates the media, deserves to be noted. This institution emerged from the National Conference, with the desire of democracy activists to establish an office that would guarantee equal access to the media for all. This was the first government office for regulating the media that was established in a country like Niger that had previously distinguished itself by a total lack of pluralism in the press. Its establishment was accompanied by an exponential growth in the media sector during the democratization process. With the CSC, Niger has established an independent state entity, managed by professionals in the field, with the mandated responsibility to ensure a better management of the communications sector in a democratic context.

A Dynamic Civil Society and the Structuring of Public Space

Niger has gradually come to project an image of a country with a dynamic and visible civil society. This, however, has not been easy to achieve. It has rather been the result of a slow evolution over time and shaped by the often turbulent events that have marked the country's socio-economic and political life since 1991 (Tidjani Alou 2006).

If it is true that Niger's current civil society was born in the 1990s with the wave of democratization in the country, it is also possible to find its roots in a more distant past. Indeed, many associations pursuing various goals have existed in the country since independence in the early 1960s. These associations were called *amicales* (friendship clubs), an intentionally innocuous designation as the first forms of independent associations began to emerge after the colonial period. In this early period, it is also worth noting the establishment of the association of Nigerien students (*Union des Scolaires Nigeriens*, USN), with independence in 1960.

Through its activities, this organization distinguished itself as a strong voice of criticism against the newly emerging forms of rule that followed decolonization. It maintained this line of protest against various government policies, especially in the field of education. With the exception of this academic organization, most other associations in the early decades of independence were either professional or recreational. They were, in this sense, quite different from today's civil society organizations, which are active in various aspects of social and economic life. These new forms of social organization came into existence in the 1990s, born in the politics of the sovereign National Conference, and maintaining their dynamism since then thanks to a favorable legal framework at the national level and the strong external support they have received from Niger's financial and technical "partners" who have regularly allocated a significant share of their assistance programs to civil society.

The resulting Nigerien "civil society" in fact consists of a heterogeneous number of nonprofit organizations lumped together under this terminology. Civil society, however, remains a recurrent notion in political discourse. In Niger, it has maintained its status as a vigorous symbol of democracy given its role in organizing or stimulating regular debates, thus contributing to the emergence of a public forum. Indeed, workers' and students' unions have played a major role in promoting democracy. At key historic moments, such associations and unions have led notable activism in the public arena, defending major causes such as democratic processes or fighting the rise in cost of living. Such activities have to a large degree rendered civil society visible; it has become a full-fledged central actor in Niger's public life.

Simultaneously, however, much public ambivalence remains about the actions of civil society. On the one hand, leaders of civil society organizations have often been denounced as "per diem hunters," or other practices through which they personally profit from the activities of their associations. The reality of this frequent tendency has contributed to a negative image of civil society, with many criticizing organizations for not working for the common good but rather for the sole benefit of their leaders. But this is only one of the faces of civil society; the other face is a virtuous one with selfless members who work for common goals and the greater good in public life. This contrasting vision of civil society persists largely thanks to the initiatives undertaken by organizations renowned for their commitment to the struggle for democracy.

In addition to the ups and downs of a fledgling civil society, a crucially important new dynamic born of the politics of democratization is the amplification that the media regularly provide to political struggles, social disputes, and routine political debate. Since the early 1990s, Niger's media environment has become and remains extremely open, with a varied and highly politicized written press (both paper and digital), more than a dozen private TV stations, and about twenty radio stations including an array of highly diverse international radio stations (RFI, BBC, Radio China, Africa No. 1). To this should be added the increasingly central role of social media in recent years; the elections of 2016 clearly demonstrated their capacity to influence opinions and representations.

Crucially, these social dynamics and public debates in the context of the intense politics of democratic debate in Niger's turbulent trajectory have had an important impact on the building of state institutions. Gradually over the period, and as a means of managing the issues raised by these dynamics, successive Nigerien governments have created administrative entities specifically entrusted with the oversight of recognizing and regulating these organizations. Thus, the "Office of Public Liberties" of the Ministry of the Interior monitors associations, while the "Office of NGOs and Developmental Associations" within the Ministry of Community Development monitor non-governmental organizations. As for the media, they are overseen by a multi-actor regulatory office whose mandate is the protection of freedom of information and of the press.

Anchoring Human Rights in Institutions

Another new domain for state intervention that emerged from the process of democratization in Niger was in the field of human rights. The principles of human rights have thus been enshrined in the various democratic constitutions of Niger, which reference among its norms the Universal Declaration of Human Rights of 1948 and the African Charter of Human Rights of 1981. These references, for example, appear in the Preamble to the Seventh Republic's constitution of 2010, as well as in the article devoted to the rights and obligations of human beings. Importantly, these legal instruments can *ipso facto* be used to challenge government officials, who also have an obligation to inform citizens about their rights.

The embracing of this new policy domain via the politics of democratization was accompanied by a series of institutional reforms and innovations with significant effects on the state. In 1998, the government established an office of human rights within the Ministry of Justice, thus dedicating a specific office and a team of civil servants to the management of this new policy domain. In addition, training on human rights was instituted for judges so as to conform to this new context. Furthermore, the 1999 constitution of the Fifth Republic mandated the establishment of a National Commission on Human Rights and Liberty, something that was accomplished in 2000 and which was to continue under the subsequent republics.

DYNAMICS OF TERRITORIAL OVERSIGHT

The development of a capacity for territorial oversight is part and parcel of the process of rooting the state in Niger's plural societies, and hence key to state building. In fact, this is a multidimensional dynamic that involves various sectors of activities that have historically been central to the state, but which have also significantly evolved and expanded in interaction with— and at times driven by—the politics of democratization. In the following section I focus on two axes: on the one hand, on the decentralization and de-concentration of power as strategies for anchoring democracy in Nigerien societies; and on the other hand, on the erection of a system of justice as an inseparable component of the establishment of rule of law.

Decentralization and De-concentration as a Means of Solidifying Democracy and the State

Niger is a vast country, with an area of 1,267,000 square kilometers. Perhaps largely for this reason, it is also widely described as a country where governmental administrative presence and oversight has been very limited. This territory was long governed by an administrative reform law of 1964, which redefined the orientation and administrative structures of the colonial territorial units for the newly independent Republic of Niger. The administrative framework thus established was to be maintained without any significant transformations until the inception of the decentralization process in 2004. Four years later, in 2008, Niger passed a law establishing a new structure for the organization and administration of the territory of the Republic of Niger. In fact, as elsewhere in the region, this reform was driven by an understanding of decentralization as a key component of the democratization process, accompanied by de-concentration as a way to strengthen the state's presence across the national territory, and consequently a necessary component of a successful decentralization policy.

A component of the decentralization process begun in 2004 was the establishment of municipalities in various parts of the country. In March 2012, Niger finalized the elaboration of a reference document guiding its decentralization policy, *le code général des collectivités territoriales.* "Communes," especially those in rural areas, constitute the first markers of a continuous physical presence of the State. The Code defines three types of communes in Niger: rural communes, urban communes, and cities. Mayors achieve power in these communes via elections, but they are also at the same time the representatives of the state in their municipalities. Consequently, if local governments promote local democracy in Niger, they also allow the promotion and expansion of a state presence in villages and other localities. Most fundamentally, the extension of public services (especially in health and education) to the local level allows the state administration to gain closer proximity to citizens. Democratization in rural areas of Niger has accompanied the self-administration of local governments through institutions which thus gain in legitimacy, even if it must be recognized that this dynamic remains very limited in villages located far from the centers of most basic services.

Similar comments could be made about the policy enacted in the name of the de-concentration of power. While the basic framework for the organization of the national territory did not change, there is an important shift in the terminology. The old *arrondissements* created by the 1964 reform were thus transformed into *départments,* each headed by a prefect. In addition, their numbers were increased as the former *postes administratifs* were also transformed into departments. The units previously referred to as *départments* were transformed into regions, each headed by a governor. What is important to note here is that these changes signified an increase in the number of *départments,* each with its own administration and resources. The process thus helped to promote the establishment of better roots for the state in rural areas, allowing in turn for stronger oversight of the national territory. These dynamics born out of the politics of democratization have augmented the state's influence over local populations, and decreased the distance between citizens and state administrative structures.

In this context, it becomes clear that the democratization of rural areas in Niger has simultaneously enabled the state to take root and to increase its presence in socio-economic areas that had previously been the domain of traditional chiefs, and where the state's presence was historically limited to the village elementary school teacher or the nurse.

Construction of Justice and the Rule of Law

Democratization places justice at the heart of state institutions. For a long time the standard perception, in Niger and its neighbors, was one of the judiciary as a repressive arm of the state, a mere instrument in the hands of the rulers. This perception is rooted first in the history of colonial systems of justice, and later in that of postcolonial justice in the predemocratic era. Breaking with this perception, the democratization process introduced a new vigor to the debate on the question of justice, thanks to the stated goals of spreading the rule of law and the expansion of a judicial system in support of that effort. (Issa Abdourhamane 2006)

The examination of the evolution of this branch of government in Niger supports the conclusion that the democratic process in the country has in fact allowed a judicial apparatus to come to exist. On the one hand, the domains of action of the judiciary have progressively been extended to new fields; on the other hand, the judicial infrastructure has continuously grown to include new courts created in municipalities while also extending the jurisdiction of existing judicial institutions. In its origins, the justice system was in essence focused on criminal justice. Subsequently, it became more diversified by covering new areas such as civil justice, which came to represent a signifi-cant segment of the justice system. Criminal and civil justice thus represent the two faces of this core institution in the construction of democracy.

Increasing Specialization of the Judiciary

Progressively, the judiciary has tended to increased specialization as a result of the increased number of judges and the complexity of the litigations to be adjudicated. This specialization began in the labor sector, and later imple-mented in the juvenile justice system. This specialization has also extended to the litigation of administrative and economic issues (as with, for example, the creation of a section on economics in the Tribunal of Niamey) as well as commercial (with the establishment of a separate Commercial Tribunal). These developments have been promoted with the goal of rendering the justice system fairer and more accessible.

Furthermore, and further reinforcing these dynamics, Niger has established several distinct jurisdictional "orders." The judicial order (the most complete and inclusive of these orders) has at its highest court the *Cour de Cassation* (the highest court of appeals for civil and criminal matters). The administra-tive order, which inherited the role of the former administrative chamber of the Supreme Court, has at its summit the *Conseil d'Etat* (state council); an Accounting Court (*Cour des Comptes*) oversees the integrity of government accounts; a Constitutional Court is charged with defending the constitution and renders decisions on the constitutionality of laws and adjudicates electoral dis-putes; and a special High Court of Justice (*Haute Cour de Justice*) established to prosecute cases involving cabinet ministers and members of parliament.

Expanding Judicial Institutions across the Country

For a long time, the existence of state judicial institutions in Niger did not go beyond major urban centers; the various orders of the legal system were all concentrated in the capital city of Niamey. Since the beginning of the democratic process in Niger, the presence of the state judicial system has gradually been extended to other urban and semi-urban centers with the end goal of bringing these institutions closer to citizens. Thus, a second Court of Appeals has been established in the eastern city of Zinder. In addition, the largest city of each department now has at least one judge to discharge this essential function of a state marked by the rule of law, and there are currently efforts to extend this presence to municipalities. As a critical element in attempting to ensure the establishment of the rule of law, the gradual deployment of judges across the country in the democratic period has also contributed to the strengthening of the state across the national territory.

The Increased Assertiveness of the Judiciary

A notable characteristic of the judicial system during the democratization period has been the fact that members of the judiciary have become more assertive. Judges have come to play central political roles in the decisions they have rendered on major political and legal cases. They also distinguished themselves by their role in adjudicating electoral conflicts since the creation of the CENI in 1994. Concomitantly, attorneys have become important players in the judicial system, at the core of the institutionalized adjudication of disputes. Indeed, the profession of lawyer has tended to gain "star" prestige as the position has become more popularly known in the context of applying the guarantee of a right to a defense attorney as part of the rule of law initiative. Notably, and even if the majority of them remain based in the capital city, the number of lawyers in the country has increased and there is growing emphasis on the need to ensure accessibility to legal defense across the country.

Notaries have also come to play an increasingly active role in the legal system. As notarizing documents has become a required formality in many processes, notaries are at the heart of some of the most important transactions in the country's socioeconomic life. There is a growing demand for notaries in urban areas, and in the discourse about the protection of individual and collective liberties in the context of democratization, there is awareness of the necessity to extend this to other urban centers and to rural areas.

CONCLUDING THOUGHTS

Throughout this chapter, I have attempted to highlight the "trickle down" effects of the democratization process in Niger in terms of their impact on the dynamics of political and administrative institutionalization. The evidence, I believe, largely points to the importance of this dynamic. But it also raises further questions about the more potentially damaging effects of democratization on states in the region, opening fertile ground for further research.

As noted in the introduction, the very nature of the democratization occurring in African countries, and its consequences on administrative and political developments, remain an area of debate and contention. There have been questions and critiques about the models of institutional transfers, often characterized by a great deal of imitation, which are shaping the future of these countries. Many administrative and political institutions that have been adopted are not products of local history, and some wonder if the ownership of these institutions by African societies is sustainable. And the forms that such ownership have taken raises problems of their own; undoubtedly, the most striking of these remains the degree of politicization of the civil service in the context of electoral competition, and the perverse effects of this politicization on the autonomy of the state. This autonomy is also compromised by the high rate of unionization of bureaucracies, a fact that places significant limits on the state's capabilities to act. Furthermore, the expansion of non-state sectors result in a heavy loss of competent human resources within the state, further raising questions about the efficacy and capacity of the state as these positions are filled with more politically supportive public servants. Finally, as many have noted, the politics of democratization have also been accompanied at times by the rapid growth of spaces of corruption within government, which tend to promote new dynamics that considerably erode state structures.

All of these questions clearly place the importance of considering the effects on the state at the heart of any analysis of political and administrative dynamics, and they push us to ponder the long-term institutional impact of the ongoing democratization processes on state building in rapidly changing societies. In Niger, I have argued, the seemingly turbulent history of democratization processes over some three decades has, perhaps paradoxically, had significant and important effects in terms of the expansion of a republican conception of the state, the extension of the state's realm of action into new sectors, and the further territorial anchoring of the state. To be sure, this has been accompanied by some of the more problematic dynamics suggested in these concluding comments. The future trajectory of the development of state capacity will be shaped by the push and pull of these competing and at times contradictory dynamics, all in the context of a continued quest for developing democracy.

REFERENCES

Acte fondamental n°21 defining the jurisdiction of public authorities during the transitional government, National Registry of Niger, Special issue, number 5, of November 1, 1991.

Apard, Élodie. 2015. "Les modalités de la transition démocratique au Niger: l'expérience de la conférence nationale." In: *Pouvoirs anciens, pouvoirs modernes de l'Afrique d'aujourd'hui*. Bernard Salvaing, ed. Rennes: Presses universitaires de Rennes.

Bierschenk , Thomas and Jean-Pierre Olivier de Sardan, eds. 2014. *States at Work: Dynamics of African Bureaucracies*. Leiden: Brill.

Buijtenhuijs Robert and Elly Rijnierse E. 1993. *Democratization in Sub-Saharan Africa (1989-1992): An Overview of the Literature*. Leiden: African Studies Centre.

Buijtenhuijs Robert and Céline Thiriot C. 1995. *Democratization in Sub-Saharan Africa 1992-95: An Overview of the Literature*. Leiden: African Studies Centre

Charlick, Robert. 1991. *Niger: Personal Rule and Survival in the Sahel*. Boulder: Westview Press.

Diamond, Larry J and Mark F. Plattner, eds. 2010. *Democratization in Africa. Progress and Retreat*. Baltimore: John Hopkins University press (2nd edition).

Djibo, Mamoudou. 2001. *Les transformations politiques au Niger à la veille de l'indépendance*. Paris: L'Harmattan.

Gazibo, Mamoudou. 2005. *Les Paradoxes de la démocratisation en Afrique*. Montréal: Presses de l'Université de Montréal.

Gazibo, Mamoudou. 2010. *Introduction à la politique africaine*. Montréal: Presses de l'Université de Montréal.

Gervais, Myriam. 1997. "Niger: Regime Change, Economic Crisis, and Perpetuation of Privilege." In *Political Reform in Francophone Africa*. John F. Clark and David E. Gardinier, eds. Boulder: Westview Press.

Goujon, Alexandra, 2015. *Les démocraties. Institutions, fonctionnement et défis*. Paris: Armand Colin.

Grégoire, Emmanuel. 1995. "Cohabitation au Niger." *Afrique contemporaine*, 175, juillet–septembre, 43–51.

Guillaumont, Patrick and Sylviane Guillaumont, eds. 2000. *Ajustement structurel, ajustement informel. Cas du Niger*. Paris : L'Harmattan.

Idrissa Kimba. 2001. *Le Niger: Etat et démocratie*. Paris: Karthala.

Illiassou Ali and Mahaman Tidjani Alou. 1994. "Processus électoral et démocratisation au Niger." *Politique Africaine*, 53, 128–132.

Issa Abdourhamane, Boubacar. 1996. *Crise institutionnelle et démocratisation au Niger*. Bordeaux: Centre d'Etudes d'Afrique Noire (CEAN).

Issa Abdourhamane, Boubacar. 2006. "Justice et consolidation démocratique au Niger." In *Gouverner les sociétés africaines : Acteurs et institutions*. Patrick Quantin, ed. Paris: Karthala.

Lagroye, Jacques and Michel Offerle. 2011. *Sociologie de l'institution*. Paris: Belin.

Laouel Kader, Mahamadou and Dodo Aïchatou Mindaoudou. 1993. "Les lacunes juridiques de l'Acte fondamental n° 21 portant organisation des pouvoirs publics au Niger." *Revue juridique et politique,* 47(1), 109–119.

Levitsky, Steven and Lucan A. Way. 2010. *Competitive Authoritarianism: Hybrid Regimes after the Cold War*. Cambridge: Cambridge University Press.

Liman-Tinguiri, Mamadou Kiari. 1990. "Crise et Ajustement Structurel au Niger (1982–1988)." *Politique africaine*, 38, 76–86.

Loada, Augustin and Jonathan Wheatley. 2014. *Transitions démocratiques en Afrique de l'Ouest. Processus constitutionnels, société civile et institutions démocratiques.* Paris: L'Harmattan.

Maignan, Jean-Claude. 2000. *La difficile démocratisation au Niger.* Paris: Centre des Hautes Etudes sur l'Afrique et l'Asie Modernes (CHEA).

Mamoudou Abdoulaye. 2010. *Le Niger au rythme des élections. Chronique politique.* Niamey: NIN.

Médard Jean-François. 1991. *Etats d'Afrique noire.* Paris: Karthala.

Niandou Souley, Abdoulaye. 1990. "l'Armée et le pouvoir au Niger." *Politique africaine*, 38, 40–50.

Quantin, Patrick. 2010. "L'Afrique: l'art d'étirer un concept." In *La démocratie. Histoire, théories, pratiques.* Holleindre Jean-Vincent and Benoit Richard, eds. Paris: Sciences Humaines. 293–301.

Raynal Jean-Jacques. 1993. *Les institutions politiques du Niger.* Paris: Sépia.

Robinson, Pearl T. 1991. "Niger: Anatomy of a Neo-traditionalist Corporatist State." *Comparative Politics*, 24(1), 1–20.

Robinson, Pearl. 1994. "The National Conference Phenomenon in Francophone Africa." *Comparative Studies in Society and History*, 36(3), 575–610.

Tankoano Amadou. 1996. "Conflits autour des règles normatives de la cohabitation au Niger: Eléments d'analyse juridique d'une crise politique (1995-1996)." *Revue camerounaise de science politique,* 2(2), septembre 1996, 91–106

Thiriot, Céline and Klaas Van Walraven. 2002. *Democratization in sub-Saharan Africa: Transitions and Turning Points: An Overview of the Literature (1995-1996).* Leiden: African Studies Centre.

Tidjani Alou, Mahaman. 2001. "La dynamique de l'Etat post-colonial au Niger." In *Niger: Etat et démocratie.* Kimba Idrissa, ed. Paris: L'Harmattan.

Tidjani Alou, Mahaman. 2006. "Niger: Mutation du politique et émergence d'un nouvel acteur social." *Alternative Sud*, 13(4).

Van Walraven, Klaas. 2013. *The Yearning for Relief: A History of the Sawaba Movement in Niger.* Leiden: Brill.

Villalón, Leonardo A. and Abdourahmane Idrissa. 2005. "Repetitive Breakdowns and a Decade of Experimentation. Institutional Choice and Unstable Democracy in Niger." In *The Fate of Africa's Democratic Experiments. Elites and Institutions.* Villalón Leonardo A. and Peter Von Doepp, eds. Bloomington and Indianapolis: Indiana University Press, 27–49.

Chapter 7

Reforming for Stability or Reforming the Instability?

Legacies of War, Democratic Struggle, and Institutional Change in Chad

Lucien Toulou

The political history of post-independence Chad is marred by crises, intractable conflicts, and extreme violence. In addition to the persistence of war, the country's institutions have been stymied by the abusive nature of the state and the lack of capacities of its agents. This context makes it difficult to fully grasp the political dynamics that have underpinned the country over the last quarter century or so, given the tendency to consider any attempt at setting up new institutions, or at bringing a new order, as a mere interlude between two cycles of instability. Although Chad is often presented as a clear case of a failed post-authoritarian transition (e.g., Buijtenhuijs 1998), one must nevertheless recognize that in the early 1990s the country's authorities had to confront the double burden of restoring political stability while attempting to put in place more democratic institutions.

The government was thus compelled to look at the transition from a different angle, or to commit to a different "ideal type" (in the Weberian sense) of transition. Political leaders had to "govern the inter-war" (Debos 2011, 412), that is to rule the country between one war and the possibility of the next. The result was a prolonged transition from repeated violence, if not exactly to peace, at least to a situation of what might be dubbed "permanent non-war," further delaying the possibility of addressing root causes of political instability and armed conflicts. As Chad's military–political elites seem to have developed a strong tendency to use violence to access and hold power, a daunting set of tasks was essential: to contain threats of violent outbreaks; to nurture a more peaceable political culture among leaders long socialized into violence and aggression; to increase political participation; to institutionalize political tolerance as the only game in town in the aftermath of war; and to promote nonviolent political competition.

After the halfhearted political overture of the early 1990s, the attempts to break free of the cycles of instability that were caused by successive waves of armed rebellions in the 2000s and into 2010 led to negotiations and even in some cases to the emergence of new rules of the game, if not to the establishment of a new political order. Yet, it is tempting to dwell on authoritarian counterwaves—given that they do in fact represent a strong trend—and to underplay or ignore the gradual shifts and small openings that have occurred within the political arena. To fully grasp the meaning of the change which occurred—or failed to—factors tempering authoritarianism and reducing political impasses should be considered. Among these are concessions made by those in power. The political agreement of August 13, 2007, which opened up possibilities for liberalizing the political space in the country represented one such concession.

It would be difficult to understand the process of institutional reform in Chad without taking into account the implementation of this landmark agreement, and it is thus at the center of the discussion in this chapter. As a means of easing the tensions that persisted in the political class while also strengthening the process of democratization, the agreement was an *ersatz* settlement between the government and some civilian opposition groups. Its importance in terms of restoring normality after years of instability was, however, limited. At the risk of falling into the "illusion of electoralism" (Karl 1986), Chad seems to have given priority to elections at the expense of more structural dimensions of democratization and the pacification of politics (Levitsky and Way 2010; Schedler 2013; Riedl 2014). The reforms that were decided upon in the wake of the agreement aimed chiefly at ensuring the survival of the group in power by renewing the conditions of its legitimacy. The question is therefore not so much one of what changed—or did not change—in Chad's political evolution over twenty years, but rather of what has motivated the main actors to promote a certain number of reforms. More specifically, how have constraints in the political environment shaped both the institutional continuities and the disruptions arising from the instability that has characterized the country since independence, and with what consequences for the state?

Over the past twenty years, efforts to develop a more democratic and peaceful political order have remained weak. This is due to a large extent to the persistence of cyclical violence fed by a constellation of rebel movements, as well as two major coup attempts against the regime. Chad has also felt the repercussions of tensions in neighboring countries on its borders, especially from Sudan (International Crisis Group 2010). More recently, terrorist activity throughout the Sahel has presented itself as an external challenge as Boko Haram has launched attacks in downtown N'Djamena from Nigeria and Cameroon, and the Chadian military has actively led counterterrorism efforts in Mali, Niger, and southern Libya. The strategy of military diplomacy adopted by Chad through its leadership role in this fight against terrorism in the entire region has earned the country an international reputation as a key counterterrorism partner. However, this new prominence has overshadowed the country's enduring precarious political and institutional situation.

The institutions that were supposed to foster new legal and political dynamics have turned into roadblocks to normalization that cannot be explained only by seasonal rebellions and the militarization of politics. In light of these issues, therefore, the task at hand is to examine Chad's contemporary evolution through the lens of a temporary, precarious, and uncertain situation, rather than expecting consistency and sustainability. This means that despite the reconfiguration of the legal framework and the political landscape of the country, the relative institutionalization (or not) of the rules of the game and of their founding norms seems not to be contingent only on the country's stability or instability. The calculations of the players and the fact that reforms are subordinated to the shifting needs of those in power must also be taken into consideration.

This chapter analyzes the political evolution of Chad over the last two decades. It focuses on the impact of the institutional reforms that came out of the political agreement of August 13, 2007, arguably the most consensual bipartisan arrangement adopted in the country since the National Conference of 1993. The August 13, 2007, Agreement was aimed at easing the enduring tensions within the political class and strengthening the democratization process. It provided a new framework for reshaping the relations between leading political groups, away from armed confrontation, and allowed for the improvement of the electoral system and the advent of a new political dispensation. Its scope was, however, limited to improved conditions for the elections and its impact curbed by the opposition boycott of the 2011 presidential election. The reluctance of the country's president to give up on some of his powers and prerogatives, as well as the presence of powerful vested interests in maintaining the status quo, coalesced into only paying lip service to the fundamental changes that would be needed for the country to come to term with repeated instability and violent conflict.

Taking stock of the achievements and shortcomings of this agreement, I argue that institutional reforms in Chad neither contribute to breaking the recurring cycle of violence nor catalyze new political dynamics. Rather than building foundations for long-term stability, largely cosmetic reforms inevitably sow the seeds of recurring cycles of contestation and violence. In this context, any analysis of Chad's institutional reforms should capture both political and historical obstacles—such as the country's legacy of instability—and also elite behavior as demonstrated in a lack of political will. Such an analysis must address what might be called the "constrained concessions" made by political actors in an attempt to preempt or resist more substantive political reforms that appear to threaten their political survival.

This approach does not limit itself to an institutional analysis of Chad's political evolution in recent years. That is, the analysis does not focus exclusively on the formal and legal dimensions of the dynamics of the institutionalization of norms in relation to the type of political regime in place, the political institutions in force, or the voting rules or the party system, as an approach based on historical institutionalism would entail (Hall and Taylor 1997; Stone 1992). Rather, the introduction of a "strategy" variable helps to demonstrate that rules and institutions impose some limitations upon the range of existing options and lead players to choose certain repertoires of action over others. It also stresses that the attitudes of the players toward institutional change can vary depending on their positions and the resources available to them. Since institutions influence the behavior of actors—including when they are opposed to them—Chad's legacy of instability becomes interesting for our purposes only when it sheds light on the attitude of the players, either when they are constrained by the new institutions, or when they try to instrumentalize instability to use it as a political resource.

The chapter starts with the presentation of a set of developments that have marked the country's history since independence, teasing out some of their implications for the later adoption of new institutions that were supposed to foster peace and increased stability. I then discuss the general context of the political agreement of August 13, 2007. This framework, I argue, helped to shift power relations between the ruling majority and its opposition from a situation of permanent escalation of tensions to one characterized by comparative appeasement. A third section is devoted to an analysis of the shifts in the legal framework of elections, together with an examination of the electoral management system adopted by Chad. The paper stresses the main innovations of the reforms, before looking at some of the limitations of the existing institutional architecture of elections in the country. Pointing to the chiefly election-oriented provisions of the political agreement of 2007, this chapter underlines the perils of "electoralism" and the nefarious tendency to seek to secure the immediate stability of the regime at the expense of the long-term stability of the country, which helps to explain the emphasis on such provisions. The chapter also identifies opportunities for normalization that might come out of an alternative reading of this "new national pact based on the rejection of armed struggle" (International Crisis Group 2010, ii).

A DAUNTING LEGACY OF POLITICAL INSTABILITY

Chad's history since independence is a story of external and internal tensions that have beset this Sahelian state; of resort to arms by military–political players with a preference for violent means of solving conflicts; of hints at political openings regularly followed by dubious outcomes; and of noteworthy efforts to normalize politics and to end the spiral of conflict. A lingering nostalgia for the single-party era, as well as the perverse effects of "Dutch disease"—the adverse effects of a windfall in high-valued export resource— in the realm of the political economy of oil wealth, have both hindered the country's efforts to assert and build democratic institutions and to promote socioeconomic development. Oil exploitation in Chad began in 2003, raising hopes that the revenues generated would lead to poverty alleviation. While there have been significant improvements in transportation, social, and community infrastructure, the predominance of the oil sector, amidst an undiversified economy, has resulted in an economy that is vulnerable to exogenous shocks. As is the case for other countries of the Economic and Monetary Community of Central Africa (CEMAC), Chad faces recurring and severe economic crises. The loss of oil proceeds, coupled with security expenditures to root out terrorism at home and in neighboring countries, as well as governance challenges, have all negatively impacted the ability of the state to address its main development challenges.

Political reform in such a context has proven challenging, given that security is always an issue, both internally and at the borders. There is also the issue of confronting the false dilemma of a choice between changing the political regime and seeking the democratization of the political order—at the risk for incumbent rulers of losing power—or an authoritarian restoration under the guise of maintaining order and stability (Buijtenhuijs 1998), the safer option and hence the one eventually adopted by the political elite in control of the state. Unsurprisingly, this elite thus opted for the "sequentialization" (Carothers 2007) of political reform. In the name of giving priority to the consolidation of armed peace, they deferred action on human rights, on the creation of institutions that ensure the rule of law, and on the promotion of democracy. Although these attributes of democratic regimes are incompatible with an authoritarian restoration, they are well suited to brokering peace and promoting stability.

Chad gained independence from France on August 11, 1960. Since then the country's political evolution has been marked by instability and violent conflict. The political pluralism that reigned at the end of colonial rule and during the early months of independence came quickly to an end in 1962, with the emergence of single-party rule at the instigation of François Ngarta Tombalbaye, the country's first head of state. In an atmosphere of simmering violence, Tombalbaye was himself toppled by a coup in 1975, inaugurating the cycle of violent coups that entrenched the practice of forceful seizure of power and undemocratic rule into the country's contemporary politics. The violence took a turn for the worse in 1979 with the outbreak of a full-blown civil war. For over a decade, the country was subsequently torn apart by murderous conflicts, which sanctioned the domination of Chadian politics by military figures and hindered all efforts at normalization, including efforts to organize democratic elections. Given this rather daunting legacy of instability, elections were reduced to exceptions as a method for the transfer of power. Even when they seemed to renounce the call to arms in favor of a "call to the ballot box," the successive new masters of the state would only observe democratic rules and procedures when that seemed useful in the legitimation of their initial coup. Aside from the external pressures, this factor appears evident from the preamble of the current constitution.[1]

In that sense, Idriss Déby's takeover following an insurgency against Hissène Habré in 1990 opened up fresh perspectives for an easing of tensions in Chadian politics. Here, as elsewhere, the new rulers had to take into account this *zeitgeist*, while enjoying the honeymoon period that usually marks the early days of a new administration. In addition, the early 1990s began with the global changes ushered in by the end of the Cold War. It also witnessed a rapid propagation of democratic norms and values, together with the imposition of new conditionalities for development aid, which culminated in the end of single-party regimes (Daloz 1997; Banégas 1999; Gordon 1997; Chafer 1992). In addition to such external pressures and the manner in which they were handled by Idriss Déby, efforts to liberalize the political space were also encouraged by the effects of contagion and geographic proximity. Political changes in neighboring countries, where the single party had already been discarded or where sovereign national conferences had been organized, may have inspired anti-authoritarian demonstrations in Chad. In any case, such influences certainly helped dissidents to voice claims that they had been unable to express until then, and they thus compelled authorities to concede a number of political reforms.

The arrival of a new leadership led to cautious hopes that the authoritarian system of rule and the serious human rights violations that had been the hallmark of Hissène Habré's regime (1982–1990) would finally end. In this political context, a National Conference was organized in 1993 to lay the groundwork for a multiparty system (Buijtenhuijs 1997). As part of the political reforms adopted by the new regime, many political parties received formal recognition. As early as October 1991, an ordinance had been issued establishing the conditions for the creation, dissolution, and functioning of political parties. But the hopes for a true democratization process in Chad were soon dashed; in the end, the new rulers restored the government to a form of political continuity that also represented a continuity in repression.

Nonetheless, it is important both to note that Chad's present institutional configuration grows out of the initial reforms of the 1990s, and to recognize the measure of change that these reforms gradually brought about. As elsewhere in the region, the changes of those years sparked political processes of institutional change and reform that have been driven by the question of democracy and that have had an ongoing and cumulative effect on the Chadian state.

Four constant features have marked Chad's turbulent history. First, one must note the tendency to consolidate power based on the refusal to tolerate any opposition. This predisposition for repressive authoritarianism demonstrated by the country's successive governments has notably resulted in the banning of rival parties and the creation of a system of single-party rule, while also feeding an obsession with conspiracies. The fear of political intrigue, sustained in each case by the very conditions under which power was acquired to begin with, has tended to produce a primary focus on the enemy from within, followed by fears of the enemy from without. It becomes impossible to distinguish between the real and the imagined threats against rulers, and each rebellion has looked like a shadow theater in which the plots and interlinkages of the various actors are hard to disentangle.

Second, it is hard to ignore the ties—sometimes invisible—between local military–political personnel and foreign military and diplomatic actors in the outbreak and the continuation of hostilities, as well as in initiatives for peace and normalization. This intertwining of internal and external dynamics in the shifts from stability to instability, and vice versa, has been particularly notable as regards French military interventions in the country during phases of rebel attacks in the north in 1968–1970, 1978, 1986, and, to a lesser extent, as part of the military support given to Idriss Déby during the onslaught on N'Djamena by rebel forces in 2008 (Leymarie 2008; Koulamallah, 2014). Similarly, one could mention the difficult and fluctuating relations with Libya, marked by the breaking of diplomatic ties in 1971, a reconciliation attempt in 1972, the occupation of the Aouzou Strip by the Libyan army in 1973, and Libya's military intervention in 1980. Within Chad itself, characteristic events include the 1979 inter-Chadian reconciliation conference in Lagos, Nigeria, the emergence of rebel groups that were supposedly supported by Sudan in 2005, and the signature of peace agreements between these groups and the authorities in 2006 and 2007. Behind each of these seemingly domestic "Chado-Chadian" conflicts there lurk various overlapping transnational interests.

Third, to put an end to long episodes of instability, players have had to resort to the signing of opportunistic agreements and alliances that were sometimes rather peculiar and unrealistic. It is therefore not surprising that such accords have proven as weak as the governments and institutions to which they gave birth. A prime example of this is the establishment of the Transitional Government of National Unity (*Gouvernement d'Union*

Nationale de Transition, GUNT) in 1979, headed by Goukouni Oueddei, which quickly degenerated into an open war between Oueddei's troops, supported by Libya, and those of his defense minister, Hissène Habré. There have been several such "governments of national unity" since 1990, and none has been able to establish trust between the ruling power and the opposition. Complicating the situation further, a gradual straining of the country's social fabric, due in particular to the exacerbation of the North–South cleavage by civil war, seems to structure many of the relations between ethnic, regional, or religious segments of Chad's political elite—even if these have at times been reconfigured based on class interests.

Fourth, while the lack of a normalized political setting has been problematic for fostering a public debate on political reform over the past twenty years, it is worth noting that in contrast to the decade of the 1990s, the end of the 2000s was marked by a new phase in the institutional evolution of the country, due primarily to the signing of the landmark political agreement of August 13, 2007. This agreement entailed, in effect, a negotiated settlement of the deep mistrust that had developed between the various political actors in Chad, a mistrust rooted in the gradual abandonment of the opening of the political space that had begun in the early 1990s with the involvement of opposition parties. That retrogression seemed to have nipped in the bud any hope of a "concession without conversion" to the democratic process by those in power.[2] In other words, the concessions in favor of political liberalization had not changed the fundamentally authoritarian and oppressive nature of the regime, nor had they affected the ways in which an elite socialized by "living by the gun" (Debos 2016b) envisioned its own relationship to power, namely by putting a premium on force rather than on public deliberation and democratic principles. One should not expect the impossible; political liberalization cannot turn warlords into apostles of democracy overnight.

After the National Conference of 1993, the political agreement of 2007 presented an alternative framework for reorganizing relations among the ruling groups in the political system on the principle of negotiation rather than by armed confrontation. This agreement thus showed how leading political players defined the problems affecting their country, and the solutions they envisaged. It would therefore shape the horizon of their expectations for the choices that needed to be made in order to perpetuate, strengthen, and transform the existing institutional arrangement in the country.

BREAKING THE POLITICAL BIND

The political agreement of August 13, 2007, represented an effort at a transition to a new era in the relations within Chad's political class, after a period of suspicion, mistrust, and ruptures fueled in part by the history of military-political troubles. The impasse in political dialogue between the main contenders grew out of the ambiance of mistrust that had followed the presidential election of 2001, and was exacerbated by the decision by President Déby to attempt to seek a third term in the 2006 elections. Déby, who had been in power since 1990, had first won election in 1996 following the National Conference and the adoption of a new constitution, and was then reelected in 2001 in bitterly contested elections. A constitutional revision, officially approved by a 2005 referendum that was boycotted by the opposition, did away with the limit of two presidential terms that had been enshrined in the 1996 constitution, allowing Déby to once again stand for president.

Presidential term limits carry the potential for the beginnings of a culture of democracy to take root by offering the possibility of a peaceful change of government. By enshrining a time limit for the exercise of supreme executive power into the constitution, such provisions promise a periodic renewal of the elite at the top of the political system. The tensions and the disagreements that ensued after the Chadian ruling elite reneged on the constitutional promise of a legal limitation on perpetual power led many members of the democratic opposition to boycott the presidential election of May 2006.[3] Exacerbating the tense situation further, a few days earlier rebel groups had carried out an attack on the capital, N'Djamena, casting a considerable shadow over the general climate of the election.[4] Rebel movements maintained a state of insecurity over a significant portion of the national territory, notably in the eastern parts of the country, and legislative elections initially scheduled for the same period were eventually postponed.[5]

A series of discussions between the various political players, with the support of the international community, in particular the European Union, eventually helped to initiate a process of restoring trust and normalizing the political situation. A national political dialogue between the political parties of the presidential majority (i.e., those supporting Déby) and those of the so-called democratic opposition[6] was convened from April 11, to August 10, 2007, in N'Djamena. On August 13, 2007, the process concluded with the signing of a political agreement, henceforth known by that date, with the officially stated goal of strengthening Chad's democratic process. Acclaimed by virtually all Chadian political figures, the agreement laid out in detail a legal and regulatory framework that the signatories committed to adopt, so as to lay the groundwork for free and fair elections, and the normalization of Chadian politics.

A monitoring and support committee, the *Comité de suivi et d'appui de l'accord politique*, was created to oversee the implementation of the decisions and the recommendations in the Accord, and to remove any possible obstacle in that regard. This committee included representatives from both the majority and the opposition. The president, as head of state, was designated as the guarantor of the agreement, while the international community— whose support was key during the negotiation debates—was to play the role of facilitator. The implementation of the agreement, however, was hampered by many misunderstandings among political actors, and was further marred by the security situation in the east as well as the persistence of rebel attacks, including an attack on N'Djamena that almost succeeded in overthrowing the president in February 2008. Inevitably, these events had an impact on the electoral process and the other planned institutional reforms. Originally scheduled for 2008, then for 2009, the first post-agreement elections eventually took place only in 2011.

On the other hand, in the aftermath of a rebel incursion into the capital in early 2008, there was a relative easing of political tensions. After the ordeal of violence that had threatened them all, the rapprochement between the political players took the form of an *ersatz* government of national unity, including the appointment of several ministers from the so-called democratic opposition. One of the immediate tasks that this new government set out to accomplish was the adoption of the legal and regulatory provisions of the political agreement of August 13. These provisions were concerned in particular with the electoral management body that was to be established, the planned changes in the electoral code, the census which would establish the electoral rolls, and the general climate of the elections. In addition to the committee set up to monitor and support the political agreement, the most emblematic institutional reforms to come out of this dialogue between the ruling majority and the opposition was a revised independent national electoral commission (*Commission Électorale Nationale Indépendante*, CENI), with enhanced responsibilities and a new composition that provided it with much greater legitimacy.

A NEW FRAMEWORK FOR THE
ORGANIZATION OF ELECTIONS

The negotiations that led to the conclusion of the political agreement of August 13, 2007, aimed at a resumption of the dialogue that had been broken by disputes over elections in 2001, 2002, and 2006. The main goal was to lay the groundwork for credible elections and to thus ensure progress toward political stability and social peace. The establishment of new institutions to reinforce the democratic process was, therefore, a crucial step. Moreover, the new elections were expected to curtail the risks of outbreaks of violence, and to help develop a culture of political tolerance and peaceful competition for power. In sum, they were to organize a transition from violence to peace and a break from the habitus of worsening instability that seemed to arise from the cleavages that had marked previous elections.

With the return to a situation of relative stability in the country and at the borders, the elections revived the struggles over the control of oil revenue and the modes of redistribution of these resources. They also bore the potential for inflaming existing antagonisms and creating new sources of tension. The political agreement of August 13, 2007, however, provided for new possibilities for legitimation by improving the conditions for the organization of elections, and hence their credibility. Indeed, a consensus seemed to have appeared among those conducting the electoral process (including electoral authorities, political parties, and civil society) on the function of the texts that had been adopted in the process of defusing the political dilemma created by the boycott of the 2006 presidential polls (Toulou and Soukolgue 2013). Significant changes made to the electoral code dealt with provisions for the voting rights of the military, nomadic populations, and the Chadian diaspora—issues which had long been sources of tension between the ruling majority and the opposition. Provisions for voting for travelers, voting by proxy, the participation of party representatives in the deliberations of the CENI, and the use of the single ballot were all additional issues included in the reform.

In the past, nomadic populations and members of the Chadian diaspora had four days during which they could vote, while other voters had only one day.[7] Contrary to previous elections, all citizens voted on the same day in 2011 and in the municipal elections of 2012. This reform of the length of the voting period had the benefit of assuaging the suspicions of voter fraud on the part of nomadic and diaspora voters.[8] In terms of voting mechanics, the single ballot principle was adopted for all elections.[9] This change, however, required significant efforts in terms of voter training. The efforts in this regard, however, proved insufficient given the difficulty of the problem, and the rate of invalid votes was unusually high in both the legislative and the presidential elections of 2011.

On the other hand, the new electoral code established clear electoral systems, which vary for presidential, legislative, and local elections. As is the case across the region, Chad's president is elected by a majority two-round system. In order to be elected in the first round a candidate must receive an absolute majority of votes cast. If no candidate reaches this threshold, a second-round runoff is held between the top two candidates in the first round. The provisions of the constitution of May 31, 1996, as revised by the referendum of 2005, stipulates that the president can be reelected—meaning that Chad's constitution no longer limits the number of presidential terms. In the case of legislative and local elections, a list system is used, with each list including the same number of candidates as seats to be filled. In distributing seats, a combination of majority system and proportional representation is used. If a list wins an absolute majority of the votes cast in a district, it is awarded all of the seats. Otherwise, seats are awarded on a proportional system, using the largest remainder formula.

These changes in the electoral code have had some positive effects, including the fact that proportional representation has allowed for new parties to be represented in parliament and municipal councils, and that there has been an increase in the number of female deputies. Following the legislative elections of February 13, 2011, thirty-one parties were represented in the National Assembly, as compared to fewer than fifteen in the previous legislature. Additionally, many women candidates found themselves well positioned on party lists, and sometimes even at the top of the lists. Thus, the National Assembly increased from nine women out of 155 seats (5.8 percent) after the 2002 elections, to twenty-eight women out of 188 deputies (14.9 percent) following the 2011 elections.

Moreover, the composition of municipal councils is rather heterogeneous given the diversity of parties which won seats in many municipalities, to such an extent that gridlock ensued in the processes of choosing executive positions in some town halls following the communal elections of January 22, 2012. These elections were an important step in the decentralization process that has slowly gotten underway in the country. The decision to pursue decentralization was first evoked in a resolution of the 1993 National Conference that called for efforts to establish a "strongly decentralized unitary state" (*un État unitaire fortement décentralisé*). The 1996 constitution confirmed this option and defined some of the ways in which to proceed by requiring the creation of four levels of decentralized territorial collectivities: the region, the department, the commune, and the rural community. Although a body of rules was gradually adopted, the decentralization process ran into several difficulties, such as a lack of progress in the transfer of central state competencies, the financial autonomy of the local collectivities, the place of the traditional chieftaincy, and the weakness of the technical and financial capacities of local institutions (Tchad Eco 2014, 1).

The handling of elections in Chad has also evolved in an administrative sense. The country has moved from a mixed to a comparatively more independent model of election management body. The law of August 4, 2009, modifying the electoral code provided for the composition of the revised version of the electoral commission, a significant step in the running of elections in the country. This law provides for majority-opposition balance in the CENI, with increased powers and the technical assistance of a permanent electoral office, the *Bureau Permanent des Élections* (BPE). This innovation briefly led to hopes that Chad would install a permanent electoral administration, but that did not occur. While the BPE is intended to ensure some continuity in the management of elections between electoral cycles, the CENI, which actually organizes and supervises all elections, remained a temporary institution in the revised form, and is only constituted for each electoral cycle. The lack of a permanent election management body is not conducive to the preservation of the institutional memory and long-term capacity development in the planning and conduct of electoral processes.

Prior to the legislative elections of February 13, 2011, the Ministry for Territorial Administration oversaw and managed the electoral process along with the CENI. The latter had thirty-one members appointed by the government and the political parties, with the government choosing sixteen. Under this mixed regime, a division within the Ministry organized the elections, while the CENI monitored, supervised, and announced the results. Until the 2006 elections, voter registration also came under the jurisdiction of the Ministry for Territorial Administration through a national commission for the electoral census. That commission was tasked with preparing the lists that would be used in the organization of elections. Even though the commission included people from diverse political backgrounds, the fact that it was based in the Ministry meant that it failed to win the trust of all political players, in particular those in the opposition. Thus, in 2001, the opposition requested and later obtained the cancellation of the electoral census. As for the CENI, its composition lacked balance since the ruling party and its allies chose two-thirds of the members.

The misgivings of a portion of the opposition with respect to the existing CENI model had led to a boycott of the presidential election of 2006. There was a significant negative impact on voter turnout, as well as a decrease in the confidence of stakeholders in the electoral process. Reform of the CENI was thus an important part of the 2007 Accord, notably by eliminating the imbalance in representation through the adoption of opposition and majority parity in the membership of the organization, with fifteen seats for each. The chairman of the body was also to be selected from that point on, from people known for their political neutrality and independence (as enshrined in Point 1 of the August 2007 accord).

The electoral commission also had a new task. While the previous commission was mandated to only deal with the voting operations, the reform expanded the CENI's purview to overseeing the entire electoral process, from voter registration to elections, as well as the post-elections process. The CENI is assisted by the permanent electoral bureau, the BPE, a technical body with a dual role. During electoral periods, the BPE is part of the electoral commission, serving as its secretariat, whereas in between elections it falls under the tutelage of the Ministry for Territorial Administration and oversees voter registration and management of the electoral lists.

In 2009 a law established a charter for political parties, with the view of better regulating the creation and activities of parties in the country. While recognizing the rights of citizens to join political groups, the law requires that political parties have a genuine national base and that they contribute to the promotion of democratic values by renouncing any resort to violence in the conquest of power. The charter also includes some efforts to ensure greater participation of women in politics. Thus Article 54 of the charter specifies the formula for the distribution of annual state subsidies to political parties: 15 percent for parties that took part in the most recent elections at all levels; 40 percent to be distributed proportionally among parties represented in the National Assembly; 35 percent to be distributed among parties represented on municipal councils, again in proportion to their representation; and 10 percent reserved for parties with women deputies in the National Assembly, proportional to their number.

The charter did not receive its implementation decree until the entry into force of a new charter issued through a presidential ordinance (and not a National Assembly vote) in May 2018. Problematically, it did not regulate campaign financing in a comprehensive way. The charter only indicated, in Article 148, that political parties were to be financed by their own means and with a subsidy from the state. The charter also specified, in its Article 51, that parties could receive outside assistance, provided that such assistance did no harm to national integrity, independence, or sovereignty. Nothing was said about the use of public resources or the ways in which parties needed to report their handling of public subsidies. This silence on the funding of political parties is all the more cause for concern given the fierce debate over the question of hidden financing and, in particular, over the use of state resources by the ruling party. Unfortunately, the new charter for political parties did not adequately address these shortcomings.

Finally, a law adopted in 2009 defines the "relations between political parties and their elected militants." Specifically, the law tackled the issue of "political nomadism," or "floor-crossing," the change of political party by elected officials while in office—a practice which had long been a major concern for the opposition.[10] The new law now requires that those in elected positions remain affiliated with the party under which they were elected, or else lose their seat. Another law adopted the same year established a formal status for the opposition for the first time. Defining political opposition as the parties, or groups of parties, that are neither represented in government nor support the government's policies, the law designates as "leader of the opposition" the chair of the opposition party that has the most deputies in the National Assembly.

MIXED CONSEQUENCES OF THE REFORMS

While the reforms of Chad's electoral system that followed the political agreement of August 13, 2007, marked real progress, they also faced some limitations. The most significant of these involved the institutions that organize elections and the legal provisions that frame them, in particular those in the electoral code. Overall, Chadian political actors seemed content with the general structure of electoral administration that was promoted by the reforms (Toulou and Soukolgué 2013). The CENI, however, has had a number of operational problems that have considerably impaired its effectiveness throughout the electoral process. This is perhaps unsurprising; despite the reform of its legal framework, the CENI remained first and foremost a political organization, made up of representatives of the political parties, who do not always have experience in electoral matters. In a move to address this issue, representatives of civil society organizations were appointed to the Commission in 2013. While a tripartite composition of the CENI (majority–opposition–civil society) was regarded as a positive step toward more independence and inclusivity of the Chad's electoral administration, this change did not however contribute to better election management, as attested by the contestation by opposition parties of the outcome of the 2016 presidential election won by incumbent Déby.

Article 39 of the electoral code also created local representative offices of the CENI—established according to the same partisan formula as the national level CENI—and gives these local offices the power to appoint the members of the polling stations. The code also specifies that this should be done in a way that conforms to the majority-opposition parity rule, as much as possible. Political parties, however, have not always complied with the law's provisions, often selecting electoral agents by collusion and within family circles, with no regard to the required criteria—for instance, with regards to level of formal education. This haphazard selection of polling staff has resulted in the inadequate administration of the electoral process, notably in the completion of the required transcripts (*process-verbaux*). The ensuing errors have led to the invalidation of thousands of recorded results, notably during the legislative election of 2011, thereby depriving voters registered in the invalidated polling stations of the possibility of having their votes count in the election of deputies.

Moreover, the voter census to establish electoral lists has been one of the weakest links in the arrangements for handling of elections that came out of the political agreement. This has stemmed not so much from uncertainties in the modus operandi, but rather from the manner in which the census was carried out. While the agreement initially prescribed a "biometric" voter registration process,[11] time and funding constraints eventually led political players to accept a more classic method of compiling the electoral lists. After a pilot census in some districts, an initial registration was conducted in May and June 2010, across the national territory as well as abroad. Over six thousand census officers worked to register nearly five million voters out of a total population of eleven million. The CENI made considerable efforts to raise awareness within the citizenry, but the registration process did not kindle much enthusiasm, despite the involvement of civil society organizations in the operation. At one point, members of the government and top-level administrative staff called on people to register. Census workers were recruited, trained, and deployed, often belatedly, in the regional CENI offices, but the selection process and the low level of training led to quite unsatisfactory results. The same was true for entry clerks, whose technical competence proved quite limited. These shortcomings explain in part the difficulties faced by many voters in finding their name on voter registries or on the voter list on voting day in 2011 (European Union 2011, 17). A biometric voter registration eventually took place in 2015, resulting in the registration of 6,298,801 voters compared to 4,830,144 in 2011. Yet this system did not lead to a more accurate electoral roll acceptable by all contestants (Debos 2016a).

The technical failings of the electoral body at such a late stage in the electoral process in 2011 might well have been a cause in the delays that marred the elections. A similar observation was made with regard to the cascade training of branch managers by delegates from the central CENI, and of voting station officers by branch managers. The accumulation of so many technical anomalies called into question the effectiveness of the new decentralized institutions for electoral administration. It also led to questions about the professionalism of that administration, beyond the legal guarantees of independence that it claimed were part of its operation.

Simultaneously, the political nature of the CENI's composition had some effects on its effectiveness in the field. According to the 2008 law, the CENI was made up of thirty-one members at the national level. The branches have fifteen members per region, thirteen per department, and eleven per commune, as well as for each foreign diplomatic and consular post. The CENI thus mobilized a total of 4,870 members (CENI 2012, 28). Given such a bloated electoral administration, it is not surprising that it proved to be severely ineffective in decision-making and operational activities, precisely in domains in which the law had intended to allow it to gain political credibility through a balance in its membership.

Paradoxically, the political nature of CENI and its bloated composition did not facilitate interaction between the body that handled elections and the political parties. A 2013 law reinforced the bloated nature of the CENI, raising the numbers of its members to forty-one, including seventeen representatives of the majority, seventeen from the opposition, six from civil society, and a commission's chair appointed upon agreement by the three groups based on his or her competence, experience and moral integrity. While the August 2007 political agreement stipulated that the "monitoring and support committee" emanates from the agreement, that institution often behaved as if it were the CENI that emanated from the committee. It sometimes over-stepped its powers, such as when it tried to secure the removal of the CENI's chairman in December 2011 (European Union 2011, 13), or in cases when it interfered with activities and decision-making of the CENI, including the selection of its branch members (CENI 2012, 83–84).

Furthermore, the Permanent Electoral Office (BPE), which was the main innovation of the institutional architecture for elections, has had limitations. One of its major weaknesses has been human resources. The belated delivery of voter registries can be traced back to a lack of essential administrative skills in the handling of electoral matters. This was true also of errors on voter cards, which disoriented many citizens and had an impact on voter turnout. Moreover, the hybrid nature of the BPE has proven to be problematic. Its incorporation into the Ministry for Territorial Administration in the periods between elections inevitably raised misgivings and protests among members of the political opposition and civil society. Given that the basic mission of the BPE was to keep the electoral registry up to date, it was unsurprising that its connection to a ministerial department led by an official from the ruling party has raised doubts as to the reliability of the registries, which have been by far the main point of contention between the majority and the opposition in electoral matters. A lack of close relations between CENI and BPE has been noted, as well as the lack of a clear definition of the powers of the BPE beyond the fact that it was an operational organization for the electoral census.

The new electoral code was widely criticized for the many gaps and inad-equacies that negatively affected the administration of elections in 2011 and 2012. Among these were complaints of "repetition of certain provisions, inaccuracy of certain terms that were used, delays in relation to activities to conduct that were too long," and more (CENI 2012, 79). These complaints led to changes before the 2011 elections in no fewer than eighteen provisions that were judged to have marred the consistency of the text. While some saw positive signs in this flexibility and willingness to make changes among legislators, there was also something disturbing about the instability of the much-touted new electoral legal framework over such a short timespan. The law that created the CENI also had a substantial deficiency, in that it made no provision for the establishment of CENI branches in sub-prefectures, a necessary element for the organization of elections at the local level. These branches had to be created *ex nihilo* by a decree of May 2010 that appointed the members of the sub-prefectural branches of the CENI, pending a law that was eventually adopted in November that year to rectify the issue.

In sum, some of the problems that the political agreement of August 13, 2007, was intended to solve have in fact persisted. First, the boycott of the presidential election in 2011 by the main leaders of the opposition demonstrated the failure of the political agreement to put in place a permanent, credible, and professional electoral administration that would enjoy the trust of stakeholders in the electoral process. Second, the hold of the ruling party on state institutions was an obstacle to the electoral administration's efforts to guarantee a modicum of equality and fairness in political competition. The 2007 political agreement was eventually replaced and distorted by a 2013 agreement providing for a framework for political dialogue, and whose main responsibilities was to ensure the smooth running of the elections, starting with the 2016 presidential poll. Unlike with previous polls which were boycotted by the main opposition parties, all major candidates took part in this one, a sign that they seemingly found the pre-electoral environment and conditions more conducive for their participation into the contest, despite the government's decision not to meet their demand for the use of biometric voter verification kits at polling stations on polling day. While the voting process was calm and orderly, the reelection of incumbent Idris Déby Itno was strongly contested by his opponents, who did not accept the outcome of the vote and made allegations of counting irregularities. The ensuing post-electoral scenario was a zero-sum game. Its main features included the consolidation of the overwhelming domination of the ruling party over the political space, the restriction on freedoms, no meaningful role for the opposition, and limited prospects for a constructive dialogue among the members of the political class.

MISSED OPPORTUNITIES FOR NORMALIZATION AND THE SHOWCASE EFFECT OF THE LEGACY OF WAR

The parties to the political agreement of 2007 thus failed to extend or strengthen the place of democratic structures in the country's governance. The implementation of the agreement gave the impression that the authorities were taking back with one hand that which they were offering with the other. In this sense, it is striking that the President of the Republic was designated as the guarantor of the agreement, when there was wide agreement that he had been one of the sources of the country's political impasse. The failure of the National Conference to establish better democratic foundations in 1993, the bad conditions for the organization of elections throughout Déby's tenure, and the removal of presidential term limits had all been major roadblocks to democratization that had been set up by the ruling regime itself. Faced with threats from rebel movements and the reality of legitimacy deficit, the Chadian president had signed the agreement in what was clearly a "constrained concession" (Conrad 2011); he had little choice under the circumstances. In the end, one should not have expected a change in the fundamental conditions of the political system on the basis of the reforms undertaken since the early 1990s.

The political agreement of August 2007 thus in fact hardly changed the nature of the regime. Rather, it reinforced the "perils of presidentialism" (Linz 1990) by bolstering the tendency of state institutions to take their cues from the executive branch, and by in effect reinforcing the "rigid control over the national political space by President Déby" (International Crisis Group 2010). Respect for human rights, an essential aspect of the rule of law, has often been an object of serious concern. As had been pointed out prior to the agreement by an independent expert from the United Nations, "there is no systematic policy of human rights violation in Chad, and yet such rights are constantly violated. Under-development is structural; democracy is just a formality; the Government does not practice good governance. Nothing is done to overcome these obstacles. There is neither development nor democracy, nor respect for human rights" (United Nations 2005, 2). These remarks remained largely valid following the 2007 agreement. Given the legacy of instability in the country, and the repressive nature of state institutions, the issue of human rights was not even placed on the table when the reforms were discussed.

In this context, the implementation of the political agreement did not include any measures that would put an end to impunity. With the exception of a European Union program that aimed to strengthen the capacities of the judicial system and to improve the work environment for employees, judicial system reform has clearly not been a priority. The independence of the judicial system has remained dubious, and the country's capacity to establish the rule of law remains uncertain. One important illustration of this was the lack of any progress in the investigations into the disappearance of Ibni Oumar Mahamat Saleh—the secretary general of the *Parti pour les libertés et le développement* (PLD) and spokesperson of the main opposition coalition, the *Coordination des partis pour la défense de la Constitution* (CPDC)—in the aftermath of the rebel attacks on N'Djamena in February 2008.

The army, a central actor in wars and armed interventions in other countries, as well as in the internal repression of dissidents and opponents, was kept at the margins of reforms, except for a strikingly minimalist demand for the "depoliticization and demilitarization" of territorial administration, noted in point 4.1 of the agreement: "In this view, will be appointed to the position of chief of administrative circumscription, persons with sufficient experience and probity." It is true that a halfhearted reform process of

Chad's army was started in 2005, but it has been impeded by in-built legal problems, beyond the often-noted practical issues of dealing with bloated numbers and inadequate training. To end protracted instability in the country, rebel groups and warring clans that entered into a peace settlement with the authorities were recurrently integrated into the armed forces, therefore expanding the army.

A government official from the president's circle went so far as to assert that "Chad's national army counts in its ranks traders, students, herders, women, and dead people. They were recruited by high-ranking officers and commanders of military districts, were unlawfully and fraudulently promoted to ranks ranging from lieutenant to colonel" (*Jeune Afrique* 2011). In 2011, out of twelve thousand men and women identified by a commission for the *réorganisation de l'armée* (reorganization of the military), fewer than five thousand were considered fit for service and sent to training centers (*Jeune Afrique* 2011). The overall objective of this clean-up process was to retrench, reorganize, and professionalize an army whose bloated number of staff was the consequence of the successive civil wars that had brought the country to the brink of collapse. Central to the challenges of building the Chadian state is the fact that the military continues to occupy a prominent position in politics, not only due to the recruitment of a portion of the elite into armed movements and the cyclical rebellions of independent Chad, but also importantly because the army remains one of the prime pools for recruitment into the system of territorial administration.

Chad's army has been used in different capacities and in a variety of military theaters. Analyzing the central place of the armed forces in Chad, Marielle Debos suggests that the use of force to confront recurrent rebellions and engage in repression should be seen not so much as an obstacle to state formation, but rather as an integral part of its historical trajectory (Debos 2013, 2016). However, the way Chad's military is viewed, both internally and externally, has changed. "Armed expertise" was acquired during combat against Libya in the desert, and later against rebels coming in from Sudan. Though this might be understood as one of the consequences of state failure and collapse, it is also a process of accumulation of power and capacity. Chad's army intervened in Mali, in early 2013, to fight jihadist movements. It was deployed in the Central African Republic in 2014 to help return that country to stability. It was also sent into Cameroon in early 2015 to participate in the struggle against the Islamist armed group Boko Haram of Nigeria. Over the years, the country's strategic role as a stabilization agent in the Sahel has gained prominence. Today, the country hosts a counterterrorism multinational joint task force, which also includes military units from Cameroon, Niger, and Nigeria. The efficiency and fearlessness of Chad's soldiers is often cited in all these theaters of operations, and underline the increased role of the military in the country's foreign policy, with consequent implications for state-building and capacity.

This military commitment and recognition provides state authorities with a "showcase effect," which helps to unite the nation around the military, and which can be mobilized as a symbol for regained national pride. The authorities thus benefit from a new source of legitimacy (Magrin 2013); beyond the revenue from the oil rents that finance military expenditures, they benefit from a form of diplomatic rent that allows them to delay action on internal issues of democracy, good governance, and development. The rise of violent extremism currently poses a major threat to the country's peace and security, especially in the Lake Chad Basin. The loss of oil proceeds coupled with security expenditures to root out terrorism at home and in neighboring countries, as well as governance issues, negatively impact the capacities of the state to address its main development challenges and divert resources from the fight against extreme poverty and the reduction of gender inequalities.

This "showcase effect" of warfare has another limitation. In 2014, Chad was compelled to remove its soldiers from the Central African Republic following accusations of extortion of civilians. Behind the myth of the fearlessness of the Chadian soldier lurks the question of his professionalism, which led to the downgrading of Chad's troops in military theaters such as the multinational peacekeeping exercises of the United Nations in Mali and the Central African Republic, where protection of the lives of civilians and respect for human rights are essential requirements.

Chad's army could only become professional within the framework of a general reform of the security sector. Such a reform would need to emphasize issues related to human rights and the rule of law and address the question of the administrative and political subordination of the army to civilian authority. In Chad, as elsewhere, a reform of the state cannot take place without calling into question the privileges of military men who have been converted, by presidential fiat, into civilian administrators, or without basing the socialization of the elite on something other than the use of force. This is also true of the depoliticization of the civil service. To be successful, the latter requires that the authorities commit to a process of separation of the presidential party from the state apparatus, while also basing the recruitment and advancement of state personnel on merit, not on party loyalty.

When the government organized a so-called Inclusive National Forum on institutional reforms in March 2018, separation of powers suffered a major setback and the spirit of compromise, which was the hallmark of the 2007 political agreement, collapsed. In principle the objective of the forum was to endorse fundamental changes to the country's governance framework, but this forum was the epitome of everything that went wrong with this government-led institutional reform process. The slim expectation that it could represent an opportunity to forge broader consensus on issues of national interest was tested, and laid to rest, as significant changes were undertaken summarily, and without a broad consensus. The expansion of presidential prerogatives, which was regarded as the main outcome of the forum, ultimately mirrored the various shortcomings of the process. It was criticized for its lack of transparency, inclusiveness and legitimacy. As a result, it did not contribute to defusing tensions or to ending political polarization, much less to building strong democratic institutions.

With the abolition of the prime minister's office, the chronic low degree of legislative independence inherent to the very nature of the political system, the weakening of the judiciary, and the introduction of a two-term limit, the specter of a one-man rule hovered over the forum from beginning to end, making the president the unique center of power. Generally, the introduction of a two-term limit is hailed as an opportune solution to curb the power of incumbent presidents and as an important milestone for a potentially peaceful power transition. Yet, the 2018 reinstating of the presidential term limits which had been scrapped in 2005 was seen as a ploy that would allow President Déby to continue to run the country unchallenged for twelve more years. The changeover was achieved by the adoption of a new constitution on April 30, 2018, prescribing term limits—but allowing the current president to be elected for two additional mandates. Déby could therefore in theory rule the country until 2033—a feat that would keep him in power for a total of forty-three years. What was perceived as an overt attempt to prolong an already long tenure of the president (nearly twenty-seven years in office at that point) was accompanied by a dramatic expansion of the constitutional powers of the president

In a very short time span, the new constitution was put together by the president's office rather than by the technical drafting committee appointed after the forum. The draft constitution was endorsed by a cabinet meeting in April 2018 and immediately submitted to the National Assembly for a vote, and then promulgated by the president. The entry into force of the new constitution stirred controversy in the country over the legality and legitimacy of its adoption by the National Assembly. A day before the constitution was promulgated, the Constitutional Council rejected a petition filed by opposition parties, who insisted that given the scope and depth of amendments made to the constitution, it needed to be adopted through a referendum rather than by the National Assembly, which was overwhelmingly dominated by the ruling party. While the government insisted that it was legal for the National Assembly to adopt the new constitution, many groups in the country, including the Catholic bishops, civil society organizations, and jurists argued that the scope of changes introduced into Chad's governance framework should have been endorsed by the majority of the population through a referendum.

Widely seen as illegitimate, the new constitution further tightened the president's grip on power. The abolition of the post of prime minister and the absence of a deputy president allow for the expanded concentration of power, and arbitrary and institutional bottlenecks. It is therefore certain to erode an already precarious balance of power between different branches of government, and increase the danger that state institutions will be stymied by highly centralized, overwhelming, constitutionally unchecked, and unbalanced presidential powers. With the abolition of the office of prime minister, the president has become both head of government and of the public administration. The arguments advanced in favor of this change were that it would be a quicker, straightforward, and more efficient way to run the country, and that it would render the president more accountable to the population who elected him. But with this, the interface between the government and the National Assembly was gone, and an institutional buffer which has played a major role in regulating the interactions between the executive, other branches of government and different stakeholders in the country—while also ensuring a delicate balance between the representation of northern and southern communities in the country—was eliminated. The new round of institutional reforms in which Chad engaged in 2018 thus further eroded the promise of democratic progress that seemed to emerge from the political agreement of August 13, 2007.

CONCLUSION

Over the course of the debate on democratic reform since the early 1990s, a state has begun to be built in Chad, within the context of—and in spite of—the instability that has characterized the country since independence. It is difficult to make sense of the institutional shifts that have accompanied this process of "normalization" and state-building without taking into account the effects of the legacy of war. The twofold transition from authoritarian rule and from civil war has not led to a successful political normalization or the institutionalization of an established political system. This is the ongoing consequence of the cyclical nature of rebellion, of tensions with neighboring countries, of persistent contestation of electoral processes, of the weakness of public institutions, and of the low degree of confidence among the citizenry in the state's capacity to claim a monopoly on legitimate physical violence across the national territory.

Given this heavy legacy of instability, Chad's rulers have, for a long time, resorted to armed violence. After prolonged periods of violent conflict, long hoped-for elections have sometimes led to unrealistic expectations; expectations that do not adequately account for what the leading political players in fact can and want to do for the country's normalization. While voting is often presented as a ritual renouncement of violence, whereby the ballot becomes a weapon against bullets, in fact the historical record in places that are transitioning from instability to political normalization does not often suggest the possibility for successfully holding legitimate elections. Nevertheless, the political agreement of August 13, 2007, negotiated after a difficult period of suspicion, mistrust, and consensus-breaking, in fact helped to reunite Chad's political class around the issue of universal suffrage. The comparatively peaceful organization of the legislative elections of February 13, 2011, the presidential election of April 25, 2011, and the local elections of January 22, 2012, would not have been possible without a commitment from the main stakeholders in the electoral process to accept the consequences of the relevant provisions of the agreement.

However, democratization does not stop at the organizing of elections, of course, and many other aspects of the democratic struggle in Chad will continue to shape the process of state building, and prospects for stability. In this regard, one might note that the demilitarization and depoliticization of the state administration, issues which the political agreement identified as essential to the electoral process, were not the object of any specific measures. Similarly, while political parties from both the majority and the established opposition signed the agreement, it did not include the rebel movements or civil society organizations. The agreement also remained silent on other basic elements of democratization, such as human rights, the rule of law, and the fight against impunity, elements which are crucial to ending the cycle of instability in the country and hold major implications for the future of state building in Chad.

The boycott of the 2011 presidential election by segments of the opposition broke the consensus on the conditions for the organization of voting. There were disagreements on the lessons to be drawn from that election. No common vision has ultimately emerged as to the kinds of actions that should be taken to better organize future elections, or how to conduct the necessary reforms that would end the era of war and cyclical violence by laying the framework for a genuine normalization of politics in the country. As a result, the reforms that are essential to the establishment of the rule of law and respect for human rights, separation and balance of powers, and a deeper reform of the security sector all remain a preserve of the president. No real change is possible in any of these domains without his dedicated political will, in addition to pressures from the opposition, civil society groups, and external actors. In the context of the widespread Sahelian security crisis that followed the 2012 collapse of Mali, however, external pressures are unlikely, given the diplomatic rent that accrues from Chad's military commitment to the fight against terrorism in the region.

No meaningful political dialogue has taken place in the country since the signing of the 2007 political agreement. Rather than participating in the 2017–2018 government-led institutional reform process, opposition parties called for a political dialogue to discuss some of the main issues confronting the country, including civil liberties, election management and the fight against corruption. There is no trust between the majority and the opposition. In addition to grievances related to the contestation of the outcome of the 2016 presidential election and the restriction of the political space, this mistrust is the result of conflicting agendas and understandings of the notion of political dialogue within the framework of the political, economic and security situation of Chad. While incumbent authorities present the institutional reform process as an opportunity for the country to come together and to agree on the key institutional changes that are needed, opposition parties advocated for a more ambitious and much wider debate, with outside facilitation, which they claimed could iron out the main differences between the majority and the opposition on the issues of concern. These divergent views reflect the widening gap that exists between the ruling regime, opposition parties, and independent civil society organizations on the major challenges confronting the country and the kind of solutions to develop in order to address them.

By and large, neither the National Conference of 1993 nor the political agreement of August 13, 2007, fundamentally changed the militaristic and repressive nature of the Chadian regime, nor did they modify the basic parameters of political power in Chad. The 2017–2018 institutional reform process was thus another missed opportunity to forge a national consensus on the fundamental changes needed for the country to come to term with its long history of instability and military authoritarianism. To a large extent, the establishment of a "full presidential regime" with the adoption of the new constitution in May 2018 represents a move to the highest stage of personal rule. Chad was thus poised to slide into a "one-man state," which could be considered a continuation of the defunct one-party state by other means. The semblance of political continuity and leadership stability in the short term might lead some to conclude that the status quo will endure, but an entrenched political regime does not necessarily mean political stability for a country, and the decline of political domination might start with its apotheosis. The long history of instability, the legacy of war, as well as political longevity and lack of a culture of leadership succession amidst weak institutions, are instead the perfect recipe for a regime breakdown, with the risk of fueling further instability in the country. In this context, only much broader and fundamental reforms, including through the development of strong institutions and the nurturing of a democratic culture, can bring about systemic political transformation in Chad.

NOTES

1. Without losing sight of the important role of external pressures and the compromises that had grown out of the national conference, this was the essence of the spirit of the preamble to the Chadian constitution of 1996, which calls on citizens to "resist and . . . to disobey any individual, groups of individuals, or state body that might seize power by force."

2. I borrow Richard Joseph's (1997) term here, from his typology of the different possible "conversions" undergone by incumbent elites in the process of transition to democracy. Joseph distinguishes between "apparent conversion," "feigned conversion," "concession without conversion," and "deposing before conversion."

3. In the end five candidates stood for this election: the incumbent President Idriss Déby, the Minister of Agriculture Albert Pahimi Padacké and three candidates from small parties allied with Déby's: Delwa Kassiré Koumakoye, Brahim Koullamalah, and Mahamat Abdoulaye.

4. This was the first rebel incursion led by Mahamat Nour, who would subsequently become minister of defense following a political agreement, before again taking up arms against the regime a few years later.

5. The failure to hold elections to replace the sitting legislature was to lead political actors to twice prolong deputies' term in office. The legislature's mandate was only to end in 2011.

6. The Accord of August 13, 2007, resulted in the definitive division of the Chadian political spectrum into two camps: the presidential majority and the democratic opposition. In contrast to the military opposition, especially as embodied in the constellation of rebel movements in the decade of the 2000s, the so-called democratic opposition is far from being a united force. Most of the groups around which it has been organized have been unstable, and have floundered following inevitable leadership squabbles. The mix of parties espousing a "unitary" versus "federalist" vision for Chad, to mention only one of the many cleavages, reduces this opposition to a disparate collection of political actors without a common ideological base or a shared political program. It is unsurprising, therefore, that the opposition has difficulties in presenting itself as a credible alternative to the ruling party, and that it enjoys only limited room for maneuver.

7. Nomadic populations regularly move between the northern and the southern parts of the country, following the seasons and the extension of grazing areas. Official estimates put the number of nomads at 165,175 in Chad. They represent an important electoral stake, as does the community of Chadians in the diaspora, estimated at 240,000 voters.

8. This had long been a bone of contention. In 2001, for example, the vote of the Chadian diaspora had been annulled by the Constitutional Council following reports by elections monitors deployed by Chadian civil society organizations in such countries as Sudan, the Central African Republic, and Cameroon.

9. A single ballot format lists all candidates or party lists in a district, and the voter is required to mark his or her choice. This contrasts with the multiple ballot system commonly used in the region, which involves a separate ballot sheet for each candidate or party from which the voter much choose one to cast.

10. The debate on this law was highly contentious, with the presidential majority parties, which were often reinforced by defections to their side by opposition deputies, and opposition parties, who are the main losers in this phenomenon, on opposite sides of the debate. It took the intervention of jurists from the International Organisation of La Francophonie to find a compromise, and to secure a resolution on the constitutionality of the law.

11. As part of its efforts to modernize its electoral system, Chad introduced biometric technology capturing fingerprints to register voters.

REFERENCES

Banégas, Richard. 1999. "La démocratie est-elle un produit d'importation en Afrique? L'exemple du Bénin." In Christophe Jaffrelot, ed., *Democraties d'ailleurs*. Paris: Karthala, 509–541.

Buijtenhuijs, Robert. 1997. *La conférence nationale du Tchad: un essai d'histoire immediate*. Paris: Karthala.

Buijtenhuijs, Robert. 1998. *Transition et élections au Tchad 1993–1997: restauration autoritaire et recomposition politique*. Paris: Karthala.

Carothers, Thomas. 2007. "The 'Sequencing' Fallacy." *Journal of Democracy* 18(1): 12–27.

CENI (Commission Électorale Nationale Indépendante). 2012. *Rapport général sur le processus électoral 2009-2012*. N'Djamena. Government document; CENI.

Chafer, Tony. 1992. "French African Policy: Towards Change." *African Affairs* 91: 37–51.

Conrad, Courtenay R. 2011. "Constrained Concessions: Beneficent Dictatorial Responses to the Domestic Political Opposition." *International Studies Quarterly* 55(4): 1167–1187.

Daloz, Jean-Pascal. 1997. "Le temps mondial au sud du Sahara: de la représentation à la ressource politique." In Zaki Laïdi, ed., *Le temps Mondial*. Brussels: Complexe, 143–167.

Debos, Marielle. 2011. "Living by the Gun in Chad: Armed Violence as a Practical Occupation." *Journal of Modern African Studies* 49(3): 409–428.

Debos, Marielle. 2013. *Le métier des armes au Tchad. Le gouvernement de l'entreguerres*. Paris: Karthala.

Debos, Marielle. 2016a. "Biometric Voting in Chad: New Technology, Same Old Political Tricks." *The Conversation*, 4 May.

Debos, Marielle. 2016b. *Living by the Gun in Chad: Combatants, Impunity and State Formation*. London: Zed books.

European Union. 2011. "Mission d'observation électorale de l'Union Européenne au Tchad." *Rapport final sur les élections législatives du 13 février 2011*.

Gordon, David. 1997. "On Promoting Democracy in Africa: The International Dimensions." In Marina Ottaway Boulder, ed., *Democracy in Africa: The Hard Road Ahead*. Boulder: Lynne Rienner Publishers, 159–162.

Hall, Peter A. and Rosemary C. R. Taylor. 1997. "La science politique et les trois néo-institutionnalismes." *Revue française de science politique* 47(3–4): 469–495.

International Crisis Group. 2010. "Tchad: au-delà de l'apaisement." Rapport Afrique No. 162.

Jeune Afrique. 2011. "Tchad: l'opération 'nettoyage' de l'armée a commence." 10 november.

Joseph, Richard. 1997. "Democratization in Africa after 1989: Comparative and Theoretical Perspectives." *Comparative Politics* 29(3): 363–382.

Karl, Terry Lynn. 1986. "Imposing Consent? Electoralism versus Democratization in El Salvador." In Paul Drake and Eduardo Silva, eds., *Elections and Democratization in Latin America, 1980–1985*. San Diego: Center for Iberian and Latin American Studies, University of California, 9–36.

Koulamallah, Abderaman. 2014. *La Bataille de N'Djamena*. Paris: L'Harmattan.

Levitsky, Steven and Lucan A. Way. 2010. *Competitive Authoritarianism: Hybrid Regimes After the Cold War*. New York: Cambridge University Press.

Leymarie, Philippe. 2008. "De N'Djamena à Kaboul, opérations françaises secrètes." *Le Monde diplomatique*, March.

Linz, Juan J. 1990. "The Perils of Presidentialism." *Journal of Democracy* 1: 51–69.

Magrin, Géraud. 2013. "Les ressorts de l'intervention militaire tchadienne au Mali (2013)." *EchoGéo: Sur le Vif*.

Riedl, Rachel Beatty. 2014. *Authoritarian Origins of Democratic Party Systems in Africa*. Cambridge: Cambridge University Press.

Schedler, Andreas. 2013. *The Politics of Uncertainty: Sustaining and Subverting Electoral Authoritarianism*. Oxford: Oxford University Press.

Stone, Alec. 1992. "Le 'néo-institutionnalisme': défis conceptuels et méthodologiques." *Politix* 40: 155–168.

Tchad Eco. 2014. "Le bimestriel du CROSET n° 2 du 1er novembre au 31 décembre 2014: Décentralisation et soutenabilité de l'économie tchadienne."

Toulou, Lucien and Baïdessou Soukolgue. 2013. *Comprendre l'organisation des élections au Tchad*. N'Djamena: EISA/IDT.

United Nations. 2005. *Rapport sur la situation des droits de l'homme au Tchad établi par l'Experte indépendante Mónica Pinto*. United Nations.

Chapter 8

The Dialectics of Democratization and Stability in the Sahel

Rahmane Idrissa

As with so many dynamic historical processes, the best analytical framework for examining democratization has to be a dialectical one, even though scholars of democratization have generally favored a static linear framework for understanding the phenomenon. "Transitologists," as they are called—following a 1970 article by Dankwart Rustow[1]—have tended to like a model of "stages of transition" from dictatorship to democracy, with the intervening possibilities of stagnation or regression producing difficult-to-categorize regimes that are neither fish nor fowl (but that make good material for many academic typologies). This notion of linear transition is not in itself inaccurate. Transitions to democracy do occur, and any such transitional passage from one point to another has an element of linear progress to it.

But, there is also a fundamental problem here. To elaborate an analytical model from this common sense fact implies a somewhat naive belief in the actual existence—somewhere in the world—of "full democracies" and "full dictatorships," in which all political processes and parameters converge to create perfect alignments of the stars in a democratic or a dictatorial constellation. This is clearly a normative delusion; no real-world complex political system could realistically have such uniform qualities. Even Denmark or Sweden have elements of authoritarianism—let alone a country as large and conflicted as the United States—and much as many academic liberals can label China or Saudi Arabia for their grim authoritarianism, even such countries do comport some elements of democracy, in perhaps unexpected ways.

The papers collected in this volume collectively serve as a corrective against this delusion. The workshop with the authors that first gave rise to this volume, and the editorial processes of reading, translating, and editing the chapters, have reinforced our premises that studying linear "transitions" makes much less sense than focusing on the dialectical tensions between democracy and authoritarianism in any given political system. Such tensions might be graver in some cases—and at some points in time—than in others. And they might, at certain junctures, appear more favorable to democracy than to authoritarianism, or vice versa.

Among the cases studied in this book, Burkina Faso offers a good lesson of this important point. From the transitologist's viewpoint, the country was languishing in a limbo of "competitive authoritarianism" (Levitsky and Way 2010) or "electoral authoritarianism" (Schedler 2013) until the insurrection of 2014, which suddenly—literally overnight—transformed it into something resembling "full democracy." It is difficult to make sense of this abrupt change within the framework of a linear model of change. By contrast, Augustin Loada argues in this volume that the Burkinabè political system before 2014 was in fact characterized by a deep struggle between forces that were favorable to democracy and forces sustaining authoritarianism. The actors driving such forces were not necessarily pro-democracy or pro-dictatorship in a principled sense of such phrases. In most cases, they were in fact pursuing specific political interests, all while claiming to support the normative regime of democracy. But in their wrangling, a gradual dialectical progress in the direction of *more* democracy began to emerge; even the efforts deployed by the authoritarian leadership to attempt to rein in this movement—though they led to apparent democratic setbacks—ultimately only made the revolution more abrupt and more radical. This obviously does not mean that Burkina Faso has since then become a full democracy, but rather that the tension between authoritarianism and democracy has now tipped strongly in favor of the latter.

In this concluding chapter, I propose to explore the implications of this dialectical model of analysis for the central concern of this book: the relationship between a quarter century of democratic political struggles and the strength of political institutions in the Sahel. The hypothesis of interest is that, in the specific context of the Sahel in the late twentieth and early twenty-first century, dialectical progress toward democracy is a function of the strengthening of a political consensus around the democratic nature of political institutions. The failure of national development in the 1970s–1980s and the externally imposed political and economic governance reforms that coincided with democratization in the early 1990s endowed political institutions—the legislature, the judiciary, the constitution and others—with a central role in providing rulers with the legitimacy that they otherwise lacked. While democratic institutions do not necessarily bring about economic prosperity, they shore up political stability, which is the minimal condition for any form of social or economic progress. With regard to the upheavals of democratization described in the case studies in this volume, it might seem unconvincing to postulate a relationship between democratic institutions and political stability in the context of these countries. Yet the historical background that I summarize in the section that follows lays out my reasons for arguing that such a relationship does in fact exist.

If Sahelian rulers depend on democratic institutions for legitimacy and the resulting political stability, they have nevertheless often demonstrated authoritarian impulses that can be partly traced to the political experiences of their countries in the first decades of independence. Erosion of legitimacy and political instability do not then derive from democratic institutions, but rather, quite to the contrary, from the actions of authoritarian leaders who weaken or breach the political consensus around the democratic nature and operation of key institutions. In other words, the more both incumbent and opposition leaders consensually agree on respecting democratic institutions, the stronger those institutions grow, the more legitimate elected leaders become, and the more stable the political system ends up being. But since each of these points depends on the political struggles and settlements that take shape in any given context, its progress cannot be linear. It will hinge, at every juncture, on the results of struggles in the political arena, and obliges political analysts to do what they often prefer not to do: privilege the empirical messiness of history over the conceptual elegance of theory. The authors of our case studies have delved deeply into the messiness of history and, since conclusions are best kept short, I have the luxury of summarizing some theoretical pointers in what follows. These considerations do not have the elegance and parsimony of a conclusive theory, and I will return, by way of illustration, to the messy historical facts. But my aim is to provide a relatively cogent theoretical perspective.

This chapter has three sections. The first provides historical information that is important for making sense of what democratization means exactly for the political development of the Sahel countries. The second section lays out the theoretical perspective I propose by returning to some of the cases studied in the book. I end by offering a short *précis* on theoretical pointers.

FIVE PHASES IN A BACKGROUND

The origins of democracy in the Sahel are colonial. This is of course an African paradox, but perhaps less so if one thinks dialectically. There are at least five phases in the trajectory of democracy in the Sahel since the colonial era.

First, there is the fact that the Sahel was colonized by the French Third Republic, a liberal democracy in a rigorous sense of the term, as it possessed a "minimal state" and strong democratic institutions. Those institutions were in fact so strong that the government was able to function without a formal constitution, but rather on the basis of pragmatic constitutional laws, adopted in the 1870s, that arranged for the relations between political institutions and organized universal male suffrage. The state was strictly limited to its so-called regalian functions—minting currency, finance, law and order, war, and diplomacy. The state could not engage in social and economic policy, since its conservative founders wished above all to guarantee extensive economic freedom to the propertied classes, without undue care for troublesome proletarians. However, it sought its legitimacy in upholding some of the democratic principles of the French Revolution, including the classical "negative" citizens' rights (those rights not to be kept in check by the powers that be), equality before the law, and anticlericalism (Garrigues 2011; De Thy 2017)

The political domination of the Sahel by this regime led to some incongruous outcomes. Familiarity with democratic principles rapidly grew in the region, first in Senegal, where they were widely known in the "four communes" that constituted France's earliest establishments on the continent, and then—in ways that colonial rulers vainly came to wish that they could control—in other parts of the region. On the other hand, given the conservative nature of the Third Republic, its "mission" in Africa could not be social and economic development but rather economic exploitation, that is, to make Africa safe and pliable for the ventures of France's capitalist classes. This obviously entailed the need for an authoritarian form of governance, in practice, a "disciplinary" version of the metropolitan minimal state. In the colonies, the play of regalian functions was not reined in or regulated by democratic state institutions such as those set up by the constitutional laws of the 1870s in France itself. As a result, forces of opposition that developed in the colonies tended to clamor for the extension of democracy in the empire through the elaboration of representative institutions, the rule of law, and democratic control of executive power. The Popular Front government of 1936–1937, which broke the Third Republic consensus on not developing social policy, toyed with the idea of satisfying such demands, but eventually did not do it—bowing to pressure from colonial governors, who represented the authoritarian principle of *le commandement* in the colonies (Koerner 1974).

In the second phase, the French Fourth Republic—proclaimed in 1946—contrasted with the previous regime not only in having a constitution but also in the more socially committed and progressive state that it enshrined. This postwar state was entrusted with the mission of developing and coordinating social and economic policy, including in the colonies. The Fourth Republic also held a more "positive" conception of citizens' rights and equality, extending these deep into the social and colonial domains. It was in this sense more democratic than the Third Republic—even if less economically liberal, given the extensive authority to intervene in economic matters, and the social guarantees offered by the state. This by no means implies that colonial authoritarianism had vanished overnight, but it certainly found the new terrain—in which colonial subjects were granted widening political rights—less hospitable than before. It was this new political dispensation that became the cradle of the Sahelian states. The Fourth Republic was replaced in 1958 with a Fifth Republic, but this was more of a constitutional shift—fusing presidentialism with parliamentarism to give rise to a "semi-presidential" political system—than a clean philosophical break with the previous regime.

This was often marred by high-handed French intervention. According to historian Van Walraven (2013), for example, Niger was the victim of the first African coup d'état, at the hands of French governor Colombani, in 1958. Yet generally the Sahelian states came to independence in 1960 with strong democratic institutions, reflective of the democratic progress made in France under the Fourth Republic. In particular, state institutions were tailored to support substantive citizens' rights, not just in the liberal domain of so-called negative rights, but also in the progressive field of "positive rights" (social and economic rights).

Yet, and this is the third phase, within a few years authoritarianism had completely done away with democratic governance throughout the Sahel. The very powers that the state received to support, protect, and extend citizens' rights were used to overturn them. For instance, the state mission of social and economic policy offered authoritarians the convenient possibility of punishing or rewarding citizens in accordance with their docility, or lack of it. The state was generally instrumentalized by leaders bent on control and intolerant of opposition, a process that unmistakably weakened its institutions, often to the benefit of single party structures, which became the nerve centers of decision-making. But even here—and despite the picture of unmitigated despotism that can be found in the literature characterizing this period—the fall of democracy was not complete. Given the colonial roots of this development, there was a certain determinism at play that shaped a variety of outcomes across the Sahel.

In that regard, the two extremes, in the Sahel, were probably Senegal and Chad. As France's first colony in West Africa, Senegal had long been more exposed than other Sahelian countries to democratic governance. This was particularly true in the so-called four communes of its coastline, which were ruled as fragments of the French Republic and not as possessions subject to colonial authoritarianism (Johnson 1971). Moreover, as the headquarters of the administration of the *Afrique Occidentale Française* (AOF) the colonial federation that included all of the Sahel (except for Chad), Senegal inherited from colonialism a larger, more mature, and more complex state apparatus than the other countries of the region. It was consequently not possible to subsume the state under the single party *Union Progressiste Sénégalaise* of President Senghor in the authoritarian 1960s. Chad, at the other end of the spectrum, was a remote dependency of *Afrique Equatoriale Française*, the less "evolved" central African counterpart of the AOF, with a tiny adminis-trative structure in 1960 and a mode of governance that remained, throughout the colonial era, more militaristic than anywhere else in the Sahel. As a result, at independence President Tombalbaye was able to fully instrumentalize a ramshackle state and put it at the service of his idea of how Chad should develop. But he did this at the cost of violent and chronic instability.

A country like Niger sits in-between these two extremes. For instance, when endeavoring to expunge the strong political opposition of the Sawaba party—the one that fell victim to Governor Colombani's coup of 1958— Niger's single party, the *Parti Progressiste Nigérien*, felt compelled to create "special courts" (*juridictions d'exception*) to "deal" with its opponents and avoid any risky reliance on the normal operation of the rule of law. This suggests that democratic norms survived to an extent that was uncomfort-able to the rulers, even as a successful career in the state apparatus strongly depended on toeing the party line and being a card-carrying member of the "party-state" (*parti-Etat*), the revealing moniker of the single party. Then there is the special case of Mauritania, which proclaimed an Islamic Republic at independence, thereby formally breaking with the Francophone democratic standard (which entailed constitutional secularism), although not necessar-ily with the erstwhile reliance of colonial authoritarianism on the country's maraboutic élites.

The fourth phase in this history is the period of military rule, which came about everywhere in the Sahel, except Senegal. To a very large extent, this military backlash was a direct result of the weakening of state institutions. Writing in that period, Lavroff claims that African armies were "rational and efficient" institutions comparable to their counterparts in the developed world, unlike other state institutions, which he describes as hamstrung by their ties to "traditional society" (Lavroff 1972). This was an interpretation rooted in the then-prevailing modernization theory of comparative politics, and it quickly proved erroneous as the 1970s wore on, but there is certainly something to the notion that the armies were more robust autonomous institutions, since they were generally less affected by the political manipulations that neutered other institutions (the judiciary, parliament, and the civil service). In other words, the armies came out relatively unscathed by the debacle of the state that resulted from authoritarian manhandling. They were thus able to move in when the crisis of the development models adopted by the Sahelian countries left the rulers in direct confrontation with a discontented population—without the buffer of state institutions to channel and organize anger and malaise. In every case, this scenario played out in ways that can be easily documented.

The first to fall, in 1966, was Maurice Yaméogo of Upper Volta (Burkina Faso), following strident protests from the bureaucratic class—the social milieu to which he belonged—after he cut their salaries steeply. In fact,

Yaméogo was toppled by a popular insurrection, with the military taking over after a power vacuum appeared at the top of the state as a result of social troubles. Modibo Keita of Mali was next in line, after his socialist model of development floundered and his government fell into disarray, with infighting between "pragmatists" and "doctrinaires" amid growing social troubles. In 1968, the military ousted him, characteristically retaining the "pragmatist" wing of his regime afterward. Niger's Hamani Diori was himself removed by the military following the great Sahel drought of the early 1970s and at a time when his regime had so lost its way that he convened the first full party congress in years in an effort to overhaul it. The event was scheduled for May 1974, but was preempted in April by the coup that ended his regime. The following year, Chad's François Tombalbaye was felled by the bullets of a group of gendarmes after he had spent several months—in a period of severe economic and political crisis—moving people around in the army trying to prevent that very outcome. Things seemed to be going more or less better for Mauritania's Ould Daddah, thanks largely to income flowing from the iron mines of Zouérat, when he chose to strike an alliance with Morocco to partition the then-Spanish (later Western) Sahara. In response, the POLISARIO Front for the liberation of Western Sahara attacked the Zouérat area, conveniently located near their bases of operation, and thoroughly disrupted Mauritania's lifeline industry. In the ensuing economic crisis, Ould Daddah was bloodlessly flushed out by the military in 1977.

The Senegalese exception to this pattern seems to corroborate the underlying rule that a nexus of stronger state institutions and more democracy made such military outcomes unlikely. In the late 1960s, just like his colleagues in other Sahelian countries, Senghor faced a severe crisis in the model of national development. Sensing a loss of legitimacy, he grew paranoid and arrested several dignitaries of his party and of the government amid mounting social malaise, accusing them of plotting a coup. Eventually, however, he chose to let off steam by reinstating multiparty democracy in 1976–1978 (the dignitaries were released on the heels of this reform). The return to constitutional democracy was limited by the fact that only four parties were permitted to exist, but the reform nevertheless proved to be an effective means to calm the crisis of legitimacy. In 1980, the cash-strapped Senegalese state requested the assistance of the International Monetary Fund (IMF). In April of that year, Senghor gave an address to the nation in which he grimly pronounced the end of "the African party" (*la fête africaine est finie*) (Diop and Diouf 2000), before resigning in December and thus escaping any abrupt removal by popular insurgency or a coup.

The fifth phase served as the prelude to the current era of democratization. In the 1980s, the search for ways to address worsening economic conditions led to the adoption of periodic institutional innovations, or "restorations," that fostered dynamics favorable to democracy. Again, this did not happen in a linear fashion—progressive or regressive. The most unclassifiable case is that of Burkina Faso, where a revolutionary experiment—in this volume Loada refers to this as a *régime d'exception*, the normative phrase within the Francophone democracy lexicon for military rule—included elements of a radical democracy that were far more substantive than what obtains today in the Sahel (or indeed in other parts of the world), but that was developed by authoritarian political means in the period from 1983 to 1987. This authoritarianism proved as adverse to the development of strong, autonomous state institutions as any. Yet its compelling promotion of democratic values contributed to making life less easy for the authoritarian President Compaoré in post-revolutionary Burkina and, through the power of memory, it fueled some of the forces that led to his eventual downfall in 2014.

Pearl T. Robinson (1992) has chronicled some aspects of a similar, though more low-key, experiment in neighboring Niger, where a gradual return to "republican" norms, that is, state institutions consonant with the upholding of citizens' rights—substituted "participatory democracy" for the *régime d'exception* that had been installed in the coup of 1974. In this process, between 1982 and 1989 Niger's dictators granted a series of freedoms of expression and association that required liberal democratic institutions for their full exercise, thus empowering people from the country's bureaucratic class to vocally demand them.

In this volume, Zekeria Ould Ahmed Salem also discusses the unconventional adoption of municipal elections without political parties that was organized by Mauritania's Ould Taya in 1986—an action that must be understood as an experiment in trying to secure more legitimacy for the authoritarian government through some limited democratic participation. Such examples, of which there are others, suggest that by the 1980s the Sahel's authoritarian leaders were aware that they needed to root their power in state institutions, and that this would require a degree of democratic exercise. However, until the early 1990s, the direction taken was certainly not an embrace of liberal democracy—not even in Senegal. Indeed, we can refer to this fifth period as a "prelude" only with the wisdom of hindsight; leading actors at that point were groping toward something else, and most political analysts believed that, in the Sahel, just as in the rest of Africa, democracy was simply not in the cards.

THE MANY WAYS FORWARD
AND SOME DEVIATIONS

I will not return here to a history of democratization in the Sahel since the early 1990s; each of the case studies in this volume describes those processes in rich detail. My purpose in this section is rather to analyze the contemporary situations explored by the authors in light of the dialectical theory illustrated by the broad historical perspective I have provided above.

Sahelian democratizations occurred at an inauspicious time for state institutions in Africa. The prolonged years of economic decline and political stasis that had begun in the 1970s had convinced many political analysts that state institutions in African contexts could not be taken seriously.[2] Their conclusions were reinforced with the international trend toward promoting "thin" states in the developing countries under the aegis of the IMF in the 1980s. If international institutions did not necessarily share the theoretical radicalism of political scientists on the subject of the "African state," they were glad that they could draw on their scholarship to legitimate their structural adjustment "restructuring," which consisted mostly of scrapping "developmental" institutions (including development banks, agricultural credit facilities and extension, subsidies for farmers' cooperatives, industry, and trade parastatals). Thus, by the early 1990s, states in the Sahel, shorn of such organizations, had lost much of their ability to conduct social and economic policy. In fact, while many of them "imported" a version of the constitution of the French Fifth Republic, their situation became in some sense closer to that of the Third Republic. They retained their regalian powers and were encouraged to focus on institutions—such as those connected to the rule of law—that were valuable to business, but they were also forced to slash commitments to education and health and to abandoning the project of national development.

The Stage of Democratization

These shifts led to ambiguous outcomes. On one level, the thinning of the state has had a negative impact on the strategies of authoritarian control that political scientists describe within the analytical framework of "neo-patrimonialism" (Pitcher et al. 2009; Wai 2012). The patrimony that grounded those strategies is state resources, which under the erstwhile "developmental state" were more diverse and considerable than following their pruning by structural adjustment. But, as we shall see below, authoritarians, chased away from one feeding ground, managed to find another one within the new order of things. At another level, the weakening of the state coincided with the rise of the politics of democratization, with consequent negative implications for how democracy performed, as well as for popular perceptions of what it means. This in turn has stimulated antidemocratic trends such as the populism that characterized attacks on the constitutions of Niger and Senegal in the late 2000s.

The reforms of the state described earlier set—or at least shaped—the stage for democratization. In the previous era, governments had striven to draw legitimacy from economic and social policies, packaged as national development. In the new era, economic policy is outsourced to the IMF and the World Bank, while social policy has become primarily a matter for international aid, performed by nongovernmental organizations, international charities, cooperation agencies of rich countries, and United Nations agencies (Mann 2014). In this context, it is hard to gauge the legitimacy of Sahelian rulers. In principle, legitimacy might derive from the will of the population expressed via the vote, but—and although this has varied—voting has generally proven a limited source of legitimacy in all the countries studied here. Aside from a generally low turnout in democratic polls, voting is heavily manipulated by incumbents in some of the countries, sometimes through coercive tactics or intimidation,[3] while opposition parties also routinely engage in foul behavior.[4] If electoral victory allows rulers to stake a claim to democratic legitimacy, however dubious, their performance is severely constrained both by the barebones institutional environment of their "restructured" states, and by their accountability to international financial organizations and other foreign "partners." Since there is little convergence between the latter's programs and the expectations and aspirations of their respective citizenries, the legitimacy of the leaders is thus further eroded.

Yet if, in the past, the erosion of legitimacy had almost systematically led to regime-changing popular insurgencies and coups, such outcomes have become more unlikely and appear unsustainable in contemporary contexts. Disruptive social anger does boil up—as it did several times in Mali in the 1990s (leading to the burning down of the National Assembly and President Konaré's house in 1993), in Niger in 2005, in Burkina Faso in 2006. And coups did happen: in Niger, with remarkable regularity (1996, 1999, 2010), in Mauritania (attempted in 2003 and 2004, successful in 2005 and 2008), in Mali, amid a national security crisis (2012), and in Chad, in the form of (unsuccessful) armed attacks. But in the countries where democratic institutions were more entrenched (Mali, Niger, and Senegal) or where they have grown sturdier through a dialectical confrontation between incumbents and opposition (Burkina), not only did institutions not collapse, but they also channeled the malaise back into expressions more favorable to democracy.

These evolutions are not straightforward. In the next subsection, I compare the case of Mali—where the politics of democratization as they played out meant that institutions were in some sense underused—to the case of Niger— where different political dynamics led them to be overused. The contrasting processes were to have strikingly different implications for the elaboration of resilient state institutions, and hence for political stability.

Institutions: Underuse and Overuse

In Mali, despite serious social troubles that can be traced to structural adjustment as well as to foul play from opposition parties, President Alpha Oumar

Konaré (1992–2002) maintained his commitment to democratic institutions and to free elections—which the opposition chose to boycott each time—and retired peacefully from national politics after his second term. His unwillingness to manipulate institutions in order to stay in power strengthened them, in contrast to the debilitation of state institutions under the country's previous authoritarian regimes. However, the fact that opposition parties sought to delegitimize him by withholding participation in the political process also meant that institutions could not mature through the play of democratic politics. This continued in a different manner under Konaré's successor, Amadou Toumani Touré (see Villalón and Idrissa 2005b).

Toumani Touré was widely admired for his key role in the founding of Mali's democracy in 1991–1992, and the political class felt compelled to treat him well. This enabled Toumani Touré to develop a governance system of so-called consensus, but one that revolved around his persona. As a system of cooptation and corruption, it was a case of soft authoritarianism (though the word sounds almost too harsh for how Toumani Touré in fact practiced it) and it did not directly imperil democratic institutions. Unlike "true" authoritarian rulers, Toumani Touré did not try to control and neutralize challengers by manipulating and deliberately weakening institutions. Instead, he fostered informal political relations to conciliate potential challengers, forestalling the need to forcibly exclude them from the political arena through more brutal strategies. This foggy way of circumventing democratic institutions was certainly not good for democracy, but it did not lead to authoritarian rule either. Rather, this continued underuse of democratic institutions led to a form of institutional atrophy, which goes a long way toward explaining some of the more shocking aspects of the Malian political disarray of 2012–2013. Rather than sparking popular mobilization and a national rallying around democratic institutions, Mali's response to attacks from jihadist theocrats and Tuareg irredentists was an ill-planned coup followed by a popular insurrection leading to the brutalization of interim president Dioncounda Traoré in May 2012. It is important to note, however, that while there is a clear relationship between the decades-long underuse of democratic institutions and this severe bout of instability, Mali has nevertheless remained on the democratic side of the Sahel spectrum of governance.

In Niger, it was the very respect for democratic institutions that initially led to a course of events that proved dangerous for democracy. Under the country's Third Republic (1993–1996), there were no attempts by leaders to monopolize power by manipulating and circumventing democratic institutions. Instead, the major political players all tried to gain the upper hand by using, in all legal ways possible, the powers and prerogatives that the institutions gave them, which they did by scrupulously respecting the forms and procedures specified in the law. The objective was still the full monopoly of power, but it was to be achieved through playing by the rules. However, since such an objective was in fact problematic in a democracy—where power is generally dispersed and limited—the rules and institutions were overused, and the political leaders produced an institutional gridlock.

The result was that within just a few years of the adoption of democratic institutions, the government found itself log-jammed as a president and a prime minister from two opposing parties each made full use of their pre-rogatives to hinder the other, and soon nothing could get done. Eventually, after many months of this situation, and with no solution in sight, the military resolved the impasse with a coup, to the relief of the populace. Unfortunately for democracy in Niger, the coup maker, Baré Maïnassara, had a different approach to democratic institutions than the politicians he forced out of power. Not only did he think—like other authoritarian rulers—that institu-tions could be manipulated at will to yield desired results with little concern for political reality, but he was also remarkably heavy-handed in how he did it. In one instance, he sent armed and turbaned men to seize ballot boxes after a vote, which led to a fight between the masked ballot box snatchers and the staff of the electoral commission. But this very roughness was a sign of the entrenchment of Niger's democratic institutions. After Baré Maïnassara was killed in a coup in 1999, the institutions of the Third Republic were reinstated (as the Fifth Republic, 1999–2010; Baré Maïnassara had dubbed his rule the Fourth). Indeed, the institutions were further strengthened in a constitution that drew lessons both from the gridlock of 1995 and from the ways in which Baré Maïnassara had forced the constitutional chamber of the Supreme Court to annul election results in April 1999 (the action that triggered the coup against him) (see Villalon and Idrissa 2005a).

The Fifth Republic was an institutional success, but it harbored an enemy within, in no less than the person of President Mamadou Tandja, the man to whom it twice handed power via elections, in 1999 and 2004. Nigerien con-stitutionalism was by then firmly locked into the notion of the two-term limit for the presidency, yet Tandja came to wish to break that lock and remain in power. The institutions of the Fifth Republic—in particular the legislature and the Constitutional Court (created in lieu of the earlier and less autonomous constitutional chamber of the Supreme Court)—resisted his schemes. In the end, Tandja was reduced to undertaking a "constitutional coup," suspending the Constitution of the Fifth Republic even though he had no prerogative to do so, and hurriedly organizing a constitutional "referendum" to install a new regime (the "Sixth Republic") in 2009. In the face of massive dissatisfaction and protest, his attempted return to an authoritarian regime with a democratic veneer was short-lived; Tandja was removed by the military in January 2010. Just as in 1999, the army opted to remain in charge only long enough to again oversee the restoration of democratic institutions—with the Seventh Republic being largely a reversion to the Fifth Republic.

This complicated story suggests ambivalent lessons for democratic institutions in Niger. On the one hand, it shows a remarkable "stickiness" of such institutions in the country's political framework. Repeated attacks by authoritarians only saw democratic institutions snap back to their former importance, indeed oftentimes reinforced in the process. After the Baré Maïnassara fiasco, even military coups took on the air of police operations in favor of democracy. On the other hand, Tandja's attempt to remain in power drew genuine support from some large sectors of Nigerien society, clearly not just because of a belief in his leadership, but also due to his criticism of democracy. If the institutions themselves appear necessary to most Nigeriens—Tandja himself felt compelled to put in place mock democratic institutions under his Sixth Republic—the political class and the lack of economic progress were easy targets for a populist discourse that stirred up vague hope for something better.

Moreover, after this episode, Niger's political class returned to its old habit of working institutions to the hilt. In recent years, the boundary between overuse and abuse has been blurred, as President Mahamadou Issoufou manipulated the judiciary to exclude a powerful challenger from the political arena, and win his second term in inequitable polls. The case of Niger therefore still poses the question of what happens to democracy when institutional mechanisms, though supported by a strong democratic consensus, are hobbled by the authoritarian impulse. I will return to this question (and others) in the final section below. But before getting there, I discuss the cases of Chad and Mauritania to further explore the relations between these two factors: the democratic consensus and the authoritarian impulse.

Institutions: The Authoritarian Impulse and Democratic Consensus

In all the cases studied in this book, what unfolded throughout the era of democratic politics was a dialectical struggle between those in power—those intent on *controlling* the process so as to remain in power—and those out of it—who sought to *exploit* the process to acquire it. A third group claimed to hold both to account (especially those in power), as members of "civil society."

In the French language texts of the case studies, those in power are often metonymically called "the power" (*le pouvoir*), a useful meaning of the word that does not exist in English, and that is both more precise and more objective than either "regime" or "government." In particular, unlike these two words, this is a term that marks the context of democratization. Under an authoritarian dispensation, the fact that there was no open political arena outside of the ruling system meant there was no need—or at least there was not much of one—to delineate the field of power. Under democratization, the major shift came from the emergence of such an open political arena, which became a space of competition for *le pouvoir*, for remaining or becoming *le pouvoir*. In the Sahel, given the lack of resources for a more substantive concept of democracy, competition concentrated on institutions, and institutions have thus become the deciding factor in where a country falls on the democratization spectrum, between authoritarianism and democracy.

Democratization in the Sahel started as an event, the adoption or restoration—via constitutional referendums or revisions—of formal institutions that opened up the political arena and set out to regulate relations between rulers and the ruled on the basis of elections, rule of law, and political freedoms. In some countries, such as Chad, Mali, and Niger, this event was orchestrated in the form of a "national conference" (see Nzouankeu 1993; Robinson 1994). Once this adoption or restoration is proclaimed, *le pouvoir* emerges both as something that can be challenged in an attempt to displace it, and something that will fight back. A struggle for power, *le pouvoir*, is inherent in democratization. As I have argued earlier, all Sahelian countries have inherited a dangerous memory of how far such fighting or struggles can take them: that is, to a willful instrumentalization of institutions in ways that eventually devitalize them and lead to authoritarian rule. This memory is not discrete; it does not stop at a certain category of people. Those in the opposition, once they come to power, are able to resort to the strategies that it inspires, as is exemplified by the cases of former President Wade of Senegal, or President Issoufou of Niger.

Counterpoising this authoritarian dynamic, democracy can benefit from the strength of the consensus on institutions that may develop across the political class and civil society in specific ways, according to the ways in which the politics of democratization are played out in different national contexts. The two cases where the democratic consensus appears to be particularly difficult illustrate this point well: Chad, which has clearly failed to establish a viable consensus, and Mauritania, which was somewhat more successful despite long odds.

Like Mali and Niger, Chad "transitioned" to democracy through a national conference. However, the event had different implications for the three countries. In Mali, the national conference was organized after the removal of the authoritarian ruler via the classic combination of popular insurgency and a resulting coup. In Niger, the authoritarian ruler quietly left power immediately after the conference, which he did not attempt (or did not manage) to control. In Chad, by contrast, President Idris Déby was in power before, during, and after the conference, and remained in place almost thirty years later. Not only did he engage in ruthless institutional manipulation and interference, but a preoccupation with state security in the ever-militarized politics of Chad—in addition to geopolitical threats from neighboring Libya and Sudan—continuously called into question the fragile consensuses that began to emerge at some junctures. This dynamic is particularly marked in the aftermath of the landmark 2007 political agreement, as discussed by Lucien Toulou in his chapter in this volume. It is characteristic that, in the context of Chad, a distinction has to be made between a "democratic opposition," which inhabits the official if constricted political stage set up by the national conference in 1993, and the armed oppositions that cyclically aimed to remove Déby by force. This latter subversive form of opposition nevertheless feeds into the democratic consensus, given the fact that Déby unilaterally scrapped the two-term limit for the presidency in 2005, signaling an intention to remain in power indefinitely and bend institutions to adjust them to his will.

In Mauritania, during the first fourteen years of democratization (1991–2005), the consensus around democratic institutions was even weaker than in Chad. From the outset, democratization was tarnished by a case of gross constitutional fraud. The institutional reforms that led to democracy were first presented, in early 1991, in a constitution that was endorsed by the opposition and civil society, before being subjected to a referendum in July 1991. But the constitutional text promulgated after the referendum included an addendum that stipulated that the pre-democracy laws of Mauritania would remain in force until they were abolished following certain constitutional procedures. This backhanded coda—formally fraudulent in view of the referendum process—flouted the consensus that had been built around the constitution. It gave to *le pouvoir* the means to stall or delay any of the institutional reforms that would in fact give meaning to democratization. As a result, a genuine consensus became possible only after President Ould Taya was removed by a coup in 2005. In the months following the coup, the military conducted the "transition" process in such a way that a democratic consensus did take hold in the country, as Zekeria Ould Ahmed Salem argues in this volume. However, in a series of events that are reminiscent of what happened in Niger under its Third Republic, Mauritania's political class then went on to engage in byzantine political maneuverings that put the fledgling institutions under considerable stress, and eventually provoked yet another intervention of the army in late 2008.

The case of Mauritania, since that event, is one of a restored democracy with a lively political stage. The new ruler, President Ould Abdel Aziz (2009–2019), did not attempt to overturn the key elements of political democracy, such as freedom of the press, expression, and opposition; and democratic institutions are still functioning. If a vocal section of the opposition withheld participation in the political process and refused to consider Ould Abdel Aziz a democratically legitimate ruler, their continuous protest actions—which stoked particularly high hopes of a new "democratic revolution" during the so-called Arab Spring—failed to dislodge him. To a large extent, this seems to have been due to a broader consensus about the genuineness of the country's democratic institutions than at least the radical opposition—there is also a more moderate opposition—cares to admit. Moreover, there was the fact of a two-term limit to the presidency, an institutional provision which was in fact respected when Ould Abdel Aziz stepped aside and presidential elections brought Mohamed Ould Ghazouani to power in June 2019. As a result of all this, Mauritania's democratic consensus still holds, even if it remains challenged and fragile given the contestation of the radical opposition. Yet in a sense, and as we have seen in other cases, this very political agitation may contribute to the strengthening of the institutions. This is particularly the case since it obliges *le pouvoir* to demonstrate that it is playing by the rules in an effort to preserve political stability at a time when the geostrategic threat of terrorism in the Sahel is particularly ominous for Mauritania.

TOWARD A THEORETICAL FRAMEWORK

My purpose in this chapter has not been to attempt a full theory of the relationship between democratization and state institutions in the Sahel and Africa, but rather to derive a few pointers from the lessons offered by the case studies to lay the groundwork for a perspective that may be useful for those interested in building such a theory. In this light, I return here to the questions of dialectical progress, democratic consensus, and authoritarian impulse.

A dialectical progress is one in which movement depends on a concatenation of action and reaction, involving therefore a struggle to push forward, or pull backward. The direction taken in the progress will depend on the strength of the forces that push forward, relative to the strength of those that pull backward. These contending forces can be identified in each of the cases examined here, even if storylines are rarely as clear-cut as in the dialectical movements detected by Marxists, for whom certain social classes become backward-pulling forces while others emerge as forward-pushing forces at specific historical junctures in the progression toward communism. It is easy, for example, to portray the military as an inevitably backward-pulling force in the progress toward democratization. Yet looking at the grain of empirical history, one may be surprised to find that it has in fact played unexpected roles in some cases, and at some points.

Thus, as a bulwark of Idriss Déby's authoritarian governance in Chad, the military is certainly a backward-pulling force in that country. But in Niger, it played a backward-pulling force with the coup of Baré Maïnassara in 1996, and then turned into a distinctive forward-pushing force in later events. In Mauritania, its position is even more complicated, as it appears to involve both dynamics at the same time. On the other hand, one may assume, from a conventional view of democratization, that civil society is by definition a forward-pushing force. Yet, as some researchers have found, it can play more ambiguous roles and fall for the neo-patrimonial strategies of authoritarian leaders (Fatton 1995). In this volume, Loada underlines how some civil society actors in Burkina Faso were drawn into this trap, in situations that were not unique to this country. Any theoretical framework must, therefore, account for the variations in why and how specific actors, or categories of actors, play one of these two roles in democratization.

Because of this difficulty of identifying specific actors with stable roles in the movement of democratization—given that even "democratic" opposition leaders can become authoritarian rulers once in power—I would suggest that a more fruitful theoretical approach would be to contrast more abstract factors, namely the democratic consensus and the authoritarian impulse. These are also difficult factors to conceptualize, especially the latter—and indeed it may necessitate a more nuanced terminology.

The democratic consensus can be conceptualized as a measurement of democratization, in the sense in which "transitologists" envision such benchmark instruments. In the Sahelian countries, popular adherence to democracy, as surveyed for instance by Afrobarometer, does not in reality tell us much about the "success" of transitions to democracy. As one article in the South African newspaper *Mail & Guardian* analyzing the results of the surveys puts it, "Africa loves 'democracy,' but also likes its military dictators, one-party rule, and Big Men" (Mungai 2014). This catholic embrace of both democracy and authoritarianism should not be considered a judgment on African public opinion, but rather—as any reader of Walter Lippmann's *Phantom Public* will well understand—an account of the "bewildered herd" character of the general public anywhere (1993, 145). In this light, it seems more pertinent to assess the behavior of the sections of society directly involved in the political arena, namely: incumbents, opposition, and civil society.

If transition starts with the opening up of the political arena through the adoption of democratic institutions, it cannot be said to be effective until a consensus emerges, across those sections of society, that the institutions are really democratic. This consensus is best studied according to the context, since—at least as far as I understand the matter at this point—there are no clear, "objective" criteria through which to gauge it across countries. Perhaps a yardstick with which to determine the *failure* of such a consensus to emerge is one means to measure the strength of the authoritarian impulse, as it manages to take control of institutions and renders them more or less meaningless. Conversely, when the authoritarian impulse founders or backfires, we know that the consensus must have grown stronger. Thus, as we have seen, consensus was impossible in Mauritania's democratization in 1991–2005 but grew afterward. It remains factitious in Chad to date. It developed to the point of undermining the authoritarian ruler's hold on power in Burkina Faso. And it is constantly hobbled in Niger by both incumbent leaders and by the opposition.

If we can manage to elaborate a robust, elegant, and parsimonious theoretical framework on the bases of these observations, I believe we will be able to draw insights from careful political studies of the kind collected in this book. These in turn yield important lessons for how the intimate, dialectical movement of democratic politics shapes institutions in varied national contexts, with diverging and consequential implications for the strength and stability of states.

NOTES

1. See also Schmitter 2014.

2. States in Africa were variously described as unworkable "importations" from the West (Badie 2000), "vacuous and ineffectual" ersatz versions of the modern "Weberian (Western) state" (Chabal and Daloz 1999), clearinghouses for the "politics of the belly" distinctive of "African historicity" (Bayart 1993), or "balloons suspended in mid-air" with no moorings in society (Hyden 1983).

3. In Niger, in 1998, President Baré Maïnassara had ballot boxes forcibly seized, suspended the proclamation of results to "reverse" them, and compelled the constitutional chamber of the Supreme Court to annul results he did not like. In Mauritania, in 2003, President Ould Taya arrested his principal challenger, Ould Haidalla, prior to the polls, releasing him only on the eve of the first round of the presidential election. In 2015, President Issoufou of Niger similarly arrested his principal challenger Amadou and kept him in jail until the end of the vote, while harassing and jailing many of the opposing party bigwigs.

4. Aside from fraud, discussed by Loada in the case of Burkina and also denounced in Niger's media for the tainted vote of 2015, one could point out the dogged refusal of Mali's opposition parties to participate in the political process during the two terms of President Konaré, followed by the support they showed to the questionable "consensus" governance of President Toumani Touré. In Senegal, opposition figures allowed themselves to be coopted on a large scale in an endemic case of "political transhumance."

REFERENCES

Badie, Bertrand. 2000. *The Imported State. The Westernization of the Political Order.* Stanford: Stanford University Press.

Bayart, Jean-François. 1993. *The State in Africa: The Politics of the Belly.* London and New York: Longman.

Chabal, Patrick and Jean-Pascal Daloz. 1999. *Africa Works. Disorder as Political Instrument.* Bloomington, IN: Indiana University Press.

De Thy, Ludovic. 2017. "L'écriture des lois constitutionnelles de 1875. La fondation de l'ordre constitutionnel de la IIIe République." Unpublished doctoral dissertation, Université de Bourgogne.

Diop, Momar-Coumba and Mamadou Diouf. 2000. "Sénégal: par-delà la succession Senghor-Diouf." In *Les Figures du politique en Afrique: des pouvoirs hérités aux pouvoirs élus*, edited by M-C Diop and M. Diouf, 139–188. Paris: Karthala.

Fatton, Robert. 1995. "Africa in the Age of Democratization: The Civic Limitations of Civil Society." *African Studies Review,* 38(2), 67–99.

Garrigues, Jean. 2011. *Les Patrons et la politique.* Paris: Perrin.

Hyden, Goran. 1983. *No Shortcuts to Progress: African Development Management in Perspective.* Cambridge: Cambridge University Press.

Johnson, G. Wesley Jr. 1971. *The Emergence of Black Politics in Senegal. The Struggle for Power in the Four Communes 1900-1920.* Stanford: Stanford University Press.

Koerner, Francis. 1974. "Le Front populaire et la question coloniale à Madagascar. Le climat politique en 1936." *Revue française d'histoire d'outre-mer,* 61(224), 436–454.

Lavroff, Dimitri-Georges. 1972. "Régimes militaires et développement politique en Afrique noire." *Revue française de science politique,* 5, 973–991.

Levitsky, Steven and Way, Lucan A. 2010. *Competitive Authoritarianism: Hybrid Regimes after the Cold War.* Cambridge: Cambridge University.

Lippmann, Walter. 1993. *The Phantom Public.* New Brunswick and London: Transaction Publishers.

Mann, Greg. 2014. *From Empires to NGOs in the West African Sahel: The Road to Nongovernmentality* (African Studies Series). Cambridge: Cambridge University Press.

Mungai, Christine. 2014. "Africa loves 'democracy,' but also likes its military dictators, one-party rule, and Big Men." *Mail & Guardian Africa,* 21 October 2014.

Nzouankeu, Jacques Mariel. 1993. "The Role of the National Conference in the Transition to Democracy in Africa: The Cases of Benin and Mali." *Issue: A Journal of Opinion,* 21(1/2), 44–50.

Pitcher, Anne, Mary H. Moran and Michael Johnston. 2009. Rethinking Patrimonialism and Neopatrimonialism in Africa. *African Studies Review,* 52(1), 125–156.

Robinson, Pearl T. 1992. "Grassroots Legitimation of Military Governance in Burkina Faso and Niger." In *Governance and Politics in Africa*, edited by Goran Hyden and Michael Bratton, 143–162. Boulder, CO: Lynne Rienner.

Robinson, Pearl. 1994. "The National Conference Phenomenon in Francophone Africa." *Comparative Studies in Society and History,* 36(3), 575–610.

Rustow, Dankwart. 1970. "Transitions to Democracy: Towards a Dynamic Model." *Comparative Politics,* 2(3), 337–367.

Schedler, Andreas. 2013. *The Politics of Uncertainty: Sustaining and Subverting Electoral Authoritarianism.* Oxford: Oxford University Press.

Schmitter, Philippe C. 2014. "Reflections on 'Transitology': Before and After." In *Reflections on Uneven Democracies: The Legacy of Guillermo O'Donnell*, edited by Daniel M. Brinks, Marcelo Leiras and Scott Mainwaring, 71–86. Baltimore, MD: Johns Hopkins University Press.

Van Walraven, Klaas. 2013. *The Yearning for Relief. A History of the Sawaba Movement in Niger*. Leiden: Brill.

Villalón, Leonardo A., and Abdourahmane Idrissa. 2005a. "Repetitive Breakdowns and a Decade of Experimentation: Institutional Choices and Unstable Democracy in Niger." In *The Fate of Africa's Democratic Experiments: Elites and Institutions in Comparative Perspective*, edited by Leonardo A. Villalón, and Peter VonDoepp, 27–48. Bloomington, IN: Indiana University Press.

Villalón, Leonardo A. and Abdourahmane Idrissa. 2005b. "The Tribulations of a Successful Transition: Institutional Dynamics and Elite Rivalry in Mali." In *The Fate of Africa's Democratic Experiments: Elites and Institutions in Comparative Perspective*, edited by Leonardo A. Villalón and Peter von Doepp, 49–74. Bloomington, IN: Indiana University Press.

Wai, Zubairu. 2012. "Neo-Patrimonialism and the Discourse of State Failure in Africa." *Review of African Political Economy,* 39(131), 27–43.

Index

About the Contributors

Leonardo A. Villalón is professor of African politics and dean of the International Center at the University of Florida, where he also coordinates the Sahel Research Group. From 2002 to 2011 he served as director of the university's Center for African Studies. He has worked extensively across the countries of the Sahel, including as codirector of the "Trans-Saharan Elections Project" (TSEP), involving exchanges on electoral issues with six Sahelian countries, and as principal investigator of the research project: "Political Reform, Socio-Religious Change, and Stability in the African Sahel." He has published numerous works on the Sahel and is editor of the forthcoming *Oxford Handbook of the African Sahel*.

Zekeria Ould Ahmed Salem is associate professor of political science at Northwestern University and director of the Institute for the Study of Islamic Thought in Africa in the Program of African Studies. Until 2017, he was professor of political science at the University of Nouakchott, Mauritania. He earned his PhD from the Université de Lyon, France, in 1996. From 2005 to 2007, he served as secretary general of the Ministry of Higher Education, and then of the Ministry of Rural Development in Mauritania. He is the author of numerous works, including the book *Prêcher dans le désert: Savoirs, violences et changement social en République Islamique de Mauritanie*. In 2010–2011, he was a Fulbright visiting professor at the University of Florida.

Ismaïla Madior Fall is professor of law and political science at Cheikh Anta Diop University in Dakar, Senegal, where he also served as director of the Centre de recherche, d'étude et de documentation sur les institutions et les législations africaines (CREDILA). Fall is a member of several international research networks including the Network of African Constitutionalists headquartered in Johannesburg. He has published extensively on constitutionalism, the process of democratization in francophone African countries, elections, and party system institutionalization. He was appointed minister of state in Senegal in April 2019, having served as minister of justice from 2017 to 2019, and previously as special political advisor to President Macky Sall.

Moumouni Soumano is executive director of the Centre Malien pour le Dialogue Interpartis et la Démocratie, which aims to strengthen the capacity of political parties and the framework of democracy in Mali. He also teaches law and political science at the Université des Sciences Juridiques et Politiques de Bamako in Mali. He holds a doctorate in public law from the Université Paris XIII. He has consulted extensively on capacity-building for democratic institutions, including the National Assembly, electoral bodies and political parties, and has published widely on these topics.

Augustin Loada is professor of public law and political science at the University of Ouagadougou, Burkina Faso, where he has also served as dean of the faculty of law and political science. He is founding director of the Centre pour la Gouvernance Démocratique (CGD) in Ouagadougou. He is the author of numerous works on such topics as elections in Burkina Faso, political regimes, good governance, and decentralization. From 2014 to 2015 he served as minister of public service in the transitional government of Burkina Faso. In 2019, he founded a new political party, Le Mouvement Patriotique pour le Salut (MPS).

Mahaman Tidjani Alou is professor of political science at the Université Abdou Moumouni in Niamey, where he has also served as dean. He is a senior researcher and cofounder of the Laboratoire d'Etudes et de Recherche sur les Dynamiques Sociales et le Développement Local (LASDEL), of which he served as director from 2001 to 2007. He has published widely on the state in Africa, on north–south cooperation, decentralization, political elites, and development policies. He holds a PhD in political science from the University of Bordeaux. He has served as political advisor to the Nigerien prime minister, as well as on the commission that drafted the 2010 Constitution for the Seventh Republic. Since 2017, he has served as president of the scientific advisory council of the Centre National d'Etudes Stratégiques et de Sécurité (CNESS).

Lucien Toulou is currently team leader for peace consolidation and support to democratic institutions with UNDP in the Democratic Republic of the Congo (DRC). From 2016 to 2018, he was chief technical advisor for elections with UNDP in Chad. Previously, he was programme director with the Electoral Institute for Democracy in Africa (EISA). He has served as EISA's country director in Chad, Madagascar and DRC. Toulou holds a PhD in political science from Sciences Po-University of Bordeaux IV, France, and has taught political science at the Catholic University of Central Africa in Yaoundé, Cameroon. In addition to works on issues related to elections and democratic governance in Africa, he has developed numerous training manuals and handbooks in election administration, election observation, voter information, conflict mediation, party poll watching, and for female candidates standing for elections.

Rahmane Idrissa is senior researcher in the African Studies Centre at the University of Leiden in the Netherlands. His doctorate in political science, with a concentration on democratization and political Islam in Africa, was obtained at the University of Florida. Idrissa's research expertise ranges from issues of states, institutions, and democratization in Africa to Salafi radicalism in the Sahel and current projects on the history of state formation in Africa.

Idrissa is the founder of EPGA, a think tank in political economy in Niger, and a member of the Niamey-based social science laboratory LASDEL. He is the author of *The Politics of Islam in the Sahel: Between Persuasion and Violence* (2017).

9 781498 570015